WORK, CULTURE AND SOCIETY

WORK, CULTURE AND SOCIETY

Edited by

Rosemary Deem and Graeme Salaman

Open University Press

Milton Keynes · Philadelphia

Open University Press
Open University Educational Enterprises Limited
12 Cofferidge Close
Stony Stratford
Milton Keynes MK11 1BY, England

and
242 Cherry Street
Philadelphia PA 19106, USA

First published 1985

This book is derived from the Open University course DE325:
Work and Society © The Open University 1985. Adapted and
revised material © the editors and contributors 1985.

British Library Cataloguing in Publication Data
Work, culture, society.
   1. Work—Social aspects
   I. Deem, Rosemary   II. Salaman, Graeme
   306'.36   HD6955

ISBN 0–335–15135–3 Pbk
ISBN 0–335–15136–1

Library of Congress Cataloging in Publication Data
Work, Culture and Society.
      Bibliography: P.
Includes Index.
      1. Work—Social Aspects.   2. Industrial Relations.
      3. Industrial Sociology.   I. Deem, Rosemary.
      II. Salaman, Graeme.
      HD4904.W644   1985   306'.36   85–11542

ISBN 0–335–15136–1
ISBN 0–335–15135–3 (pbk.)

52,196

Typeset by S & S Press, Abingdon, Oxfordshire
Printed and bound in Great Britain by
Biddles Ltd, Guildford and King's Lynn

Contents

List of Figures and Tables

Acknowledgements

The Editors would like to thank Stephen Barr of Open University Press whose idea this volume was. All of the chapters in the book are adapted versions of units originally written for the Open University course DE325 Work and Society, and we are grateful to the University for giving permission to allow us to publish in this form. We should like to show our appreciation to members of the course team, whose comments on drafts of the original units were extremely helpful in producing these adapted versions here, and many thanks too to those who typed and transformed much amended typescripts, including especially Marie Day. Grateful acknowledgement is also made to Marco Polo Press for permission to reproduce pp. 76–80 from M. Kahn-Ackerman, *China: Within the Outer Gate*, trans. D. Fernbach, 1982. Finally, the author of the chapter on 'Work outside the capitalist framework: the case of China' would like to thank, in particular, his colleague, Martin Lockett, for his help and co-operation in compiling the original course unit.

Work outside the capitalist framework: the case of China
Craig Littler

Acknowledgements
This chapter draws on work that I have done jointly with my colleague, Martin Lockett, whom I should like to thank for his help and co-operation.

Grateful acknowledgement is also made to Marco Polo Press for permission to reproduce pp. 76–80 from M. Kahn-Ackermann, *China: Within the Outer Gate*, trans. D. Fernbach, 1982.

List of Contributors

Rosemary Deem is a Lecturer in the School of Education, the Open University, and has published work on women and education and the sociology of leisure. Graeme Salaman is a Senior Lecturer in Sociology, Faculty of Social Sciences, the Open University, and has many publications in the field of the sociology of work.

Peter Hamilton is a Lecturer in Sociology, Faculty of Social Sciences, the Open University, and has published on sociological theory and agricultural work.

Elizabeth Garnsey is a Lecturer in Management Studies in the Engineering dept., University of Cambridge, and her publications include work on the division of labour, occupational structure and social stratification.

Stephen Wood is a Lecturer in the Department of Industrial Relations, London School of Economics, and his publications are mostly in the area of the sociology of work.

Craig Littler is a Lecturer in the School of Social and Industrial Administration, Griffith University, Australia, and has published work on industrial sociology, the labour process and China.

Mary Maynard is Lecturer in Sociology, University of York, and her published work includes sociological analyses of gender and race.

Ruth Finnegan is a Reader in Comparative Social Institutions, Faculty of Social Sciences, the Open University, and her publications include anthropology and work on the informal economy.

Introduction

This volume is a contribution to the sociological understanding of work. There may be those who feel that a study of work, when around four million people are denied employment, is somewhat academic. And there may also be those who are predisposed to feel that sociology, as an intellectual enterprise is now irrelevant, even discredited. This volume is intended as a vigorous rebuttal of these reservations, and as a spirited demonstration of their falsity.

Seeking to advance a sociological analysis of work, or indeed of anything, is to court umpopularity with those who benefit from existing structures of power, privilege and consciousness: for genuine sociology does not accept the propriety or normality or legitimacy of things *as they are*. Instead it is interested in questioning these 'normal' arrangements, asking: what are they, exactly? Why are things arranged like this? Who benefits from this state of affairs? Most important of all perhaps, sociology questions the very heart of existing institutions: the way we define and understand them. The sociologist is not prepared to accept things simply because they seem normal, accepted or the 'way things always have been'. It is a direct sign of the value of a sociological analysis that it questions the unquestionable, exposes the sacrosanct. Consequently, it is possible to say that an indication of the potential importance of sociology – particularly in Britain in the late eighties – is its unpopularity among the powerful.

This essential sociological approach involves an analysis of two, discrete but closely interrelated elements. Its iconoclasm inheres in its insistence on the relationship between the two: the structural and the ideological. Or practices, institutions, relationships, the distribution of power and privilege on the one hand, and ideas, values, beliefs on the other. Such an agenda can indeed make for unpopular research and debate. A ready example can be found in organizational employment, in particular, in the controversial issue of managers' rights to manage. This is a slogan which is frequently deployed in disputes. It argues that workers' *rights* (such as they are) are at best in the area of the financial; issues of control, decision-making, job design, company policy, etc., are not only *best* left to management (on grounds that they are expertly and professionally equipped for such matters) but *should* be left to management. Thus, the slogan argues, there is a moral basis to management authority. Such injunctions are of interest to sociologists. They would be interested to identify the elements of this 'right'; to compare it to other bases of man- agement authority ('expertise', ownership, etc.) and they would seek to relate such ideas to shifting strategies of management/worker relation- ship, and in particular to the intervention of the state (with its own read- ily accessible vocabulary of moral language) in industrial relationships. The ever-sceptical sociologist would also seek to contrast the language used to legitimize workers' attempts to resist management power with the vocabulary used to attack workers' organizations: while one opposes workers with the vocabulary of management *rights*, the other attacks in the name of democracy – a democracy in union organization which is seen as quite tolerable in the enterprise as a whole. The sociologist sees the vocabularies of rights and democracy then not as their exponents regard – as self-evident and acceptable values (for this would be to fail to get beneath the surface language to the structures of interest which lie below) – but as efforts to mobilize available structures of legitimizing ideas in order to retain power, or undermine resistance.

In this volume, there is no analysis of the vocabularies of industrial con- flict, or of the changing bases of management authority; this example is simply to illustrate the argument that the essential concerns of sociology – and of a sociology of work – make it unpopular with those who would prefer that we accept their judgement, their authority, without question or resistance.

It should follow from this view of sociology's mission, that it is not merely academic and irrelevant to present a collection of essays in the sociology of work at a time of massive, large-scale unemployment. The sociology of work is not simply concerned with paid employment. The definition of work is much broader than that. The vast majority of those who are unemployed still work – as do many others who are not employed but who for various reasons do not regard themselves as unemployed because they are unable or do not wish to seek paid work. Unpaid work covers a wide range of activities and obligations, from domestic chores and gardening to children and voluntary work.

Hence in this volume unpaid work is subject to the same processes of sociological analysis as paid employment (that unpaid work has for so long been invisible to many male academic sociologists tells us something about the relation of power and dominant ideologies inside the discipline itself). Held up for particular examination here is the case of housework;

who does it, what it consists of, and the power relationships which surround it. There is also a detailed exploration of the boundaries between paid and unpaid work on the margins, or outside the formal economy altogether, and the relevant chapter demonstrates that marginal work is of much more than marginal importance.

The second reason for our conviction of the relevance of a sociology of work is quite simply that we are persuaded that no analysis of work or of employment – or indeed of unemployment – can properly and usefully occur without a close analysis of the relationship between work, unemployment and the society within which they occur. Studying work reveals the major dynamics and structures of society; it shows us society at work. Many of the essays in this collection demonstrate this. The essay on factory work, for example, looks at the relationship between internal structures of control and hierarchy, and the wider structures of class relationships and industrial societies. The chapter on leisure, work and unemployment considers the shifting nature of these three aspects of contemporary life and looks at the social and economic conditions under which the boundaries between all three move or are blurred. The chapter on China poses the question of whether societies like China differ essentially from capitalist ones, considering especially the relationship between the economy, the national culture and work organization. Work organization itself is given detailed treatment in a separate chapter, which examines the forces that influence the design of jobs and the extent to which these forces emanate from the priorities of the society and economy in which occupations are located. Labour market structure and workplace divisions are singled out for discussion in a further chapter which deals with the ways in which labour markets are systematically segmented, creating not one but a number of discrete markets, each with different experiences of privilege and for deprivation. And in the chapter on agricultural work there is an attempt to make clear the importance and relevance of such work to our understanding even of industrial societies where agriculture is often forgotten about.

Clearly these articles differ widely – most obviously in their subject matter but also in the manner of their approach to their subjects. But they share one major characteristic, which places them at the heart of the sociological enterprise: they seek to unravel the relationship between work – various kinds of work – and society. Most significantly they seek to relate workplace inequalities and hierarchies to the systematic inequalities of the host society – and particularly, but not solely, to class structure.

The essays collected together in this volume are closely based on units written for a third level Open University sociology course entitled Work and Society. Regretfully, shortage of space made it impossible to include all the materials produced for that course; yet in a very real sense the essays included here have a collective authorship, since their course originals were subjected to thorough and often structural criticism and comments. It is for this reason that the authors included in this volume would like to record their debt to the support and encouragement of: Richard Brown, Christine Edwards, Richard Hyman, Kenneth Thompson, David Dunkerley, Margaret Kiloh and Robert Bocock.

The essays have not been chosen to give representative or thorough coverage to all sorts of work, or all forms of theories of work. They have been selected because they address key, current issues in the sociological understanding of work. Each essay, in its own way, identifies and treats a major issue of theoretical importance and dispute. But this does not mean that the selection offered here is *merely* academic, for by identifying issues of theoretical significance, this selection also targets issues of great practical significance, the origins of work forms, the class basis of factory control and the inequalities of labour market segmentation, the relationship between work and leisure, the nature of housework, etc. Through their analysis of theoretical and practical problems, the authors seek to bridge the gap between issues of social structure and processes and individual experience – a prime feature of good sociology. As will be seen, they do this largely through the mediating concepts of class, gender, ethnicity, inequality, hierarchy and power.

CHAPTER ONE

Factory work

GRAEME SALAMAN

This chapter argues that the structuring of factory work both reflects and is occasioned by, a basic paradox: the very circumstances which make factory work so tightly and formally structured, also tend to undermine such attempts at structuring. Factory work represents the classical, stereotypical form of work within industrial economies, even if, recently, this form of work may no longer be the most common form of work statistically.

It is the sort of work which has attracted most attention from those seeking to understand the structure and process of work organizations within industrial/capitalist economies. There are problems which follow from this: it sometimes seems as if most of the theorizing about and research into modern work forms is coloured by the assumptions, concepts and images, drawn from investigations of factory work. Yet frequently such conceptual equipment is irrelevant to the type of work under analysis. It seems that factory work is classical also in this pathological sense: many industrial sociologists seem to think there is no other sort. Nor is this all. It often appears that the stereotype of factory work is that of men working in large factories in heavy industry or on assembly lines. Yet very many factory workers are women; much factory work is in small factories employing few workers; and much factory work should be described as light – it involves the assembly of electrical components or electrical goods, food products, paper and packaging products, plastic products, etc.

In what sense then is factory work *the* stereotypical work under industrialist capitalist societies. There are a number of answers to this question.

(1) Factory work was the form of work which seemed to exemplify the principles of work organization characteristic of industrial economies. It

seemed, at the same time, to represent the most drastic break with earlier work forms and to articulate the shape of things to come. More than work in mines or agriculture or service industries, factory work represented the essentially modern forms and principles of work organization and design. Factories were also *the* characteristic work organization around which different theories seeking to explain the new work forms were developed.

(2) Factory work was a form of work which seemed to generate distinctive worker responses, of satisfaction, alienation, anomie or whatever. Early analyses of factory work suggest that this form of organization represents a break with traditional forms of exploitation or worker misery. For some this characteristic form of work-based suffering stemmed from the oppression of the line, or of technology; for others it was the isolation and alienation of the 'modern' worker. Probably for most of those who studied factory work such work clearly articulated the priority emphasized by Henry Ford: 'Machines alone do not give us mass production. Mass production is achieved by both machines *and* men. And while we have gone a long way towards perfecting our mechanical operations, we have not successfully written into our equations whatever complex factors represent Man, the human element.' It is precisely because the factory represents an attempt to achieve the synchronization of machine and man, that many researchers see it as a source of an entirely novel form of worker oppression.

(3) As a result of (1) and (2) above – that factory work articulates distinctive principles of organization and design, and that it therefore also generates distinctive forms of oppression and deprivation, it is often argued that this form of work will generate collective resistance and organized conflict; that it may indeed be the seedbed for class conflicts and ultimately for class revolution.

(4) For all these reasons, the sort of work under analysis here has been at the same time the focus of interest of both sociologists and others interested in studying work forms from an academic point of view, and practising managers with an interest in improving productivity, or morale, solving personnel problems, reducing absenteeism, or turnover. Indeed there is a connection between these two sorts of interest: practical managerial interests have frequently facilitated (and sponsored) academic interest in a direct and explicit fashion; and just as frequently, but less obviously, academic interest has tended to adopt the assumptions and problematics of managers.

The major features of factory work are two essential relationships within which factory workers are inevitably involved: relationships of control, and of employment. It is the argument of this chapter that the manner in which these two relationships are designed and applied distinguishes factory work from other sorts of work. We shall consider each relationship in turn, although it will be noted that in practice the two relationships interact with each other.

1. Control

The most obvious aspect of factory work – to observers and participants – is the extent and degree of control to which workers are exposed. Walker and Guest emphasize the fact that 'This whole complex of operations demands the perfect synchronisation of men and machines' (Walker and Guest, 1952, p. 28). This is not to say that control is necessarily the most obvious feature of factory work as it is experienced. For factory workers the most striking feature of factory work is probably boredom, and related to this, fatigue and stress. But these individual experiences derive directly from the fact of control. It is because workers are constrained to repeat short-cycle, simplified and undemanding work operations many thousands of times a day at a pace determined by a line, and in a manner specified by the tool or machine, that boredom and fatigue develop. Control is a central feature of factory organization and of worker experience. But in order to develop our consideration of these aspects of factory work we must explore two interrelated questions: why is control necessary, and what exactly is control?

(i) The subdivision of work

A major reason for control assuming such importance within factory organization is because work is subdivided. Because the work process is fragmented, because labour is divided, there automatically arises the need to reintegrate and synchronize operations. As we shall see below, in the discussion of work design within the factory system, the manner in which work is organized within the industrial factory has varied historically and still varies between societies. Certainly there were periods early on in industrialization when the factory was more of a place where workers were gathered together to continue their independent work, than a place where workers (or employees) were submitted to centralized discipline and work organization. During such early periods the owner took relatively little responsibility either for the employment of the workers in the factory (they were probably subcontracted to a gang-boss and not under the direct employment of the owner) or for the organization and control of work. Gradually, however, this arrangement was modified as owners sought to achieve greater control, at first over time-keeping, embezzlement of products or materials and productivity. Initially, efforts to improve production took the form of efforts to increase the number of hours worked. But soon these efforts were replaced by owners – or their agents, managers – attempting to improve the efficiency of work. This concern for efficiency rather than merely for the number of hours worked, and sheer output, led to concern for the design of work – i.e., for dividing and consequently reintegrating labour.

Clearly even under the early arrangement, management attempted to control workers, but this control focused largely on inculcating 'responsible' work habits among the work-force, most conspicuously in the case of their sense of time, and their time-keeping. But once managers took an interest in dividing and co-ordinating workers' work, a new urgency was added to these control initiatives. Hobsbawn points out that the early entrepreneurs believed, not without some justification, that their labour forces were largely impervious to monetary incentives, reluctant to work in the way which suited the entrepreneur or indeed to enter employment at all. It was therefore logical for employers to use compulsion, non-economic as well as economic, to recruit the labour force and to do it at work (Hobsbawn, 1968, pp. 351–2).

Interestingly Hobsbawn argues that the increasing use of machinery in the early factories served to distract entrepreneurs from the advantages that could accrue from attempts to increase workers' efficiency. That productivity could be increased through work design and regulation, rather than simply through long hours, discipline, mechanization and incentives was not immediately realized. As Hobsbawn notes, while such an attitude might not be surprising, given the staggering increases in production that could be achieved through mechanization alone, in fact, as great improvements in efficiency could be achieved through work design and work flow. The economic down-turns of the early 1870s, and particularly during the Great Depression of 1873–96, forced employers to seek new ways of increasing productivity and cutting costs. The result was that employers turned to 'intensive' rather than 'extensive' methods of increasing efficiency – i.e., rather than merely increasing hours or cutting wages, they looked for ways of increasing the efficiency with which the work was done. For the first time employers began to see the advantages of taking responsibility for work design. The result was an attitude of mind to which the ideas of Taylor (see below) and other work design specialists could appeal.

Once management took responsibility for work design it involved, in one way or another, the attempt to divide and reintegrate labour. The manner in which this was done is described below. The important point to make at this stage is that such fragmentation of work brought with it, not merely problems of discipline and security, but problems of synchronization. If workers specialize and carry out discrete aspects of a task once performed by one person, there is a need for someone else to perform the job of regulation, control, timing and integration previously performed by the craftsman as part of his normal working practice. As Marx, in a famous passage, observes: 'All combined labour on a large scale requires, more or less, a directing authority, in order to secure the harmonious working of the individual activities, and to perform the general functions that have their origin in the combined organism, as distinguished from the actions of its separate organs. A single violin player is his own conductor; an orchestra requires a separate one' (Marx, 1954, p. 313). Once labour is divided, direction and regulation become discrete and specialized functions. Indeed it is only when work is divided that management develops any specialized function at all. The fragmentation of shop-floor work and the emergence of management are separate aspects of one development.

Furthermore, work control within the factory follows from the fact that within the factory one category of person – the employers – are employing others in order to achieve a given level of production, or of profit. Employers and managers therefore have an intrinsic interest in directing employee work, and in seeking to maximize efficiency. As Marx notes: 'The labourer works under the control of the capitalist to whom his labour belongs; the capitalist taking good care that the work is done in a proper manner, and that the means of production are used with intelligence, so that there is no unnecessary waste of raw material, and no wear and tear of implements beyond what is necessarily caused by the work' (Marx, 1954, p. 180).

(ii) The direction and organization of work

The second major necessity for control within the factory follows from the fact that workers' labour is divided, but stems not from the need to reintegrate disintegrated jobs but from the need to direct and organize the work in the first place. So long as the worker is submitting to the supervision and direction of another – the employer – then there will be a need for the employer to direct and motivate the worker's labour. What this means, is that the factory worker is not selling a precise commodity or product to the employer in exchange for his or her wage: what is being exchanged is a potential, a willingness to work as the employer directs. Again, Marx noted that this is a crucial feature of work organization under capitalism (it is also a feature of much work organization under state socialism). 'What the working man sells is not directly his labour, but his *labouring power*, the temporary disposal of which he makes over to the capitalist' (Marx, 1968, p. 207).

Since workers sell only a power, a willingness to work as directed, or a potential, the employer must necessarily establish what should be done, how often, and in what manner. Employers cannot be left to their own devices, for without organization, there would be no work done since no one would know what to do once work was organized on principles other than those of established crafts.

If the first sense of factory control is the control of synchronization and integration, the second sense of control is the specification of work – that is, getting workers to do what is required of them, in the right quantities and to the right standards. Much of this can be done by rules, by job descriptions and by supervision. But much more of the specification of workers' efforts is achieved through the technology of work and through the design of work systems. A work tool, or a machine, for example a typewriter, is not only a way of increasing the quantity of output, it is also a way of standardizing the nature and quality of the output. Decisions about what to do and how to do it are now built into the machine. The worker becomes an *operative*.

(iii) The nature of relationships between management and workers

The third need for control is more contentious. Some theorists might deny it altogether. But at least in Marxist analyses of the factory it assumes major significance. It concerns the existence of an essential conflict between employees and employers, a conflict based on the discrepancy between the cost of labour and the value of labour's product. This is very clearly stated in Marx. He writes:

> The directing motive, the end and aim of capitalist production, is to extract the greatest possible amount of surplus-value, and consequently to exploit labour-power to the greatest possible extent. As the number of the co-operating labourers increases, so too does their resistance to the domination of capital, and with it, the necessity for capital to overcome this resistance by counterpressure. The control exercised by the capitalist is not only a special function, due to the nature of the social labour-process, and peculiar to that process, but it is, at the same time, a function of the exploitation of a social labour-process, and is consequently rooted in the unavoidable antagonism between the exploiter and the living and labouring raw material he exploits. (Marx, 1954, p. 313)

For Marx, control in the factory is necessitated by the class antagonisms which exist definitionally between worker and employer. As a result of this constant potential resistance, employers can never assume the willing co-operation of their work-force.

From a Weberian perspective also, conflict between worker and employer is seen as inherent in working relationships and a factor in the design and achievement of control. While disagreeing with Marx's emphasis on the extraction of surplus value as the basis for class antagonism, Weberians note that relationships between workers and employers are characterized by competition as each side seeks to improve its relative position. Hill, for example, argues that: 'Since wages are costs which affect profits and profits can be raised at the cost of wages, those whose interests lie in maximising wages are in competition with those concerned to raise profits. Both parties may be presumed to be acting in accordance with the dictates of rational economic action, but the rational appraisal of interests made by workers and managers pull in opposite directions' (Hill, 1981, p. 3).

There is a close relationship, empirically, between the perception of this conflict or competition, on the part of management, and the subsequent design of work. As Alan Fox (1974) and others have pointed out, when senior managers distrust their employees (i.e., see them as holding opposed or competitive interests) they can manifest this distrust by designing and imposing work roles which leave little scope for discretion. When this occurs of course, the distrusted employees, inhabiting work positions with little discretion or creativity, tend to respond by also recognizing a conflict of interest between them and those who design their work and dominate them. They therefore may withdraw what little commitment they had made to the enterprise. Such a withdrawal will confirm senior manager's preconceptions and add a further twist to the spiral of distrust and regulation.

These three bases of control within the factory result in different types of control. We shall now address the second major question in this section.

2. What is control?

Control within the factory has a number of different aspects. It is in fact not one process, but three, and each aspect relates to one of the factors mentioned above. The employer controls the direction, design, allocation and speed of work. The need for such control follows from the fact that management has an interest in the efficiency (profitability) of workers' work, and will therefore seek to direct precisely what work activities occur. Such control follows from the fact that in most cases, efficiency and high levels of productivity are seen as being best achieved through a system of work design which effectively separates the activities of planning and management from execution – the execution of work tasks being organized around principles of fragmentation, and simplification. Walker and Guest remark that the average mass-production factory job may be summarized as having the following ingredients: (i) mechanical pacing of work; (ii) repetitiveness; (iii) minimum skill requirement; (iv) predetermination in the use of tools and techniques; (v) minute subdivision of product worked on; (vi) surface mental attention (Walker and Guest, 1952, p. 12). Clearly a major implication of such work features is that they imply an almost total removal of decision-making discretion. This is to be placed elsewhere – in management. As F. W. Taylor, the proponent of a major school of work design known as Scientific Management, remarked:

> To work according to scientific laws , the management must take over
> and perform much of the work which is now left to the men; almost

every acts of the management which enable him to do his work better and quicker than he could otherwise. . . . Under Scientific Management the 'initiative' of the work men (that is, their hard work, their good will, and their ingenuity) is obtained with absolute uniformity and to a greater extent than is possible under the old system; and in addition to this improvement on the part of the men, the managers assume new burdens, new duties, new responsibilities never dreamed of in the past. *The managers assume, for instance, the burden of gathering together all of the traditional knowledge which in the past has been possessed by the workmen and then of classifying, tabulating, and reducing this knowledge to rules, laws, and formulae which are immensely helpful to the workmen in doing their daily work.* (Taylor, 1911, reprinted in Davis, 1972, p. 27 our emphasis)

Secondly, the fact that employers necessarily purchase from their employees only a *potential* – labour *power* – generates a need for another type of work control. Workers must be not only directed, and work content specified: they must also be *motivated*. The reason for this is simple. However stringent and precise the specification of work (in rules, procedures, technology or work design), however oppressive and rigorous the processes of supervision and quality control, there will always remain some degree of worker discretion. Employers always rely, to a greater or lesser degree, on the goodwill of the worker. The more employers try to overcome real or anticipated worker recalcitrance, through the design and imposition of tight specifications and constant surveillance, the more they are likely to need such safeguards as workers withdraw their willingness; 'working to rule', after all, is a form of resistance, not a basis for co-operation. The employer, in short, can never eliminate the need to rely upon the motivation, attitudes or work orientation of the employee. Without some degree of acquiescence, or willingness or preparedness to co-operate, the employer finds that the employee's potential is not capable of being realized in intensities and forms which she or he – the employer – desires. In other words, the subjectivity of the employee is – and must be – an inevitable ingredient in the organization of work, and in the achievement of production at work, in relations between managers and workers, capital and labour. As such it must be a central element in control relationships. As Lazonick puts it: 'The subjectivity of workers becomes an objective factor in the appropriation of surplus-value in the capitalist workplace' (Lazonick, 1978, p. 3).

A major implication of this requirement – that employers depend on employees' motivation – is that management must seek ways of ensuring that the basic conflict of interest between management and workers is not apparent to the employees. Their acquiescence must depend considerably upon their not fully appreciating the extent to which work design and work arrangements are organized to achieve interests which compete with their own. As Burawoy expresses it: 'The dilemma of capitalist control is to secure surplus value while at the same time keeping it hidden.' (Burawoy, 1978, p. 261). The practical implications of this dilemma are of considerable importance in understanding management's interest in developing or devising new forms of work design or work control which can 'tap' worker creativity and willingness. (See, for example, Littler and Salaman, 1984; Cressey and McInnes, 1980.)

Thirdly, and following from the earlier two points, the fact that relations between management and workers are often in practice and always in theory, relations of conflict or competition, means that management, while it may depend on workers, is unable fully to trust them. This introduces the need for a third element of control – supervision and surveillance. The management of worker resistance is an inevitable aspect of the management function. What this means in effect is that management cannot simply take for granted the quantity or quality of workers' work efforts. These must constantly be supervised, and workers must constantly be encouraged (or pressured) to comply with managerial dictates and requirements. The work account by Heratzi (1977) is particularly useful in illustrating this tendency. The author documents in considerable detail the way in which management attempts to ensure compliance with its production requirements, in this case through piece-rate payment systems. It is the need for supervision of quantity and quality of output which most manifests the low trust relations between management and shop floor, and which plays some part in creating the very circumstances which such supervision is designed to deal with (Fox, 1974). Management – and supervision – must take responsibility then not only for work design and organization but for overseeing work operations, for acting as a type of authority within the enterprise.

Some of these aspects of control within the factory are clearly likely to be in conflict with each other. Overt and oppressive supervision may well destroy worker acquiescence and lead to a withdrawal of goodwill. Similarly, the need to specify exactly what needs to be done, and how often, may well lead to greater problems of supervision, as workers seek to exploit what small areas of discretion remain in a largely deskilled work environment. Of particular practical management significance is the conflict between management's need for worker participation in creativity and reliability, and their anxiety that any discretion delegated to shop-floor workers might be used against management to further workers' interests (Littler and Salaman, 1984). There is evidence that this is currently a major management dilemma as Western enterprises attempt to emulate the Japanese system.

Finally, it should be noted that factory control of these three types can be achieved through a wide variety of mechanisms. As we shall see, the design of work itself is a major mechanism of control. Control can also be achieved through rules and procedures, promotion criteria, payment schemes and supervision. But other aspects of organizational functioning, ostensibly not directly concerned with control, may have implications for workers' compliance with management directives. Government policies, as the monetarist experiment of the Thatcherite government reveal, can have a direct impact on workers' willingness to oppose management or to struggle in pursuit of their own interests. Company investment strategies too can have an affect on workers' attitudes, especially when there is a chance of locating production overseas, if home-based labour fails to comply, or threatens to become too expensive.

3. The control and design of work within the factory

Numerous writers have recently debated the various ways in which control can be exercised within the corporation (see Thompson, 1984). In this chapter we will focus on the ways in which control is exercised over factory work and shop-floor employees. The first point to make is the central one: that although conceptually it is possible to separate the processes of control and of work design and organization, in practice these two processes are closely interconnected. For the vast majority of shop-floor employees, the design and organization of work represents and embodies their subordination. Some employees are controlled through rules and procedures; others are left to work according to their professional or craft judgement (suitably hedged about with constraints and safeguards to ensure their 'reliability'); but the majority, certainly of shop-floor workers, are controlled (in the sense of the direction and specification of their work efforts) through the design of work. Probably this is the most significant single characteristic of shop-floor factory work: that the work itself is designed and organized so as to minimize worker discretion and autonomy; and the necessary controls to achieve this are embodied not in rules (which can be flouted or avoided) but in the design of work itself.

We have already noted that in the early days of factory production the owner/employer took little interest in, or responsibility for, work design. To the extent that he or she was interested in levels of output, the average owner was prepared to attempt to improve these by manipulating the length of the working day, rather than by interfering in the design and organization of work. Gradually, however, this changed, as a result of the increasing size of companies, the pressures on profitability and, to some extent, the ascendancy of the industrial engineer. As Hill remarks, these industrial engineers, particularly in the USA, 'felt that the systematic application of engineering principles to factory organisation would find better ways of working and regulate labour more closely, thus raising its productivity.' (Hill, 1981, p. 24). The outcome of these pressures and convictions was Taylorism, or Scientific Management.

F. W. Taylor's Scientific Management argued a number of key principles for work design. First that the work process should be carefully and systematically analysed, and then, in the light of this analysis, broken down into single tasks, or operations. These tasks were to be made as simple as possible, such that they could be performed by (relatively) unskilled workers. Littler (1978) summarizes these principles of Scientific Management as follows: 'maximum fragmentation' of processes or jobs; the 'divorce of planning and doing' (planning now being vested in management); the worker's involvement in preparation or organization of the job; the 'minimisation of skill requirements and job-learning time' and the 'reduction of material handling to a minimum' (Littler, 1978, pp. 188–9). As Littler and many others have remarked, these principles constitute a huge impetus towards the deskilling of factory work.

A direct consequence of these principles of work design is the expansion of the role and responsibilities of management who must now take responsibility for reintegrating and co-ordinating the fragmented jobs. The control implications of Taylorism are obvious: skills, with all their implications for craftsman autonomy are destroyed, worker discretion and decision-making are reduced or eliminated; and management increasingly assumes the 'burden' of work design and work integration. The worker is now required merely to execute the demands of the manager. As Marx, much earlier, expressed it: 'The division of labour within the workshop implies the undisputed authority of the capitalist over men, that are but parts of a mechanism that belongs to him.' (Marx, 1954, p. 336).

The major work of analysis of the implications and ramifications of Scientific Management is Harry Braverman's *Labour and Monopoly Capital* (1974). (See the chapter by Stephen Wood in this volume for an elaboration of Braverman's work.) Braverman's argument specifically, is that Scientific Management is *the* stereotypical approach to work design within the capitalist enterprise, since it offers management two interrelated advantages of enormous significance: it cheapens labour by deskilling it, and thus making transfers between jobs much easier, and reducing training time; and it firmly and unequivocally vests control in management. It is therefore not simply a neutral, engineering system applied to work study and design, but a central aspect of class relations as the owners (or their agents) attempt to dominate and control those whom they are exploiting.

It is important that the broad outlines of Braverman's thesis be grasped thoroughly. As Giddens remarks:

> The crux of Braverman's thesis is that managerial control is obtained above all via the effects of the divisions of labour. It is mistaken, Braverman, argues, to talk about the division of labour in general. The 'social division of labour', which is found in all societies, has to be clearly distinguished from the 'technical division of labour', which is specific to capitalism. While the social division of labour involves the separation of

tasks devoted to the making of whole products, the technical division of labour fragments the labour task into repetitive operations carried out by different individuals. The expansion of the technical division of labour, in Braverman's view, is the most basic element in extending managerial control over labour, because knowledge of and command over the labour process are thereby progressively 'expropriated' from workers. Braverman lays a great deal of stress upon the contribution of Taylorism, or 'scientific management', to this process. In Taylorism the operations carried out by the worker are integrated into the technical design of production as a whole. . . .

Braverman shows that the rationality of technique in modern industrial enterprise is not neutral with respect to class domination. It would be difficult to exaggerate the significance of this. For if Braverman's argument is correct, industrial technique embodies the capital/wage labour relation in its very form. Class domination appears as the absent centre of the linkage Weber drew between the rationality of technique and the rationality of the (formally) most 'technically effective' type of organization, bureaucracy. It would follow that bureaucratic domination, and the concomitant powerlessness of workers, are not inevitable features of contemporary organizations; the transformation of the class relations incorporated within the 'technical division of labour' could in principle furnish the basis for the democratic reorganization of the labour process. (Giddens, 1982, pp. 38–39)

Taylor's work design principles were applied reasonably widely both in this country (largely through a consultancy firm called Bedeaux) and in the USA (see Nelson, 1975). But the concept of scientific management is important far beyond the firms in which it was initially installed, for it serves to establish the basic ideas which management approaches to work design reflect and articulate. This is not to say that Taylorism is most important simply as an ideology or theory, though some writers have argued this. It is to emphasize that the basic principles of Taylorism have actually become widespread. They are now increasingly applied both to white-collar office work and factory work (Braverman, 1974; Hill, 1981).

Following scientific management, the next significant movement in work design was that initiated by Henry Ford and known, appropriately, as Fordism. Fordism refers essentially to the development of the assembly line: the principle whereby the speed and flow of work are organized and controlled by management through the installation of a moving 'line' along which the work object moves. The assembly line is usually accompanied by a high degree of standardization. Fordism involves a further development of the control of work through the design of work; it takes Taylorism a step further. As Edwards remarks: 'The Ford line resolved technologically the essential first control system task: it provided unambiguous direction as to what operation each worker was to perform next, and it established the pace at which the worker was forced to work . . .

the line left the workers no choice about how to do their jobs' (Edwards, 1979, p. 118).

Fordism represents, Edwards argues, a distinctive form of control, which he labels technical control. The key feature of such control is that it involves 'designing machinery and planning the flow of work to minimise the problem of transforming labour power into labour as well as to maximise the purely physically-based possibilities for achieving efficiencies. . . . Technical control is structural in the sense that it is embedded in the technological structure or organisation of production' (Edwards, 1979, p. 112). The Ford line is a good example of this: once the line itself controls the pace and speed of work, the workers are no longer controlled by explicit and oppressive foremen, or by elaborate rules and procedures; they are now controlled by technology itself. Personal confrontation is transformed into resistance to the forces of technology, the remorseless, but inanimate, 'line'.

Recent years have also seen a number of developments in work design, including attempts at restructuring the assembly line and rebuilding fragmented tasks (Littler and Salaman, 1984). New technologies also offer management opportunities to re-establish managerial control. The application of electronics to information gathering and handling is occurring on an impressive and increasing scale. Management investment in new technologies, however, does not have uniform consequences for workers.

Child argues that it is possible to isolate four discrete management strategies towards labour which involve the introduction of new technology:

(i) the elimination of labour (particularly direct labour) from the production process altogether;
(ii) the translation of the use of labour from an employment to a contracting-out relationship;
(iii) the retention and development of smaller polyvalent labour forces often in combination with a 'responsible autonomy' form of control and policies aimed at enhancing normative commitment to the employer;
(iv) the intensification of direct managerial control over the labour process typically accompanied by the fragmentation and deskilling of jobs (Child, 1984).

Child notes that more than one of these strategies might be deployed within the same organization at the same time. In particular he points to the possibility of different strategies being pursued with respect to different labour markets. He argues that different strategies towards the use of new technologies will depend on decisions about whether to rely on recruitment from external labour markets, or to upgrade and develop employees from within the organization. It must, however, be remembered that managerial strategies are not simply and solely concerned with the control of labour. Essentially management wishes to put the factors of production to use in the most effective way, and to produce goods or services which are in demand in the market. An important step towards this goal is the reduction of uncertainty associated with a firm's dependence on groups or individuals.

These developments demonstrate a dilemma which continues to dominate management thinking on work design, and to explain the oscillation between relatively tight and oppressive forms of work control and design, and more 'liberal' efforts to encourage and make use of worker creativity and judgement. This is the dilemma described at the beginning of this chapter, between trust and fear, between the need for participation and acquiescence, and the pressures which lead to tight oppressive control. The capitalist employer is constantly faced with the potentially contradictory need both to exploit and oppress the work-force and to recreate the conditions which make this exploitation possible. No degree of work specification can ever remove the essential element of labour power: that it relies ultimately on the worker's willingness to co-operate. Short of removing the worker altogether the employer is sooner or later forced to seek to recover worker willingness by encouraging and harnessing their participation. Numerous management writers, particularly in the USA, have described and extolled the Japanese system of work control whereby workers' commitment is apparently achieved (with enviable consequences for productivity and quality) through the delegation of a degree of responsibility and decision-making to the workers themselves (O'Toole, 1981). Productivity, writes one influential American management expert, can be made to 'bubble up' from the shop floor through changing the organizational structure, such that worker commitment is re-engaged. Taylorism is rapidly reaching the stage where its inherent logic is so alienating that it is becoming counter-productive. 'American firms are being run out of business not slowly but quickly. . . . General Motors is experimenting with small groups of workers – "quality control circles" – to control productivity not because they like them but because they feel they must. If they don't do something new, they will be driven out of business' (Thurrow, 1981, p. 4). Hill (1981) supports this evaluation of the negative consequences of scientific management for encouraging and tapping worker participation, and adds two other consequences: it slows down the firm's response to problems because of the fragmented and unwieldy organizational superstructure, and it produces rigidities in the face of change. In order for management to overcome these pathologies, and to achieve a greater level of worker participation, some genuine degree of delegation to the worker is needed. This too carries problems for management: can they be sure that workers will use this discretionary content 'responsibly'? Will workers be satisfied, having tasted some degree of control with the relatively small amount of authority that has been delegated? Will they start questioning other aspects of management authority? One common answer to these problems is to arrange a form of work enrichment or enlargement which is more cosmetic than real.

This discussion of the problems of consent under capitalist work conditions clearly raises the issue of work structures and forms of work motivation in work organizations within non-capitalist societies. Motivation of workers is, potentially, a problem in all forms of industrial society, since all large-scale differentiated forms of work rely upon the motivation of the employee to some degree. What varies, however, is the way in which this 'problem' is solved (Thompson, 1984).

The preceding sections have considered the component elements of work control within the factory and, in particular, have noted how control in the factory is achieved through work design, especially through technologically-based forms of control. However, such methods carry certain definite and very real contradictions which are articulated in oscillations between deskilling and Taylorism on the one hand, and some degree of delegation on the other. We shall now turn our attention to the second major relationship in which workers are necessarily involved – the employment relationship – and consider, in particular, the way in which variations in the definition of the employment relationship have implications for the contradictions and tensions between principles and elements of control noted above.

4. The employment relationship within the factory

Within the factory workers exchange a willingness to expend their efforts over a set period of time in exchange for a wage. It is this basic exchange relationship – wages, and possibly other benefits in exchange for worker effort – which draws the formally free workers to the factory in the first place, and which keeps them there. By formally free we refer to the fact that workers are not constrained by law, force or indenture to work in the factory; they are formally and legally 'free' to work or not to work, and in theory free to choose where to work. (The chapter by members of the Department of Applied Economics, University of Cambridge, in this volume considers some of the limitations on this theoretical freedom.)

The 'wage effort bargain' constitutes an element – the central element – in the employment relationship, the overall agreement between employer and employee for each party to promise to supply certain commodities and rewards to the other. The effort exchange is only part of this larger relationship because, as we shall see below, on some occasions, in some societies and in some organizations this relationship is defined much more widely than a mere exchange of wages for effort.

The employment relationship within which all factory workers are inevitably involved differs from control relationships in that the latter can only occur because of the reciprocity – the contract between the two parties – implied by the former. They not only vary conceptually however; they also vary in their nature and in the methods by which they are defined and achieved. These points will be expanded below. However, while the two relationships, control and employment, are conceptually separate and are conducted through different procedures, they overlap considerably in their effects. In particular, as we shall see, the manner in which the employment relationship is defined has definite implications for the extent to which workers are controlled, most importantly for their commitment or acquiescence. Because of this effect, management can attempt to manipulate the employment relationships in order to increase worker commitment and compliance.

The employment relationship contains two reciprocal elements: what the employer offers the worker in exchange for his or her work, and how the employee defines his or her contribution – i.e., the norms which operate to determine levels of output. We shall consider these in turn.

(i) The form and extent of work rewards for factory workers

The main point to establish here is the variability in the kinds and number of rewards and facilities that management can offer its employees. For most factory workers in this country during recent years the employment relationship has been defined – on management's part – in minimal terms, in terms of the 'cash nexus'. In other words, management reduces its obligations to a minimum and offers money, and nothing apart from money, in direct and measured exchange for effort: 'The wage packet increasingly is the only link that ties the worker to a grudging commitment to his work, his [sic] bosses, and to society at large.' This cash nexus is 'a brittle strand, liable to wear thin or to snap when the dependability of earnings is threatened, or pay rises fail to keep pace with rising demands' (Westergaard, 1972, p. 162).

But if most factory workers in the 1980s in Britain find that their employer is prepared to offer only money wages, carefully measured against effort or hours of work, plus such other basic facilities or rewards as are required by law – some paid holidays, safety provision, canteen facilities, etc. – it has not always been so, nor is it always this way in other societies. For example, some nineteenth-century work organizations in Britain extended to their shop-floor employees the kinds of provisions normally offered only to white-collar staff, such as pensions, health insurance, housing and so on. One should not overestimate the pervasiveness of this pattern of employment, which by the 1890s and 1900s was restricted to a few Quaker firms and then usually only when large numbers of women and girls were employed. The point is, however, that the employment relationship was not always defined in the manner in which it is currently defined. (For other options, involving a more extensive definition of this relationship tried by employers in Britain, see Littler, 1982, chapter 7.)

In other societies, the provision by employers of non-financial rewards and facilities for shop-floor employees is more strikingly apparent. In Japan, for example, the employment relationship for full-time employees of large-scale corporations is defined very broadly. Dore remarks, on the basis of a study of Hitachi, that 'The employment relationship is not *specific* (as an exchange of labour and cash) but *diffuse* – affecting the whole man. The employer "takes care" of his employees and they respond with a general loyalty.' Dore goes on to remark that in Hitachi, welfare provision is not personal and/or arbitrary but is actually part of the employer's contractual obligation to the employees: 'The favours that count materially – the welfare benefits, the housing, the educational loans and the dormitory accommodation for one's children studying in Tokyo are all specified and contractual: their distribution rule-bound and institutionalised as employee "rights"' (Dore, 1973, pp. 270 and 274). These provisions are augmented by Hitachi employees' incorporation within a system of payment and high job security, which includes an annual increment based on seniority, merit and family responsibilities unknown amongst shop-floor factory workers in this country.

From the employers' point of view the range of benefits that can be offered vary in their nature and extent: we shall refer to this as the pervasiveness of the employment relationship – i.e., the number of facilities and rewards the employer offers or promises the obedient and congenial employee. The pervasiveness of the employment relationship varies considerably between working-class and middle-class categories even within the same organization.

Employers' attitudes towards the employment relationship are no doubt partly defined by contemporary management fashion and philosophy; but they are also part of a conscious management strategy. It is probably not only sociologists who have noticed that pervasive employment relationships can play an important part in generating worker commitment and in increasing worker dependence.

A number of writers have argued that the potential role of a pervasive employment relationship in tapping the commitment of the work-force is strongly influenced by the degree of *dependence* of the workers on the source of the welfare provision. In other words, if workers are unable to obtain the rewards offered by their employer elsewhere – from other employers or from the state – then their dependence on, and subsequent submission to, that employer will be much greater. The way in which the employment relationship is defined by management can play an important part in affecting worker commitment.

Edwards (1979) makes the same point. One of the two types of structural control which he isolates is bureaucratic control. Bureaucracy, of course, has implications for both the design of control and for the employment relationship. By bureaucratic control we refer on the one hand to control through formalized, explicit rules and procedures, to the rule of impersonal, standardized regulations which the bureaucrat simply applies as and when appropriate (i.e., a form of control), and on the other hand to a form of employment relationship emphasizing career and security for the reliable and 'responsible' employee. (For a useful discussion of these aspects of bureaucracy, and the relationship between bureaucracy and Scientific Management, see Littler, 1982.)

Edwards notes that bureaucratic control, like technical control, is embedded in the structure of the organization such that it appears to be over and above the predispositions or passions of individual senior bureaucrats. Unlike technical control, bureaucratic control is embedded not in technology, work design or work flow, but in job descriptions, rules, procedures, appraisal schemes, promotion and transfer panels, wage scales and so on: 'In its most fundamental aspect, bureaucratic control institutionalised the exercise of hierarchical power within the firm. The definition and direction of work tasks, the evaluation of worker performances, and the distribution of rewards and the imposition of punishments all came to depend upon established rules and procedures, elaborately and systematically laid out' (Edwards, 1979 p. 131).

However, for our purposes it is not the control aspects of bureaucracy that are most interesting at this stage, but its implications for the employment relationship. Clearly this form of organization has very definite effects on employee commitment, through establishing a dependence upon very specific organizational rewards: career, promotion, security, pensions, etc. To refer to Edwards again, he notes that bureaucratic forms of control encourage the 'responsible' employee to identify with the company, learn the rules and adjust his or her behaviour accordingly: to become the organization man – or woman.

(ii) Norms of effort

We shall now turn our attention to the other side of the exchange, to the factory level employees. How do they see this relationship? First, while it may be the case, as Marx and others suggest, that the employment exchange is inherently exploitative of the employee – in the sense that neither he or she can be paid the full value of a day's production because the capitalist employer must take some sufficient proportion of this value in order to finance both himself and future production and investment – this essential exploitation is invisible to the worker. As Burawoy expresses it: 'There is no separation either in time or space between necessary and surplus labor time. This distinction . . . does not appear as such in the organisation of production. It is invisible (possibly implausible too) to both worker and capitalist' (Burawoy, 1978, p. 260). He hastens to add that its effects are very apparent, but as a process it is hidden.

Secondly, workers are dependent upon capitalists, their employers. Exploited they may be, within the employment relationship, but they nevertheless depend upon this relationship for their subsistence. In other words, the experience of work, of work control and design and of the employment relationship is not sufficiently explicit and visible to encourage the factory employee to define his or her experience in terms of outright exploitation. It is not as if, like the feudal serf, the worker is being required to work a set number of days on the lord's field. The extraction of surplus happens obscurely. And the dependence of the worker on the employer for his employment (a dependence which is greatly increased during periods of recession and high unemployment) further confuses the possibility that workers will define their relationship with their employers in terms of total conflict. (None of this is to suggest that factory workers are happy; that they do not experience, on a massive scale, frustrations, work boredom, danger, insecurity, etc., or that they are not frequently greatly aggrieved by their circumstances. But the existence of such responses is not the same as an appreciation of the daily, constant exploitation as defined by Marx.)

How then do workers approach the employment relationship, or the effort exchange? All the evidence suggests that to a surprising degree, while this relationship is seen as a major arena of negotiation – bargaining over wage rates, conditions, timings of jobs, etc. – it is also defined normatively, i.e., it is not seen *purely* contractually, although it tends in this direction. Two authors who have made a study of the moral motions underpinning negotiations and expectations of the employment relationship comment that 'Relations between managers and workers, and employers and trade unions, are commonly regarded as a notably hard-headed and unsentimental area of social life. Yet the arguments of those involved in industrial relations are shot through with essentially moral terminology. In particular appeals to the idea of *fairness* abound' (Hyman and Brough, 1975, p. 1).

Custom and practice undoubtedly play an important part in determining wage norms and the extensive morality which clouds workers' attitudes towards the employment relationship. But also of relevance are larger ideological elements defining the nature (and for many the inevitability) of capitalism, the legitimacy of property, and of pay differentials; and the workers must have an appreciation of what is possible, what they are likely to be able to obtain within a particular company and within a particular historical period.

Regardless of the role of beliefs in ensuring the acquiescence of workers, it is also necessary to appreciate to what extent the *practices* of work are such as to ensure a level of co-operation. A number of authors have drawn attention to the way in which work activities – and in particular the interdependence of fragmented work activities – produces real co-operation. This is evident in Cavendish's analysis, where the work of any one worker – and therefore his or her productivity and payment – is dependent on the work of others. And this inter-worker dependence is matched by a developing working interdependence of supervision and shop-floor employees. Arguments such as these explain worker acquiescence not in terms of their ignorance, or of their having been duped by ideologies of co-operation, but in terms of the real basis of co-operation in and at work which exist even within the capitalist work process; possibilities which are precisely the explanation for management efforts to increase motivation by increasing worker participation in work decision-making.

The evidence is that workers' definitions of the employment relationship reflects (if distortedly) the definitions inherent in management's formulation of the relationship. Hobsbawm has suggested that it took workers some time to shake off pre-industrial, custom-based approaches to the effort exchange, and to replace these with more market-based calculations. They were slow to learn the 'rules of the game', he suggests, and while they began to structure union organization and strategy in more coherent and self-interested terms towards the middle of the nineteenth century, the ideal of a 'fair day's work for a fair day's pay' has never entirely disappeared.

What did play a major part in destroying traditional 'custom and practice' definitions of fair and reasonable effort–exchange agreements was the development of Taylorism. A very important, but little noted consequence of Taylorism, was that by destroying existing skilled, or craft jobs, the way was opened for new and harsher effort standards for the largely fragmented and deskilled jobs, and for which there was no historic precedent (Littler, 1978, p. 198).

5. Conclusion

This chapter has attempted to achieve a number of objectives, and has ranged quite widely over a number of issues that arise in the course of sociological discussion of factory work. We started with a consideration of the importance of factory work to sociological studies and theories of work, and to industrial, capitalist societies. It was noted that in a sense factory work had become *the* stereotypical form of work in such economies, and in sociological analyses of such economies. There are advantages and disadvantages to this: we shall consider later in the volume just how far the conceptual and theoretical approaches which have been brought to bear on this sort of work – and which have been considered in this half unit – are applicable to other sorts of work. Has industrial sociology's preoccupation with factory work left a distorting image for our analysis of other forms of work and employment?

The analysis of factory work in this chapter was conducted in terms of two basic relationships which apply – in widely differing forms – to all sorts of work, so long as the worker is in employment. The two relationships which were discussed in some detail were those of control and employment. The section on control tried to raise a number of questions: What is control in the factory? Why is it necessary? What are its constituent elements? How is control achieved? Particular emphasis was placed on the possible contradictions between the mechanisms for achieving different aspects of control, notably specification (direction), and worker acquiescence. The close relationship – at least for factory workers – between the mechanisms of control and the design of work and work technology was noted, and led to a consideration of current movements within work design.

The employment relationship was considered largely from the point of view of management definitions of management responsibilities in this relationship, and employees' definitions of what constitutes a fair and equitable exchange bargain. The role of normative factors in this equation, at least from the side of the work-force, was noted. The particular emphasis of this section was on the role of employment relationships in supporting or undermining control mechanisms. The Japanese model, briefly mentioned here, furnishes a dramatic example of the potential role of the employment relationship in establishing worker commitment.

CHAPTER TWO

Agricultural work

PETER HAMILTON

Introduction: Agriculture and industrial societies

Unlike the sorts of work referred to in most of the rest of this book, the work of the majority of the world's population is not carried out in factories, shops, offices, mines or in people's homes: the principal employer of the world's labour is *agriculture*. In general terms we can say that the primary locus of work in pre-industrial societies is the land and the domestic environment; whilst in industrial societies this locus shifts increasingly to the factory, office and shop.

Industrialization does not do away with agricultural work, of course, but it does change its *nature*, and alters the socio-economic base on which its distinctive structures and organizations are built: the family, the farm, the village, and the patterns of ownership and control of land used for growing crops. Industrialization and capitalism changed – and continue to change – the socio-economic structures in European societies within which agricultural work takes place, and agricultural work is socially organized in terms of these structures. Agricultural work is one of the oldest and most widespread types of socially organized human activities: it is thus infinitely more complex as a social form than, for example, industrial work, office work or any of the more recently developed forms of work organizations. We are primarily concerned here with agricultural work in European societies such as Britain and France, where it is possible to identify different patterns of social structure influencing the way agricultural work is organized. We are thus concerned with a discussion of European capitalist commercial farming and 'peasant' farming. ('Peasant' has an unfortunate pejorative connotation in English: but here we use the term quite technically, when talking about a small agricultural-commodity producing unit, with a work-force linked primarily by kinship ties; in other words, a peasant farm, as a social organization, is one run solely or mainly by a resident domestic group or 'household'.)

As a result of this interest in the social organization of agricultural work, we also direct our concern towards the other side of that question: the *interrelationship of work organization and patterns of inequality*. For it is clear that, with agriculture, the possession or control of property in the form of land and equipment determines certain features of work organization. The relationship between the farmer and his farm worker is a class relationship. Things are not so simple with the peasant farmer and his household – typically, his family, nuclear or extended. Whilst work organization on the capitalist commercial farm is at least formally identical to that in any other capitalist enterprise, on a peasant or family farm it clearly is not: the internal authority structure of the *domestic* group is of most importance. Evidently, we are concerned here, not with class relationships, but with kin, familial or other relationships.

In pre-capitalist and pre-industrial Europe, the fundamentally agrarian base of society and the prevalence of peasant farms largely concerned with their own subsistence meant that class relationships constituted only a minor segment of the social structure. Within industrial, capitalist societies the situation is reversed: it is social relations based on non-class forms – such as in the peasant farm – that are a minor element of the social structure. And in addition, the peasant farm is located *within* a capitalist economy that involves its members in class-related exchanges with people and organizations outside the domestic group. As you will by now have noted, we have thus come to another of the basic questions raised in this book: in looking at these two forms of agricultural work organization we are also concerned with the *kinds of relationships between those involved in work*.

However, it is only recently that the fundamentally agrarian nature of much human social organization (we must exclude primitive or 'simple' hunter-gatherer societies from consideration here) has been changed by the emergence of urban industrial societies. Although Britain, for example, saw the proportion of this active population engaged in agriculture fall below 40 per cent by the 1850s, France was still employing over 42 per cent of its work-force in farming in 1911, Italy about 58 per cent, Germany[1] around 35 per cent and the USA about 38 per cent, whilst the less developed European countries, such as Poland and Romania, continued to have more than three-quarters of their working populations in agriculture at this time. By the early 1980s the North American and West European states had almost all reduced their agricultural populations to very much lower proportions of the work-force. In Britain and the USA, farmers and agricultural workers accounted for less than 3 per cent of the active population, in France for under 10 per cent, in Italy for about 13 per cent and in West Germany some 5 per cent. Eastern Europe remains an area where large agricultural populations continue to be present –

[1] The area covered by both West and East Germany and some of France (Alsace and Lorraine).

Bulgaria, for instance, employing 33 per cent, Romania 45 per cent and Yugoslavia 37 per cent of the work-force in agriculture at the beginning of the decade. (A number of different sources, too numerous to list here, have been used for this data: e.g., UN demographic data, EEC agricultural data, national censuses and the estimates of other scholars.)

Industrialization typically generates a reduction in the farm labour force, as workers migrate towards the higher incomes offered by urban industrial work, and as new techniques are introduced, involving machines, chemicals and improved plant and animal species, which mean that more food can be produced using less labour. Furthermore, as a society becomes more industrialized and increases its per capita income, its population spends a lesser proportion of its total income on food. Economic development therefore reduces the contribution of agriculture to a nation's Gross Domestic Product – to such a point that, as in the case of Britain, a farming population of about half a million people, representing only some 2.8 per cent of the active population, produces no more than 3 per cent of GDP. The differences in the types of agricultural work which obtain in societies where 3 per cent of the population work in farming, as compared to those where 85 per cent of the population are in this sector, are necessarily rather extreme. But it is important to recognize that such differences are underpinned by clear social-structural differences which result from the predominance of either industrial or agricultural production. Those societies which are predominantly industrial exhibit a class structure based on the possession of non-landed property, and for the most part have a large urban working class, a large intermediate 'service class' of supervisors, managers, bureaucrats, etc., and a small and often vaguely defined upper class, within which are to be found the large agricultural landowners; the latter represent only a fraction of the power of the ruling class, amongst whose members will be included the much more numerous representatives of other forms of capital. By contrast, an agrarian society will most often be marked by a large peasant class, a very small urban working class and an even less significant urban middle class, all topped by the major landowners who are likely to dominate the economy and political system.

My purpose in this chapter is to discuss the organization, design and structure of agricultural work within the major industrial societies, with greatest attention being given to the social structure of agriculture in Western Europe.

Agricultural work in advanced industrial societies: empirical evidence

If we examine the types of agrarian structures which have developed in the advanced industrial societies of Western and Eastern Europe, North America, Australia and certain parts of Asia we can distinguish three main structural forms: capitalist commercial farming, collective and state farming and peasant farming. Each form involves different and distinctive types of work relationships, of the division of labour, and of land ownership and control. It is important to note, however, that in practice most advanced industrial societies exhibit a mixture of these agrarian structures. Historically, the trends of economic development have led to an expansion of the role of the first two forms, at the expense of peasant farming. In Western Europe, the gradual disappearance of peasant farmers has been accompanied by the rise of capitalist commercial farming, and it is to a more detailed examination of this that we now turn.

Agricultural employment in Western Europe: changes in the social organization of agricultural work

First, let us look at *employment* in agriculture, as this indicates some clear differences between the principal European countries. In Britain in 1900, the proportion of the total active population employed in agriculture was already down to about 10 per cent. Many historians would say that this was a direct result of the industrial revolution, which had produced a huge flow of labour into the cities, though it was also bolstered by massive increases in agricultural productivity, which came from the application of rational scientific and technological principles to farming.

In France, as we have seen earlier, 42 per cent of the work-force was employed in agriculture in the first decade of the twentieth century. In Italy the figure was about 60 per cent, whereas in Germany it had declined to about 35 per cent. Clearly, the fact that these societies were much later on the road to industrialization than Britain is an important element in explaining these statistical disparities. Industrialization, however, not only created a huge demand for labour: it is also linked very closely to what demographers call the 'demographic transition', the group of processes by which birth and death rates drop, population increases and life expectancy is extended. Thus the picture of agricultural employment around 1900 – by which time the first throes of industrialization had worked themselves out in these countries – is one in which the proportion of the work-force engaged in farming is subject to the two conflicting pressures of, on the one hand, a rapid *increase* in the rural population following on from the demographic transition, and, on the other, an industrialization process 'sucking' people out of the rural areas into the towns.

These proportions of the population engaged in agriculture need to be put a little more into context, by reference to *the social organization of work*. Crucially, perhaps, patterns of land tenure should be examined. The pattern of land tenure in Britain was one dominated by the great estates of noble and gentry landlords. In 1800 these landlords owned about three-quarters of the land: there were some English 'peasants', but they were a very insignificant proportion of the agricultural population. The great estates were farmed in substantial units by yeoman farmers on commercial and business-like lines – in Britain, as one historian has put it, 'a *capitalist* agricultural economy [sprang] ready armed from the great manorial aristocratic system' (Le Roy Ladurie, 1979, p. 134). By contrast, the rural areas of Germany, Italy and France were, with some exceptions, far less dominated by great estates of the British type. Where such estates existed, they depended less on a productive and commercially orientated class of tenant farmers than on a peasantry still, in many parts, tied to feudal customs, duties and obligations. The *predominant* form of land tenure in these countries was the small parcellized holding supporting a peasant family whose main aim was the need to ensure subsistence. Only secondarily were such families concerned to secure a cash income to purchase things which could not be produced domestically and to pay state taxes or other levies such as the tithe. Small, family-based farms are in no way inherently anti-commercial, but the problem with most of the small peasant holdings in Germany, France and Italy was that they practised a static form of agriculture which had not really changed since the feudal period and was adapted – in many ways quite rationally – to the well-known Malthusian threats of famine, death, war, epidemic and the periodic depredations of the state. The American historian Eugen Weber makes this point very forcefully in discussing the modernization of rural France:

> Since for a long time they recognized few changes indeed as suitable, the peasant masses were widely regarded as passive, stubborn and stupid. Yet we can see now that their narrow vision was the vision of frightened men in desperate circumstances; that the village was a lifeboat striving to keep afloat in heavy seas, its culture a combination of discipline and reassurance designed to keep its occupants alive. Insecurity was the rule, existence consistently marginal. Tradition, routine, vigorous adherence to the family and the community – and to their rules – alone made existence possible. The village was an association for mutual aid. Lands, pastures and ovens were generally ruled in common; dates for sowing, and harvesting, were set for one and all. Since all *had* to pull together, no deviance could be tolerated. (Weber, 1977, p. 479)

The static condition of agriculture in the peasant farming regions lasted well beyond the mid-point of demographic transition. In some cases it was supported by social, economic and political changes which were, paradoxically, a part of the industrialization and political modernization of continental Europe. In France, for example, the revolutions of 1789 and 1848 unleashed a massive subdivision of land ownership from which the peasantry were principal benefactors. De Tocqueville called the equal-inheritance laws of Napolean's state a 'land-mincing machine', but they seemd to offer the prospect of a long-dreamed-for peasant paradise – the ownership of sufficient land to guarantee security for the peasant family.

The existence of a divergent – or, more accurately, many divergent – peasant cultures in rural Europe forms another base from which to explain the differing modes of agricultural development, as between the continent and Great Britain, that are reflected in the raw employment statistics. Whereas Britain was a relatively unified society in cultural terms, France, Italy and Germany demonstrably were not. In 1900 the two latter had only recently become unitary states. France, though a unitary state for much longer, still exhibited many of the characteristics of a colonial empire, where cultures oppositional to that of the urban administrative élite were undergoing a form of subjugation. These oppositional cultures were essentially those of the rural areas, and were one of the reasons why a static agriculture based on small-scale peasant subsistence farms was able to persist until well into the twentieth century.

In England, since the agricultural system was effectively a commercial and capitalist one in most of the country, and there was consequently a high level of interpenetration of rural and urban economy, universal rational principles of time, cost, productivity, loss, work and leisure affected most areas of life (see Macfarlane, 1978). In the isolated and inward-looking peasant farming areas, on the other hand, such rationalistic ideas were slow to penetrate. Values based on specific characteristics of the local culture took a long time to be replaced by the universal and abstract values of the developing capitalist economy.

Time is a good case in point. In a traditional peasant society, concepts of time were relative to both local conditions and the eternal order of the seasons. Past and present might represent a lived continuum, and the concept of 'out-of-date' would have little meaning. Time was measured according to 'natural' and thus *variable* rhythms: peasants hoeing, for example, would take a bite from a loaf of bread, throw it in front of them, hoe up to it, bite and throw again (Weber, 1977, p. 482). Horses and oxen determined the pace of mechanical work, and the limitations of climate and the availability of natural fertilizers dictated how long land should be allowed to 'rest'. Traditional customs (which might go back as little as ten years or as long as five hundred) set aside periods when certain tasks could be performed, and were immortalized in the proverbial sayings which constituted the 'science' of traditional agricultural production. In the Auvergne, for example, during the nineteenth century, the year was divided into two: 'winter, from All Souls to St George's Day (November 1st–April 23rd) and summer, when beasts could sleep out of doors'. In the Franche-Comté, by contrast, summer was divided not into months but into 'times' – a 'time' for going outdoors, a 'time' for haymaking, a 'time' for harvesting. During autumn and winter there were 'times' for sowing and mending, and for communal gatherings (*veillées*) (cf. Weber, 1977, p. 483).

To a traditional peasant farmer, time is work, in the same way as life is work: and all life is devoted to work in order to ensure subsistence, which of course guarantees life. Thus, life is work, and work is life. But once it becomes possible to *rationalize* agricultural work, the connection is capable of being broken. Applying chemicals to the land means that it does not have to 'rest' for so long. The connection between the 'rest' of man, animals and land is changed. Using machines means that a field can be ploughed in a quarter of the time needed with horses or oxen. But once *money* and time can be linked together, the traditional harmony and unity of work break down completely. If agricultural work is conceived as work for *pay* rather than physical subsistence, then the meaning of work changes. Effort is now measured in terms of the amount of money it produces, and one major consequence is that, being precisely measurable, it can now be 'lost' – a concept which is meaningless in a society where time is a diffuse category. 'Traditional time had no fixed units of measure: there was not even a break between work and leisure. Even the loss of time (comings and goings, pauses, waiting) passed largely unnoticed because integrated in routine and unquestioned . . . land was often counted in the units of man or animal time it took to work it: not a fixed measure but one relative to conditions' (Weber, 1977, p. 482). Ritual and ceremonial activities in a traditional society have a distinct 'pay-off' in terms of their expected contribution to soil fertility, for example, or their functions as means of ensuring group cohesion and solidarity. But once effort can be measured in terms of fixed units of time, people begin to see such activities as a 'waste' of their time, and traditional customs and rituals decline.

But it is not only 'cultural' activities which change as a result of the spread of abstract and universal values about time and work: once work is expected to produce a cash revenue in relation to the effort involved, a great deal of work is seen as no longer 'worth' doing. 'Where work had once encompassed a multitude of undertakings – weeding, mending enclosures or buildings or tools, pruning or cutting trees, protecting young shoots against cattle, splitting fire wood, making rope or baskets – it was now judged by the norms of salaried labour. Tasks that did not yield ready returns in cash were considered not work but pottering, like going around the fields to look them over. Modern people paid others to do them or let them go undone' (Weber, 1977, p. 484).

It is clear that traditional practices concerned with how work is valued and perceived had a great deal to do with the relative stability of peasant farming in Europe, at least until the mid-point of the twentieth century. But once the destructive forces of the national market and the values of industrial capitalism had penetrated the main strongholds of peasant farming (a process completed between about 1950 and 1960), a massive rural exodus was set in train. By 1960 it was in full flow.

At that point in the post-war economic recovery of Europe, the proportion of the UK's total active population engaged in agriculture was down to 4 per cent. In West Germany (not, it must be remembered, the same country in geographical terms as the one mentioned in comparisons for 1900) only 13 per cent of the population was engaged in agriculture. In Italy a massive decline was in train: at the end of the Second World War 43 per cent of the population had been engaged in agriculture; by 1960 the figure was 29 per cent. In France a similar situation was occurring: by 1960, 20 per cent of the population was engaged in agriculture, although numbers were dropping at an accelerating rate. In all these continental countries the rate of decline during the period from 1900 to 1960 had been considerably greater than that in Great Britain, since there had been a massive dose of industrial expansion in the period after 1945.

The period between 1900 and 1960 was also marked by another very important type of development for the peasant farming areas of continental Europe: the shift from a type of static agriculture designed to ensure subsistence, autonomy, independence and stability to a modern form of agriculture based upon the rational application of the factors of production in order to produce commodities for a national market. As a distinctively 'commercial' approach spread through the farming regions of continental Europe, a major reorientation of the structure of agricultural holdings and the farm labour force occurred. Britain was already equipped with a predominantly commercial agriculture in 1900, and subsequently moved rapidly to a situation in which the bulk of farmland is now owned by farmers themselves. This process was already in train in 1900. The great landed estates were feeling the pinch of the agricultural depression which began in the 1880s but continued until the late 1930s. By the end of the First World War many estates were in such a parlous condition that they sold off most of their land – often to their tenants – at knock-down prices. In 1900 about 10 per cent of land was farmed by its owners; by the time of writing (in 1984) about 75 per cent is formed by owner-occupiers. The irony, indeed, is that British agriculture is becoming increasingly based on familial labour and, in that sense, is approaching ever more closely the typical forms of farming in continental Europe. Although an EEC report in 1977 noted that there had been a slight overall *increase* in the proportion of paid as opposed to self-employed labour in European farming, this had been the result of changes in only a few countries, and notably in Italy, where most small family farms in Europe were to be found. Such data still confirm the general trend towards a small number of primarily family-labour farm units, together with a smaller number of commercial capitalist farms.

Naturally, wide divergences remain. If we examine the range of farm sizes (in area terms only – these of course mask variations in business size, which can be quite extreme) we see that the proportion of small and medium-sized farms is much greater in Germany, Italy and France than it is in Great Britain. In 1974, for example, whilst farms smaller than

twenty hectares accounted for only 6 per cent of agricultural land in the
UK, in Italy they accounted for 51 per cent of land, and in Germany for
43 per cent; in France the figure was much lower, at 21 per cent. At the
other end of the scale, farms of over fifty hectares accounted for 80 per
cent of the UK total, 41 per cent of the French, 34 of the Italian, but only
16 per cent of the German.

To sum up: in each of the countries we have been looking at there has
been a rapid decline in the agricultural labour force between 1900 and
1983: the least rapid decline being in the UK, which for obvious reasons
had the least far to go. At the same time the size of farms is continually
increasing in each country, with a simultaneous constant increase in the
size point (for a given level of productivity) at which a farm is viable as a
commercial enterprise.

Having indicated in statistical terms the background to the development of agricultural work in Europe, it is now appropriate to look at
certain characteristics of the 'design of work' in capitalist commercial
farming and peasant farming. My concern here is to identify the main
features of work in each type of farming, and to suggest how each is connected to different types of social relationship amongst workers, and to
the underlying modes of social organization on which such work is
based.

Capitalist commercial farming

Changes in the sizes of farms in Western European societies have not
occurred simply as a result of personal economic forces. Trends towards
larger farms have been encouraged by the state and by farmers' organizations as a method of making farmers more 'efficient' as producers of
foodstuffs. Although the assumption that size brings various economies
of scale with it can be questioned, it has been a touchstone of much
economic policy in capitalist societies that the small farm is a 'problem'
in economic and social terms.

The intellectual background of a belief in the efficiency of large-scale
units has a respectable pedigree. The French Physiocratic economist
Quesnay, writing as early as the end of the eighteenth century, argued
that: 'Land employed for the cultivation of grain crops should be put
together as much as possible in large farms managed by wealthy farmers,
because there is less expenditure in the maintenance and repair of buildings, and proportionally much lower costs and much greater net product,
in big farms than in small farms.'

Since Quesnay's time, the merits of the large versus the small farm have
been extensively debated. But the debate has not been merely an intellectual game: for theories of the 'incorporation of agriculture within
capitalism' have had real consequences in political and economic terms,

influencing the development of state and collective farms in Eastern Europe, and the elaboration of policies designed to benefit large 'efficient' producers within Western Europe. The debate is about the transformation of agricultural work as a concomitant of capitalist industrialization.

Marx, responsible for much of the form in which this debate has been conducted, was perhaps as brilliantly one-sided in his insights about how this rural transformation would take place as he was with those devoted to transformations of the urban sector of industrial production. Yet it remains true that his inability to look beyond the case that best fitted his favourite thesis has been responsible for a certain degree of theoretical confusion about the social development of agricultural production within Western European capitalist societies. For Marx built a theory about the forms which capitalism would take in agriculture with particular regard to what was happening during his own lifetime in Britain. It is not surprising that Britain appeared to Marx to be the lead country in the rise of industrial capitalism, and perhaps no less surprising that industry's counterpart – agriculture – should be seen as similarly indicating the path for all other capitalist societies to follow.

This would not have mattered so much if Marx's ideas about capitalist development in agriculture had simply been confined to projecting trends in British farming. But instead they were directed to predictions about the demise of peasant farming which ignored the historical particularity of the British case. Furthermore, such ideas were translated into practice in a number of societies where the peasantry was thought to be a bar to agricultural progress, and led directly to the creation of state and collective farms whose results have been generally less impressive than either the peasant farms they replaced or capitalist farms.

In the realm of rural development in so-called 'Third World', Marx's ideas have received an even more severe test, as they have been adapted to the situation of peasant societies marked by colonial exploitation as well as to indigenous social and cultural conditions quite different to those in those countries of nineteenth-century Western Europe with which Marx was familiar. Hence the development of agricultural capitalism in such societies has taken forms which are at considerable variance with Marx's predictions, and has led many Marxist development theorists to make quite major modifications to the theses of classical Marxist theory. Indeed, it has even been argued that to take Marx's predictions about the capitalist development of agriculture at face value is to deny that rural development in 'underdeveloped' societies can be differentiated in any significant way from rural development in 'advanced' capitalist societies – the former being simply at a 'lower' level of the process than the latter, and thus at a predominantly 'feudal' rather than 'capitalist' stage in the development of the forces and relations of production.

Thus, despite the problems inherent in his formulations, Marx's prediction of an increasing concentration of the control of farmland in the hands of capitalist entrepreneurs, employing the dispossessed former owners of small peasant farms as agricultural labourers – whilst the landowner is stripped of his role as organizer and master of the production process, becoming no more than a 'receiver of rent' – has for over one hundred years been the focus of debate over the failure of agriculture to follow the same course as manufacturing industry. This debate has called into question the nature of peasant economy and society, of pre-capitalist modes of production, of the transition from feudalism to capitalism and of the demonstrable survival, persistence – and even expansion – of farming based on familial ownership and labour in countries such as Britain and the USA where conditions seemed the most propitious for the creation of large capitalist farms.

Central to the whole debate about *agrarian transition* – as the incorporation of agriculture within capitalism is often termed – is the role of the small or peasant farmers. Do they constitute a type of *transitional* social formation of small proprietors or 'petty commodity producers' whose future role is to become a dispossessed agricultural and urban proletariat? This formulation follows Marx's own, which may be seen as a radical rejection of the 'development problematic' *tout court*. Certain readings of Marx's writings (especially from Volumes 1 and 3 of *Capital*) indicate that he viewed the capitalist development of agriculture as an indispensable element of capitalist industrial development. It is perhaps unfortunate that Marx concentrated his attention on the historical experience of Britain in devising an analysis of capitalist agriculture. His theory of industrial capitalism, in taking Britain as a model which other societies would inevitably follow, led to the rather atypical de-peasantized agriculture of Victorian England being constituted as the prototypical form of agrarian capitalism.

For Marx, capitalist society was inevitably committed by the laws of capital formation to the concentration of the social structure into three distinct classes: rentiers, capitalists and proletariat. The two former classes would eventually merge together as they represented the interests of property and capital. In Victorian England, this type of class structure was already in evidence, especially in the industrial towns. But it was also clearly evident in the countryside, where the advantageous conditions for arable farming in the third quarter of the nineteenth century had encouraged the formation of a tripartite class structure of landowners, tenant farmers and landless agricultural labourers. It is thus not surprising that Marx should have been struck by the apparent symmetry of industrial and agrarian capitalism, and tempted into seeing contemporary rural England as the prototype of the capitalist penetration of agriculture which would eventually be generalized throughout Europe. However, far from being the model for a universal process English agrarian capitalism in its tripartite form has proved to be unique, in essence because it was only in England (and lowland England at that) that the indigenous peasantry was abolished *before* industrialization. As Newby has pointed out:

> Britain and its white-settler colonies (Canada, Australia, New Zealand and – for these purposes – the United States) are distinguished by their very absence of a peasantry, whereas in virtually every other country in the world the peasantry has survived the onslaught of *subsequent* industrialization. The value of the 'English model' of agrarian development is therefore limited in the extreme. *It is the persistence, not the disappearance, of the peasantry which has turned out to be the most distinctive feature of agricultural capitalism.* [My emphasis]

It is important to recognize that Marx's conceptualization of the peasantry constituted the other side of the coin to his model of agrarian capitalism. For Marx, movement towards the tripartite system is only possible through the concentration of land in the hands of a smaller and smaller number of landowners, and the consequent dispossession and proletarianization of peasant farmers. His writings clearly recognize a contradiction between the emergence and rapid expansion of industrial capitalism, and the evolution of a system of landownership whose origins were pre-capitalist. Capitalist society merely introduced new forms of expropriation of the surplus produced by the peasant family: taxes and money rents replaced feudal dues.

Marx's assumption that the tripartite agrarian class structure of Victorian Britain (landowners, capitalist tenant farmers and landless farm labourers) would penetrate every capitalist society has been proved false, largely because his model, Britain, had eradicated its peasantry *before* industrialization (cf. Newby, 1982, p. 7; Hamilton, 1984). Marx was unable to foresee the resilience of peasants in face of the effects of industrial capitalism, and in particular unable to forecast the dire consequences for the tripartite system of the world agricultural depression that was just beginning in the last years of his life.

For Marx, agrarian capitalism was simply a derivative of industrial capitalism. It involved three classes: rentiers (in this case the *landlords*), capitalists (the *tenant farmers*, who supplied the working capital to set up and run their farm businesses) and proletarians (the *farm labourers*, who possessed no land). When Marx was writing, Victorian 'high farming' was in its heyday, particularly in the arable east of England: a system in which the landed aristocracy and the lesser gentry derived their very considerable incomes from renting their farm land to tenant farmers, who ran large farm businesses growing corn and raising meat to supply the growing urban demand for food, and who employed a large number of landless farm workers. The landlord supplied fixed capital; his return was ground rent. The tenant supplied working capital; his return was profit. The labourers supplied their labour, its exploitation by the tenant farmer produced his profit (with the help of the weather and the soil); the labourers' return was wages, and usually precious little of those. The Norfolk four-course rotation of the period of 'high farming' was associated with a clear-cut rural social structure. At its pinnacle was the landlord (typically, at least half the landlords were of noble birth in the 1870s, for instance) whose large estate dominated the territory over which it extended. As Newby has described it, such an estate was 'a functioning centre of political and social influence', involving a 'complex set of proprietorial rights, not only over the agriculture of the estate, but over its minerals, its game, its Members of Parliament, its clergy – in short, over the entire locality and its inhabitants' (Newby, 1977, p. 33). The tenant farmers were 'sturdy yeomen' who aspired to be known as 'gentlemen' farmers and who expected to be treated with deference by the farm workers. Tenants could be evicted by a landlord at little notice, so they in turn deferred to him. At the bottom of the structure were the agricultural labourers, a poorly-paid proletariat who in the arable areas lived in village communities which were a 'hierarchical and authoritarian occupational community' (Newby, 1977, p. 45).

This occupational community was confined to the arable areas of eastern lowland Britain, and was a quintessentially *capitalist* system in its separations of rentier, capitalist and proletarian on clear economic grounds. Although similar systems existed elsewhere, however, it was not *typical* of all farming in Britain or in the other countries where it appeared. Social structures in the rural communities of other parts of Britain were dependent upon a form of agricultural production predominantly concerned with the raising of livestock, and thus a different design of work and a different form of capitalism were evident. In addition, as mentioned, the end of 'high farming' saw the collapse of the rural social structure based on three clearly differentiated classes. Tenant farmers began to buy out their landlords, especially after the 1914–18 War. In 1900 only 10 per cent of farm land in England and Wales was 'owner-occupied'; by the early 1970s about 60 per cent of land was owner-occupied, and the figure had almost certainly exceeded 75 per cent by 1983–4.

Although the tripartite system certainly existed in the pastoral and mixed-farming regions of Britain, the generally smaller scale and size of farm businesses meant that the social structure was less clear-cut. Family labour was a feature of the farming system. Landlords were rather less distant from their tenants; they in their turn were closer to their workers, who were moreover frequently related to them. The dispersed settlement patterns of pastoral areas did not encourage the physical separation of farmer and farm worker in the village community, as occurred in the nucleated settlements of the arable areas. Pastoral areas were also more resistant to economic changes in agriculture, and even less reliant upon the fickle nature of large urban markets. It would frequently be the case that the worker would himself be a smallholder, using his wages to supplement an income derived from his own small-scale farming or horticulture.

In this way, the pastoral areas were more akin to the peasant farming regions of Western Europe, where subsistence agriculture and commercial food production were combined activities. Work was less hierarchically organized, there was greater co-operation among workers because of the lesser differentiation of work tasks, and the farmer himself would frequently join in with certain activities. By contrast, the East Anglian arable farmer was typically a 'manager' who would have compromised his authority over his work-force if he had taken part in their work.

The small-scale owner-occupied family farm was prevalent in western Britain when Marx was writing, and yet he seems never to have considered the problems of applying the tripartite system to predominantly pastoral forms of agricultural production, especially in a situation of diminishing marginal returns. Despite its apparent superiority, tripartite capitalist farming was not to survive agricultural depression – either in Britain or in the other British-influenced areas where it existed, such as America, Canada and Australasia – whereas family farms were resistant to it.

The trend since 1945 has been for British agriculture to become more intensive and commercially organized, whilst diminishing in importance as a capitalist employer of wage labour. Although arable farming is once again highly prosperous, it is now dependent upon many fewer hired workers, and the farmer is much more likely to be a landowner providing both fixed and working capital. Perhaps most significantly, the farm is now quite frequently run by a majority of *family* labour, even in the richest arable areas.

In the immediate post-war period there were about 600,000 full-time agricultural workers in England and Wales. By 1980 this figure had shrunk to about 170,000. The principal sources of this dramatic change have been:

(a) a reduction in the number of farms – from about 360,000 in 1945 to about 200,000 in 1975;
(b) the impact of technological change on agricultural work;
(c) perhaps most important, the demands for labour of other sectors of the economy.

Such factors have led to a change in the labour composition of farms: total numbers of farm workers have declined more rapidly than those of farmers in recent years, and farmers themselves now constitute over one-third of the farm labour force (Winter, 1979, p. 2). The proportion of farms in the medium-size range, employing no hired labour, has increased, no doubt in response to the possibilities offered by the greater mechanization of farm work and a long-term trend towards arable farming, which is considerably less labour-intensive than stock-rearing.

Despite such changes, which suggest a progressive expansion of family *farming* quite large numbers of farm workers remain on the land: mostly low-paid[2] – although highly skilled – workers who find their occupation is accorded low status by the rest of society.

As Newby indicates in two important studies (Newby, 1977 and 1979), changes in technology and the decline in the size of the farm labour force are changing the relationship between the farm worker and his employer. Indeed, there is a continuing long-term decline in the average number of workers employed on each farm. This has two main effects. First, it has changed the nature of control of the work-force; as Newby shows, the increasingly face-to-face relationship of worker and farmer has, paradoxically, made a *paternalistic* style of management more important in modern farming. (By 'paternalistic' Newby means the tendency for the farmer to take a dominant role in many aspects of the farm worker's non-work life.) Secondly, such statistics reveal the increasing trend for farmer and farm worker to be related by kinship ties. Thus, and again somewhat paradoxically in the light of Marx's predictions about the capitalist incorporation of agriculture, capitalist commercial farming is an increasingly familial form of work organization.

The convergence of capitalist and peasant farms

If the structure of capitalist commercial farming in Great Britain during the last 100 years has become more *familial* (i.e., employing a higher ratio of kin-related workers to non-kin-related workers, 'family' workers usually being wives, sons, daughters, etc.), what trends are evident in other countries of Western Europe?

In general terms, as mentioned earlier, all the Western European nations have dramatically reduced their farm labour forces since 1945, against a background of rapidly increasing labour productivity. In countries such as France, Germany, Italy and Spain the existence of a significant peasantry has meant that the creation of a capitalist commercial farming sector has been complicated by large-scale outflows of rural labour to other economic sectors. Yet although economic development has accelerated rural exodus, it has not 'modernized' agriculture in these countries along exclusively capitalist lines.

---

[2] Although farmers' incomes increased over 45 per cent in the period 1981–3, farm workers' wages increased by less than 10 per cent in the same period. In 1984 their basic wage was increased by the Agricultural Wages Board by 4.5 per cent to £87 per week.

For example, a capitalist farming sector has existed for a long time in northern France. But although this sector has expanded since 1945, the form of French agricultural development has been characterized by the rapid 'modernization' of the peasant sector. Before the 1939–45 War French agriculture, outside the 'islands' of large-scale capitalist farming in northern France, was chiefly characterized by small-scale, traditional peasant farms – the so-called *monde paysan* – protected by state policy. After the war it became apparent that the old policies would not work, and by 1958 young 'middle' peasant leaders had taken over the French farmers' union (FNSEA) in order to promote new economic and social policies for agriculture. To put it very crudely, the FNSEA wanted to modernize French agriculture by strengthening the 'middle' peasantry and allowing the 'small' peasantry to disappear, encouraging this by grants for farm rationalization and retirement incentives to the predominantly elderly 'small' peasants.

The effectiveness of this policy can be judged by reference to the decline in the French rural and agricultural populations. Between 1954 and 1975 the agricultural population more than halved, whereas it had taken from 1906 to 1954 to decline from 40 per cent to 23 per cent. Furthermore, during this process of rapid modernization the social composition of the farm labour force has changed markedly. As in Britain, farm work has become more, not less, familial in character, as farm labourers have left agriculture at a higher rate than *chefs d'exploitation* (farmers).

In many parts of France where smaller holdings predominate, both family and hired workers have 'voted with their feet', leaving farms to be run by the farmer alone, with the help of his wife. In 1970, 90 per cent of French farms did not employ any permanent hired workers, whilst only about 3 per cent had more than one worker, and rather fewer than 9000 farms, or 0.56 per cent of the total, had more than five full-time hired workers. Thus, while the familial character of French agriculture has been strengthened, the composition of family labour has changed dramatically, for it is now predominantly the couple, rather than the couple plus their parents, offspring or other kin, who carry out all farm work. It is somewhat ironic that this situation has produced, not a reduction, but an increase, in the intensity of work which farmers perform, as they are forced to exploit more and more of their own labour in order to generate an adequate income.

The example of France, whilst unique in many of its aspects, portrays many of the trends which the other predominantly 'peasant' rural societies have experienced or are in the throes of experiencing. Although the patterns of development in Germany, Italy and Spain, for instance, have underlying in-built differences, the incorporation of peasant farmers within the capitalist economy has generated similar effects on farm structures and the social composition of farm labour.

Conclusion

The nature of agricultural work has changed dramatically in most industrial societies over the last fifty years or so. It is now carried out by a very much smaller number of people, and the Western European countries in particular have seen their villages – which were once the centres of occupational communities of great diversity – emptied of all but a few remaining farmers and agricultural workers. Despite the fact that the basic resources of agriculture remain the same, i.e., land and climate, the application of science and technology has fundamentally changed the sort of work that is done.

Despite many predictions – from Marx onwards – that agriculture would become a form of capitalist production indistinguishable in character from any other form, agriculture in Western Europe has remained obstinately singular in its reliance upon relatively small businesses run by family labour. (Indeed, where conscious attempts have been made to fulfil Marx's predictions – as in the socialist states of Eastern Europe – the creation of large capital-intensive 'factory' farms has proved relatively unsuccessful.) Although the creation of vertically integrated food-producing companies has taken place, and a number of financial institutions have invested heavily in farm land, agriculture has become, generally speaking, less dependent on hired labour and the ownership of farm land has passed increasingly into the hands of farmers themselves. This makes the categorization of farmers as either 'middle-class' or as 'peasants' a difficult conceptual issue. In certain contexts – where, for example, his whole production is destined for sale to a food-processing plant with which he has a contract – the farmer is effectively selling his labour at piece-work rates to a capitalist employer, despite the fact that he owns the means of production (his farm and equipment) and is thus a capitalist producer himself. In this context, the farmer may be seen as a worker, little different from any other craftsman who owns his own tools. Indeed, such a process of quasi-proletarianization has affected, for example, many thousands of small milk producers in countries such as France and Britain who have contracts with dairies or marketing boards to supply their output at fixed cost and have very little control over the marketing of their product (cf. Évrard, 1977; Hassan, 1982). Clearly, such farmers must be carefully differentiated from those who employ hired labour and are in charge of the marketing of their product – although it is certainly true that the existence of a politically controlled market in agricultural products does make the situation of the latter very different from that of, say, a small manufacturing business. These considerations should not blind us to the fact that agricultural workers who do not own any farm property still exist in quite large numbers and represent a distinctive sector of the working class. Their pay and conditions are, in all Western European countries, inferior to those of most of their urban counterparts, and they thus constitute a particularly exploited occupational group.

This chapter has introduced some of the main features of agricultural work, with reference to its social structure and economic base, and has indicated how it differs from most other types of work dealt with in this book. It is as well to remember that even now the majority of the world's population is still engaged in agricultural work, and that in some European countries farming still represents the largest single sector of economic activity.

CHAPTER THREE

Labour market structure and work-force divisions

ELIZABETH GARNSEY, JILL RUBERY AND FRANK WILKINSON

Introduction

This chapter is, in the simplest terms, about the process by which job seekers find employment and employers find workers. Because labour has a price (wages, fees, salaries) the supply and demand of labour are likened to exchange on a market. In the case of the market for labour, buyers have to 'hire' the resource from its owners; thus households are the sellers of labour, employers (or 'firms') the buyers. In this chapter we examine some of the influences which shape the supply of and demand for labour and the reasons why in practice there are separate or segmented labour markets, relatively cut off from each other.

In our society it is a belief which goes back at least to the eighteenth century that properly functioning labour markets ensure efficient allocation of individuals to jobs and provide incentives for people to 'invest' in their education and training. However, even ardent believers in the virtues of free markets accept that labour markets are especially prone to influences which prevent them from functioning according to textbook versions. In this chapter we do not start with the notion of a single, competitive market, as in orthodox economic analysis, but instead aim to show that there are systematic processes at work which segment labour markets, creating inequalities within the labour force which interact with and reinforce social divisions among the population at large, as between age groups, men and women, the healthy and the handicapped, nationals and aliens, the educated and the uneducated, and others. Regional differences are clearly of great importance but are not dealt with directly. In analysing labour market segmentation (LMS) we look first at the labour requirements of employers and at the factors shaping the job structure of a firm or organization within which vacancies occur, or new jobs are created. Demand for labour reflects both constraints within which employing units operate and areas of discretion open to management, providing scope for employment strategies. External constraints include the economic environment and product market, the production process, industrial structure, employment regulation and factors governing the supply of various kinds of labour. Internal constraints also operate, in the form of customs and practices, which create pressures from within on the way in which jobs can be structured and paid. Despite the limits set by the operation of constraints of this kind, the demand for labour is not entirely predetermined; employers can pursue alternative policies in providing jobs of one kind or another and in seeking alternative sources of labour. We provide a schematic summary of the factors affecting job structures and the demand for labour, and compare the analysis with that of the contingency approach in organizational theory.

We go on to look at factors differentiating demand. Primary and secondary employment conditions represent ideal types or 'poles' between which industries, firms and jobs are ranged according to the employment conditions they provide. Technologies and conditions in product markets are factors found to influence the establishment of diverse employment conditions and work contracts; often these factors interact so that the determination of employment segmentation is multi-causal. Reactions to uncertainty are a pervasive influence.

In examining the supply of labour we look at factors which structure and segment the labour force; foremost among these are processes of social reproduction, which have a major influence on the labour market position of men and women. Groups of workers whose bargaining position in the labour market is weak are identified and the reasons for their relative vulnerability is discussed. Disadvantaged workers lack access to 'job shelters' established through collective action by members of occupational and industrial groups. Reasons for the quest for job security and its effects are discussed. Bargaining among groups rather than individual competition emerges as the most prominent feature of labour market segmentation processes.

In the fourth section of the chapter we look at the ways in which supply and demand for labour shape each other in a process of mutual interaction. We examine the position of the individual seeking employment and of those already in employment and the extent to which workers become confined to particular segments of the labour market as a result of their qualifications and work experience. We also discuss the qualities employers seek in their labour force and the methods used to ensure worker co-operation and performance. In this context the assumption that the quality and potential of employees matches that of the jobs in which they are employed is questioned. The labelling of jobs as skilled or otherwise depends not only on the content of the work but on the status and bargaining position of job-holders. Because employers make use of already existing social divisions in the population in allocating low status workers to low grade jobs, job segregation and labour market segmentation give rise to little social conflict. But although they seem to be socially acceptable, these practices incur social and economic costs which are not usually reckoned up.

Finally, we discuss briefly the theoretical implications of the analysis and differences of viewpoint among writers on labour market segmentation.

Evidence on labour market structure

There are a variety of ways of obtaining evidence on labour market structure. Aggregate statistical data can be analysed to test hypotheses, an approach which has been used most extensively in the USA (Gordon *et al.*, 1982). In her book *Labour Markets, Segments and Shelters* (1976) Marcia Freedman shows that the US labour market can be divided into fourteen segments, in which earnings vary in relation to such factors as industry, size of firm, collective bargaining and social characteristics of employees. In the final chapter of the book, she draws conclusions from her statistical evidence and summarizes her argument. There are other approaches to obtaining evidence on labour market structure. Some writers consider that it is important to focus on the level of the firm, examining labour utilization through surveys and case studies. The Cambridge Labour Studies Group has used a 'grass roots' approach, which involved questioning managers about their employment practices and pay policy, and employees about their work. They used interview surveys to explore the characteristics of secondary type employment in selected industries in a variety of local labour markets (Craig *et al.*, 1982; 1984). This research is the basis for the framework of analysis used in this chapter.

It is also useful to focus on a single labour market, as did R. Blackburn and M. Mann in *The Working Class in the Labour Market* (1979) which is a study of non-qualified, male manual workers in Peterborough. Much can be learned by singling out a particular firm for special study, as in Mann's *Workers on the Move* (1973), a case-study of a firm which relocated in a period of economic boom, taking its main work-force with it. This study illustrates both the dependence of employees on the firm and its 'internal labour market' (p. 30), and the dependence of employers on their experienced work-force.

Labour markets can also be examined from a comparative and historical perspective to understand their operation. In *Dualism and Dis-Continuity in Industrial Societies* (1980) S. Berger and M. Piore present comparative material from France, Italy and the USA to illustrate the argument that strategies to deal with economic uncertainty are at the root of labour market differences on the demand side and that managers make use of existing but culturally diverse divisions in the labour force to draw on segmented labour supplies. Other writers have adopted a long-term or historical approach: Edwards, Gordon and Reich (1972; 1982) have attempted to show how American labour markets evolved over time; and Rubery (1978) has pointed out the importance of worker resistance to attempts by managers to control the labour process, and the national differences in this type of struggle. Although many of these studies are American, recent European research has shown the relevance of analysing labour markets in European countries in terms of segmentation processes (Wilkinson, 1981).

Contrasts between the labour market segmentation approach and the orthodox theory of labour markets

On the basis of evidence presented in the labour market segmentation literature a systematic critique of the orthodox theory of the labour market can be mounted. Here there is scope only to sketch the main outlines of orthodox theory in order to draw attention to the distinctive features of the labour market segmentation approach. Barbara Wootton (1955) provides a simple summary of conventional economic theory of labour market functioning for the purposes of comparing this with her own different perspective. The general neo-classical theory described by Wootton contrasts at many points with the scheme of analysis presented in this chapter. As she shows, orthodox economic theory starts with a highly simplified model of the operation of supply and demand in relation to labour, simply on the grounds that this is necessary to establish a theory which has general application. Orthodox economic theory has had a profound influence on the generally accepted view of the way labour markets function. But it is important to note that orthodox theory also embodies notions of how the labour market *should* function. Wootton puts it in this way:

> What the theory is really trying to say is, it would seem, that in a fully competitive market people get out of the productive process just about what they put into it (that is in terms of the quality of their labour and their contribution to output). If this does not happen, then it is assumed that the proper functioning of the labour market is impaired by imperfections. A properly functioning market should ensure that the wage system is, by and large, fair and acceptable, according to liberal ideals.

Analysis of the labour market in terms of segmentation processes has developed since Barbara Wootton wrote that belief in orthodox wage theory was being affected by 'halting agnosticism' among economists. We can very briefly summarize some of the ways in which labour market segmentation theory diverges from the competitive theory of wages of neo-classical economics.

For a market to operate in the accepted sense, market clearing must occur, that is excess supply and demand must be eliminated through the price mechanism, which for labour is through changes in wages or salaries. According to neo-classical theory, excess demand for labour results in a rise in wages. 'Competition between employers bidding against one another in order to get hold of the limited supply of workers available is the force that pushes wages up to the point at which both demand and supply are neatly matched' (Wootton, 1955, p. 13). This view is based on the assumption that labour is inherently scarce. But it is one of the features of the structured labour markets that there are almost always alternative supplies of labour to which employers can turn, e.g., by using immigrant workers, drawing workers from the household or relocating production. The wage mechanism need not operate as postulated if instead of raising wages in the face of scarcities employers tap new sources of labour (e.g., by providing opportunities for part-time work) to maintain supply.

There are also factors preventing an excess supply of labour resulting in a fall in wages, as postulated in neo-classical theory which holds: 'In the event that employers find themselves paying more than the rate that is . . . appropriate to a given supply of labour, some workers will fail to find employment, just as goods remain unsold if they are priced too high' (Wootton, 1955, p. 13). But the mechanisms by which unemployment is to bring about a fall in wage rates are not adequately specified. This kind of adjustment cannot take place automatically and mechanically. It depends on decisions being taken by people in specific circumstances. To simplify a complex area of analysis, employers are not free to substitute cheaper labour for the labour which is apparently being paid more than is necessary, given the existence of unemployment. Effective performance in a productive unit like a plant or firm depends above all on co-operative interaction among employees. Employers pay a 'rate for the job' which is institutionalized in most organizations. Even individual productivity payments have a range which is pre-established. The use of a 'rate for the job' has grown up partly to ensure regularity and predictability in labour costs and earnings; it also reflects difficulties in measuring the productivity of individuals independently of job characteristics. Under sufficient pressure, employers do seek wage cuts. But wages are seldom cut across the board. Under cost pressures and when new workers can be recruited at lower rates because of changing labour supply conditions, some organizations have introduced a 'two-tier' wage system with lower rates for the same job offered to more recent recruits. These arrangements are widely regarded as unfair and incompatible with the norm of equal pay for work of equal value. The alternative of reducing wages of all employees to the lower rate at which new recruits can be obtained, is likely to result in costs in reduced morale and cooperation; many employers view these costs as offsetting the benefits of lower wages for all. Thus wage rates within given establishments remain relatively unresponsive to changes in supply conditions. A more common strategy is relocation and replacement of the entire labour force. In a given region unemployment can and does co-exist with stable or rising relative wages for those in employment. It does so through the operation of influences which must be studied as part of the analysis and not dismissed as imperfections.

In this chapter we explain some of the ways in which labour mobility is systematically limited. Work experience often has the effect of confining workers to a narrow segment of employment, despite higher wages elsewhere. To account for the persistence of different wage levels, economists have postulated that net rewards other than pay are equalized by workers. It is supposed that some non-wage advantages of jobs compensate for poor pay rates, that workers are engaged in trading-off monetary for non-monetary benefits. For example, they may prefer to work in small firms in a familiar industry, because they like the work and enjoy the friendly atmosphere despite lower wages. The difficulty with the trade-off argument was long ago recognized by J. S. Mill, who pointed out that poor pay is more often than not combined with unattractive work and conditions. Mill explained this in terms of the fact that unpleasant jobs are done by workers to whom no other choices are open. 'The hardships (of an occupation) and the earnings, instead of being directly proportional as in any just arrangements of society they would be, are generally in the inverse ratio to one another' (Mill, 1862). We return at a number of points in the chapter to the theory of 'equalization of net advantage'. Like Barbara Wootton we may ask why a tendency to equality should be postulated as the natural state; this would only be so if indeed by some natural justice the labour market ensured that everyone was rewarded according to what they contributed to the productive process and had to put up with in their work.

Neo-classical theory gives great emphasis to investment in training and education as providing the scarce skills which earn rewards; it is the costs and effort of acquiring qualifications which, above all, are held to underlie differences in pay. But in practice the structure of jobs and the hierarchy of pay grades does not necessarily match up with the qualifications and experience of individual job holders. Moreover formal qualifications may not be necessary for proficiency on the job, and may instead be used to ration access to desirable jobs. On the other hand some kinds of skill and experience, though they contribute to the performance of an economic unit, are not recognized in the grading system. Unless organized groups made up of members of an occupation or organization ensure that specific qualifications are used to enhance their members' bargaining position, premiums are not always paid to those with skills and experience on which employers depend. Evidence of this kind supports the argument that labour markets include a multiplicity of groups organized (whether as trade unions, licence holders or professional bodies) to obtain job protection and pay benefits through group action. Vulnerable workers fail to find 'shelter' in the form of reasonably stable and well-paid jobs defended by group action. We identify groups from which vulnerable workers emerge in the third section of this unit.

1. The demand for labour

Jobs are made available when employers seek workers for some purpose. The market for labour takes place in the context of the overall structure of jobs. At any one time most jobs are unavailable on the market because they are already filled, and replacement is not in question. One cannot examine the market for labour without analysing the stock of jobs into which new recruitment represents the current flow. In looking at the labour requirements of units of employment we will begin by examining the factors that impinge on all firms and organizations and influence their job structures. We will then go on to see what factors differentiate units of employment and lead to diverse labour requirements and the availability of jobs with divergent features (diversified demand for labour). In the following sections we will examine the allocation of members of different social groups to diverse jobs. The first section dealing with structural factors may not initially appear to have much to do with the divisions in the work-force which is the subject of this chapter. However, here we present some of the concepts which make up 'building blocks' of the analysis. Social divisions exist within the structures which make up the economy. We try to emphasize that the 'building blocks' (e.g., the notion of 'industrial structure') used to describe features of the economy are simply concepts, and where they denote empirically observable patterns these are ultimately the outcome of human decisions and relationships.

Factors shaping the structure of jobs

The structure of jobs in the economy at large reflects the total outcome of job structures within individual units of employment, i.e. firms, institutions and organizations. There is, of course, great diversity as between such micro-units of employment; in studying labour market structure one must have a basis for identifying common factors shaping demand at the micro level as well as the means of differentiating between such units according to their labour requirements. Writers on labour market segmentation have been developing a framework which makes this possible and which views the firm (or employing unit) as a social organization within which collective behaviour occurs and collective goals are pursued. In contrast, orthodox economics is concerned with the behaviour of rational individuals pursuing their own ends.

Much discussion uses phrases like 'the impact of technology on industry and society' as if to imply that job design and work hierarchies are inevitable consequences of forces which cannot be resisted. This approach obscures the fact that all social arrangements are the outcome of choices, which are shaped by the aims and objectives of those making binding decisions. This also applies to the structure of jobs and wages. To a considerable extent employers have to operate within bounds set by constraints over which they have little direct control. But there are also extensive areas of discretion which enable them to select employment strategies. Demand for labour reflects both *constraints* and *areas of discretion*. The structure of jobs is not automatically determined but is the outcome of specific decisions selected from a range of options by employers; in examining empirical material relevant to this point it is important to look out for evidence on the choices available to employers over the provision of jobs.

External constraints

External pressures bearing on job structures include the following factors:

(i) *The basic production process*
For the production of a given set of items, and in the absence of research and development facilities, firms or organizations may have little option but to make use of available production equipment which calls for a specific skill mix from the labour force. Within any industry the job structures of firms have a good deal in common where the same production process is used for the output of a common product. These constraints stem from the prior stage of *equipment design*, which in part determines *job design* within the firm. This topic is discussed further in Chapter 4. Equipment design takes place in an economic context and under the influence of cost structures which include relative labour costs. If unskilled labour is less expensive than skilled labour the desire to reduce the skill component in the manning of the equipment will influence equipment design. Although (from the firm's perspective at a given point in time) production methods are externally determined, production design is not an autonomous development. The interaction between labour costs, technology and other factors affecting job design are highly complex and are not the subject of the present unit, but it is essential to be critically aware of the implications of the notion that *technical methods of*

production constitute a constraint on employers which may wrongly be taken to imply that technology is a purely independent force. Even the choice of whether to introduce new technology or continue to use older methods of production will have a profound effect on demand for labour.

(ii) Economic environment

Firms operate within an *economic environment* which shapes the alternatives open to employers. In the widest sense the level of economic activity will determine demand for their product or services; other economic factors limit their options, including the firm's cost structure (the cost of materials and transport, etc.) and the availability and terms of credit. The industry may be expanding or declining in response to demand for the product or services. These factors interact with the technical features of production to determine the proportion of total costs made up of labour costs. For example, in a highly capital-intensive industry like chemical processing, wages and salaries make up a much smaller proportion of total costs than in the clothing industry, and this will influence personnel and staffing policy within the industry. A major influence is the state of demand in the *product market* for goods produced by the firm, i.e. the supply of and demand for the output of the firm, and the extent to which this demand is met by other firms. This in turn reflects competition between producing firms. The nature of the product market also provides the main link between (i) technolgical conditions and (ii) the economic environment. Firms are not necessarily passive in the face of product markets, however. They can exercise choice over their product range and to some extent shape product markets by sales and marketing strategies.

(iii) Industrial structure

This is the size and relationship of the economic units which make up an industry, and which partly determines the degree of control over the product market which individual producers exercise. If there are many highly competitive units operating on small profit margins, firms will be less able to control the range and price of their output and will be limited in their ability to pay the work-force; hence they may provide only relatively insecure and low-paid jobs. Where a few firms control the market they will in contrast face a different set of options in structuring jobs and pay.

(iv) Employment regulations.

Employment regulations constitute another major set of constraints in a wide variety of areas. These include the prohibition of child labour, health and safety rules, planning regulations, etc. They type of employment contract which may be drawn up, dismissal procedures, working conditions, etc., must remain within legal bounds if the unit operates within the formal economy. Unregistered employment within the informal economy occurs to bypass regulations and tax requirements. Frequently firms use one type of employment contract for internal employees but also make use of other labour to which their contractual obligations are limited. There is the option of the use of subcontracted, temporary or self-employed labour and other job forms which intentionally or otherwise bypass regulations designed to protect employees.

(v) Institutional constraints

Employers face institutional constraints which affect the supply of labour. The major institutions which create such constraints are the system of education and training, and labour organizations and professional bodies, which register and regulate the use of labour. We will be discussing the influence of these bodies in more detail when we examine the labour supply, but here we should note the importance of national and regional regulations and agreements which affect employers' use of labour and provision of jobs.

Internal constraints

In addition to the external pressures which shape job structures within units of employment, internal constraints limit employers' options in designing jobs and taking on workers. Institutional forms, customs and practices evolve which make these social units viable and which create internal constraints on the ways in which jobs can be structured and paid. These limits are adhered to partly through the strength of institutional practices which prevent the development of alternative structures and arrangements. The observance of custom and practice is also necessary to a considerable extent in order to secure the compliance of the work-force.

To a large extent, therefore, the job structure of a firm is 'historically' determined, that is, it has evolved in the course of development of the industry and firm; it can only be altered at the cost of a considerable social upheaval which entails other costs. Firms become locked into given pay and employment systems, which may be modified but are rarely radically changed. When, periodically, firms engage in a more thorough restructuring of pay and employment it is usually under the influence of major pressure from one or more of the external constraints under which they operate, as studies of firm relocation show (see, for example, Mann, 1973).

Empirical research and common sense indicate how dependent firms are on an efficient and proficient work-force. The compliance of their workers is a major requirement, and in making decisions affecting their job and pay structures, employers need to consider the firm as a social whole in which productivity results above all from efficient inter-action between employees using the available productive equipment. Employers cannot easily limit decisions to individual cases; they cannot relate in a unique way to an individual and establish his or her tasks and pay without reference to others. It may not be easy to reward individuals according to merit, adjust pay scales or even dispense with surplus labour, especially under conditions of uncertainty. The constraints under which firms operate have profound effects on productivity. Attention to the firm as a social unit also requires critical attention to be paid to the *notion of productivity*, its measurement, the ways in which it can be iden-tified and is rewarded. The notion of *individual productivity* as a basis for wage payment is called into question if *effective productivity* depends on co-operative interaction between groups using a given set of equipment. We cannot deal with this issue in detail here, but we return to it at several points in the chapter.

Alternatives and employment options: management strategies

Despite the operation of these internal and external constraints, there are also areas of discretion open to employers in selecting workers and providing jobs. Employers pursue strategies aimed at achieving their objectives and priorities, selecting their options within these areas of dis-cretion. The influence of technology on job structures is not direct. It is mediated by forms of work organization in use. The allocation of sets of tasks to a given job and the assignment of workers to given jobs can be done in a great variety of ways. Moreover, providers of jobs make deci-sion about the job structure in the knowledge that certain kinds of labour are available. Worker organizations and professional bodies play a major role in determining the structure of jobs and allocation of people to jobs – sometimes in conflict, sometimes in collaboration with manage-ment, as we shall see below.

We can summarize this discussion of the factors impinging on job structures in individual employment units using a schematic diagram (Figure 1).

In figure 1 tasks to be performed are in the first instance determined by the nature of the product or service and available technology. But other factors affect the allocation of sets of tasks to jobs and the complex pro-cesses by which occupational roles are maintained. These influences include economic factors shaping demand, costs and credit, and institu-tional factors such as trade union structure which affect the labour sup-ply. As we will see in the following section, the specific form taken by work organization and aspects of employment practice vary with worker characteristics and are shaped by labour supply factors. The chart is only schematic; in practice all relevant factors are interrelated (e.g., economic conditions and features of labour organization are interdependent). In other words the lines of influence are two-way although we emphasize here the factors impinging on job structures. Many industry characteristics which appear at first sight autonomous are in practice the collective outcome of the strategies of individual firms, e.g., the firms' product market may have been created by the sales policy pursued. Internal constraints deriving from traditional rights and practices, not shown in Figure 1, are a general and pervasive influence. It should be noted that this scheme is intentionally oversimplified for review purposes. At every point the outlook and interests of participants in the social processes summarized here are crucial precipitating factors shaping actual outcomes.

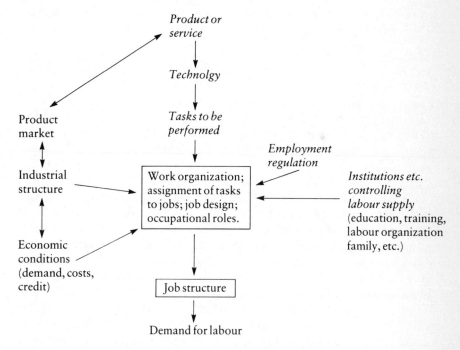

Figure 1. Factors affecting job structures in firms and organizations

The contingency approach

This scheme of analysis has features in common with contingency theory. Organizational theorists have also stressed the relationship between systems of work organization and the industrial and technological environment in which the firm operates.

> Essentially, a contingency approach is one in which it is argued that in some environments one kind of managerial practice will contribute to some desired objectives. But in other industries and circumstances entirely different results may occur. Therefore in order to be sure of the

outcome of a scheme the manager needs to consider the particular circumstances of his firm (Lupton and Bowey, 1974, p. 79)

As this quotation indicates, a managerial perspective has been adopted in the contingency approach and the effects of conflicts of interest between workers and managers (and among groups of workers) are not the focus of attention. But the need to obtain compliance and co-operation by making compromises with employees often explains the strength of custom and practice.

The emphasis on areas of discretion open to managers indicates that technology and environment do not close off all options. Managers can select policies by making choices among alternatives. Technology and environment shape the options but do not determine outcomes to the extent implied in contingency theory.

2. The differentiation of demand: primary and secondary employment

Before we examine sources of supply of labour and the interaction of supply and demand we need to examine the differentiation of demand for labour. Differences stem from variations in the constraints under which firms operate, the alternatives open to employers and the employment strategies they pursue. Complex patterns emerge within this diversity, but it is possible to classify categories of employment in the simplest terms according to whether they provide good pay, security and prospects (termed *primary employment conditions*) or fail to do so (termed *secondary employment conditions*). Diverse occupations are found within both sectors; they cannot readily be defined in terms of job content or qualifications. The starting point for the analysis of labour market segmentation is the shortage of good jobs; this rather than the shortage of 'good quality labour' is the crucial factor.

It should be noted that the use of the term 'primary' and 'secondary' to describe employment conditions is quite different from that used to describe the nature of an industry. Primary industries are raw-materials producing industries (such as agriculture and mining) while secondary industries are manufacturing industries.

The use of 'primary' and 'secondary' to describe employment conditions suggests the existence of a dual labour market (i.e., two separate labour markets) but this is a simplification. The market for labour is neither unitary nor dual. Structured patterns of demand interact with diverse sources of supply to create what can be thought of as a set of segmented markets for labour, relatively isolated from each other. In the literature on segmented labour markets variations abound on the themes of primary and secondary employment.

Primary and secondary employment conditions are essentially ideal types rather than descriptions of facts. We further need to distinguish between industries, firms (or employing organizations) and occupations; all three categories provide both relatively secure and well paid (primary type) and also insecure and badly paid (secondary type) employment. In the simplest terms *industries* which provide primary employment conditions are those consisting of a majority of *firms* (or employing organizations) providing primary employment conditions; usually these industries consist of large firms using modern technology, facing predictable demand for their products and exerting some control over their product markets. Industries providing primary sector employment are generally characterized by strong collective bargaining organizations. Industries providing secondary employment can be defined simply in terms of the absence of provision of primary conditions of employment. Within each set of industries are groups of sub-markets with boundaries which shift over time.

The most obvious evidence of the *industrial basis* for labour market segmentation (LMS) is provided by differences in pay and employment conditions for the same occupation in different industries. For occupations which are similar across industries there are systematic differences in pay and conditions; for example, haulage drivers in industries providing primary employment conditions are paid at higher rates than in industries providing secondary employment conditions.

Nevertheless, the production conditions of industries do not fully explain the provision of secure and stable jobs. Political and cultural factors affecting industries are also at work, as is shown by examining employment conditions in the same industry in different countries. There are differences in the provision of primary employment conditions in a given industry in different industrialized countries, despite similar technological and product market conditions.

Primary and secondary employment conditions

Primary and secondary type employment conditions are, we have seen, ideal types, not simple descriptions of reality. It may be helpful to think of industries, firms and jobs as ranged between two extremes which are the poles representing primary and secondary employment conditions respectively. Characteristics of industries near the 'secondary pole' include competitive product market conditions and traditional or established technology; in contrast industries ranged near the 'primary pole' exert control in their product market and use modern, innovative production methods. Firms for the most part share these characteristics of their industry but there are some which fall out of line in terms of the employment conditions they provide (that is, they offer excellent conditions in an otherwise low paying industry or poor conditions in an industry which generally provides secure well-paid jobs). Similarly, some jobs or occupations are out of line in relation to the firms and industries in which they are situated and offer employment conditions which are characteristic of the opposite pole. Jobs themselves do not always provide primary or secondary type features only; high pay and little security or low pay and security are found in combination (oil rig workers in the first case; college porters in the second, for example). A wide range of combinations is to be found of industrial, enterprise and job conditions in different markets for labour.

The issue is not simply one of terminology but of explaining differences in labour market conditions. Thus an important modification to the notion that industrial characteristics explain the availability of jobs with primary and secondary employment conditions comes from examining *firms* providing secondary employment conditions within *industries* which are largely providers of primary employment. These firms are not simply residual, i.e., left over from a previous stage of development, but play a crucial role in the industrial structure, doing subcontracted work for larger firms or providing specialist production in areas where labour costs are relatively high, for example, on labour-intensive processes. These firms are frequently risk-bearers for the industry, and may have a high rate of closure and formation. Their ability to pay good wages is limited and they often cannot provide job security. Nevertheless, some firms of this kind may adapt better to changing economic conditions than larger and more inflexible organizations.

Within firms providing good employment conditions, secondary type jobs are frequently found. There are two general patterns, primary employment conditions may be reserved for an élite, e.g., of managerial or professional staff. Alternatively a minority of workers may have secondary employment conditions in contrast with the bulk of the employees. The retail (shopping) industry provides an example of firms where a mainly male managerial hierarchy has employment conditions which contrast with those of the mass of mainly female sales workers. In many firms where most employees enjoy primary status, secondary employment conditions apply to part-time, temporary or seasonal workers, who are not treated as internal employees. But these conditions may also apply to a stable and regular category of jobs within the firm, as in the case of cleaners or canteen workers (see Craig *et al.*, 1982). The coexistence of primary and secondary jobs affords managers both workforce stability and the ability to off-load the costs of flexibility on to more vulnerable sections of the work-force. We will explore in the following sections the tendency for insecure ill-paid jobs to be held by workers with impaired bargaining capacity in the labour market.

Internal labour markets

Firms differ significantly in their internal organization and hierarchy of jobs not only because of factors beyond employers' control but because of strategies they pursue in organizing what has been termed their 'internal labour market' (Doeringer, 1967). An 'internal labour market' consists of a structure of jobs and promotion ladders, and includes the rules and processes by which personnel are selected for posts and by which wage structures are established. The 'market' is insulated from wider markets outside the employing organization and takes over some of the functions of selection and allocation of personnel, and the setting of pay levels, which are attributed to the operation of labour markets. However, internal labour markets are not concerned with matching supply and demand. Indeed insulation from external labour markets can simply be described as 'internal job structures', if the notion of an internal market creates confusion.

A major reason for the insulation of labour markets from each other relates to the pattern of recruitment and promotion within the firm's job hierarchy. Internal job structures usually have a limited number of 'ports of entry' at junior levels and promotion takes place internally. There is strict control over transfers from outside into senior positions. Where promotion from outside occurs regularly this usually reflects the operation of another labour market, such as that for managers, into which entry is controlled.

A technological explanation for sheltered internal job structures?

When internal job structures first became a subject of analysis it was believed that firms offering secure employment did so because technological developments made labour turnover especially costly for them. On-the-job experience was thought to be especially important in industries and firms providing primary employment conditions; promotion ladders were believed to develop in attempts to recruit, keep and motivate highly productive employees (Reich *et al.*, 1973). But it is inappropriate to characterize primary type firms in these terms in contrast with secondary type firms, if only for the following reasons:

(i) Mechanization often decreases learning time requirements and reduces the need for the exercise of individual initiative for many workers.
(ii) There are many examples in the UK and USA of the extension of job security and relatively high pay, which are independent of technological requirements. Examples from France and Italy have also been documented, for example, by Piore (1980).
(iii) Firms offering secondary employment conditions also depend on a stable core of employees.

Technological change has frequently been aimed at reducing learning requirements and the need for the exercise of initiative. This is a topic which is discussed further in Chapter 4. In the case of manual and lower grade white-collar workers, those firms using advanced technology in practice often require less in the way of skills acquired on the job than do firms using traditional technology. Firms providing secondary sector employment conditions rely heavily on the expertise and on-the-job experience of their workers, but they do not pay a premium nor provide job security to retain their core employees. They use paternalistic methods (a family atmosphere at work) to keep staff, and rely on the obstacles to changing jobs which prevent their experienced workers seeking higher paid employment elsewhere. What mechanization does do is to increase the productive output for which individual operations are directly or indirectly responsible, thus making *discipline, reliability and loyalty* to the employer important worker attributes, however limited the content of the job (Blackburn and Mann, 1979). These worker attributes, however, are hardly less important in traditional firms, and may in fact be more important to employers in firms providing secondary employment conditions, who cannot provide strict worker control systems or tolerate misfits or troublemakers.

So far we have found no simple technological reasons for primary employment conditions and secure internal job structures arising in some sectors of the economy and not in others. We have indicated that this diversity derives in part from differences in employers' capacity to tolerate relatively fixed wage costs and to evade uncertainty. In brief, strategies for coping with *economic uncertainties* structure the demand for labour and play an important part in determining whether primary or secondary type employment conditions are provided by employers. Wherever possible, employers providing primary employment conditions attempt to pass the costs and burdens of uncertainty on to smaller firms on a subcontract basis or by setting up satellites, while concentrating production and service provision in areas where demand is reasonably stable and predictable. These firms also establish a dual set of employment conditions, primary status being reserved for full-time internal employees while temporary, part-time and casual workers provide a buffer enabling firms to reduce their commitment to a sector of the work-force, and so vary labour costs.

Avoidance of risk and uncertainty emerges as an important source of motivation for the establishment of primary and secondary employment conditions by employers, in so far as such action is open to them. In examining the actions of those benefiting from primary employment conditions, we will find that reduction of uncertainty is also a basic objective.

The public sector

We have, by implication, dealt mainly with the private sector in this analysis of the factors structuring the demand for labour. However, the summary scheme (Figure 1) on page 51 applies also to employment in the

public sector. Economic conditions are established via government policy (through budget and wage constraints), but a similar set of forces gov-
erns the establishment of job structures which determine the categories of
labour required, or demand for labour in a given instance. For example,
in local government, economic pressures are the outcome of government
policy, but the nature of the services to be performed and the organization of work shape job design and determine what types of labour will be
required. In the past government employment has been characterized in
most countries above all by its relative stability. In France, for example,
the 'employé d'état' has a life-time job. It is to avoid the present and
future costs of providing stable employment and creating the greater collective bargaining power which such stability confers on workers that
'privatization' schemes have been launched in the UK by central and local
authorities. At the time of writing, job stability is threatened for many
government employees by technical change displacing clerical workers
and by public expenditure cuts as well as privitization policies. The latter
can be interpreted as attempts to weaken the 'labour market shelter' provided by public employment. Whether this will result in greater efficiency
under the pressure of market forces or whether it will simply establish
secondary employment conditions for public employees at the base of the
job hierarchy ladder is an open question.

Even before current cuts in public expenditure local authorities were
encouraged by budget constraints to seek new sources of labour as private employers do, and have tapped the household sector by providing
part-time work for married women at clerical and manual levels. As in
the private sector, the nature of the jobs made available is affected in part
by sources of labour available. We must now turn to examine the sources
of labour supply and their influence on job structures.

3. Labour supply: the segmentation of the labour force

Social reproduction

So far we have been concerned with structural factors affecting the
demand for labour. The supply of labour is also structured by social
institutions and by processes which differentiate groups seeking work in
the labour market. Extensive unpaid activities take place in the household and community which are prerequisites for the operation of any
labour market. The new generation is produced and prepared for working life, and services are provided to members of the existing labour force
which enable them to engage in paid employment; i.e., to become part of
the labour force. These processes, sometimes referred to as social reproduction, are ones in which the family plays a central part. Three main features of the family are relevant to labour market activities: (i) the early

training and social conditioning of the young; (ii) the care of dependants (the sick, the elderly, etc.) and the provision of other services which make workers available for paid employment; (iii) the sharing of income in a common family budget.

(i) Families not only produce the next generation of workers but also provide social conditioning which prepares the young for specific places in the occupational system. Further creation of expectations and job aspirations takes place within communities. Close differences in expectations concerning working life and standards of living are reinforced by the system of education and training which tends to confirm family influences. Expectations affect the terms on which workers make their labour available, both by influencing individual behaviour and by stimulating collective action.

(ii) The family also releases certain workers from responsibility for the care of dependants and other household obligations. Family role specialization, where one partner is the primary wage earner while the other has the main responsibility for 'servicing' the family, is partly the outcome of social conventions about the appropriate division of labour between men and women. But it is reinforced by working arrangements and requirements which demand freedom from outside commitments; it is also encouraged by internal job markets which penalize career interruptions (periods out of work) and part-time work. Freedman points out that if a couple decided that both partners should pursue modified careers with jobs compatible with shared family responsibilities, the result would be that 'neither worker could expect to hold a job with prospects for either advancement or security' because of the way in which job shelters operate (Freedman, p. 121). The situation is self-reinforcing in that expectations about future family roles shape incentives to undergo education and training and so maintain difference in the types of qualification obtained by men and women. Assumptions about family role specialization, even where these are inapplicable in individual cases, may be at the basis of the 'social exclusion' practised by some employers against women.

(iii) The relative position of men and women in the labour market is significantly influenced by the sharing of income within the family. In view of the extent to which family responsibilities impair women's bargaining position, in the majority of cases the main wage earner for the family is male. There are many circumstances where these conditions do not apply, but employers' expectations are seldom modified to take into account divergences from the traditional norm. Where the earnings of a male wage earner are not available to other family members, problems of low income and poverty predominate, as we see below in discussing inequalities associated with labour market segmentation.

Vulnerable labour market positions

We have argued that workers whose positions in the labour market are vulnerable are those most likely to be found in low-paid jobs. The bargaining position of these workers is limited by factors not affecting the majority of the labour force, such as ill health, household responsibilities, alien nationality, minority racial status, lack of employment experience or a combination of these factors. Vulnerable workers usually share two main characteristics. They are employed in a social context in which they have sources of income other than personal wages, and they are unable to exert organized control over the type of labour they supply. The connection between the costs of supporting oneself (and dependants) at an acceptable standard of living on the one hand and individual earnings on the other is severed for those who regularly draw upon pooled family income, as commonly occurs in the case of married women and young workers. The link is also broken in the case of retired workers on pensions or persons drawing a disability allowance who seek employment, and for other workers dependent in part on social security payments because they are not receiving a 'living wage'.

The case of immigrant labour is different, but not unrelated to that of indigenous low-paid workers. The inter-generational costs of social reproduction are subsidized by the country of origin which provided such maternal and child welfare provisions as were available and carried the costs of elementary or further education of immigrants. The expectations immigrants have of wages and living standards are initially determined in the poorer country of origin and the link between metropolitan work rates and immigrants' expectations is tenuous. Where ethnic communities are formed, pay expectations of members of minority groups are affected by the exclusion of their members from better paid jobs through discrimination. In contrast prime-age white males expect and are expected to be earning enough on a job to be capable of maintaining themselves and a family at a standard of living deemed acceptable in the local community. Groups of workers show a persistent unwillingness to accept pay rates below that which comes to be accepted as a reasonable level for the category of work in question (see Webb, 1926, p. 46).

Evidence on the 'working poor' shows that reliance on sources of income other than their wages, including state welfare payments, may be forced on vulnerable workers by the low wages and highly competitive conditions which prevail in the labour markets open to them (see, for example, information in Low Pay Unit Studies).

It should be emphasized that the labour market position of women is not intrinsically vulnerable but is the result of the role specialization in the family and expectations which follow therefrom. Where women supply their labour on the same conditions as men, have similar kinds of qualification and benefit from organized action in support of the pay and conditions as members of an unsegregated occupation, they may enjoy primary employment conditions. But because of the extensiveness of role specialization in the family, many employers assume that women in general have lower income needs and lesser attachment to their jobs than men, even where in individual cases this assumption is inapplicable. Access to more desirable jobs may be reduced, even for those who do not have child care responsibilities, poor health or other difficulties by managers' recruitment and promotion policies. Simply being a member of a group which includes many vulnerable workers may be a disadvantage if it leads to differential allocation to jobs.

Control over the labour supply

Vulnerable groups in the labour market differ in the reasons for their limited bargaining capacity, but they share an inability to exert collective control over the type of labour they supply. Women workers do not constitute a cohesive group and married women are socially isolated by their family responsibilities. This makes it difficult for them to organize collective action in support of improved employment conditions. The reaction of married women to inadequate remuneration has been withdrawal from the labour force where this was a feasible alternative (Humphries, 1977). Collective action by women has, however, been organized even in unfavourable circumstances as described, for example, by J. Wacjman (1983). Immigrants are vulnerable for different reasons. They are frequently brought in on work contracts which tie them to a particular employer. Even after the expiry of this period they are isolated as a group. Married women, immigrant workers and young workers are vulnerable to exclusion from jobs which are protected from competition by restrictive entry requirements. They have been unable to create institutions promoting their collective interests and must rely on government to legislate in their favour on grounds of equity, through the influence of such groups as the Civil Liberties commissions, the Low Pay Unit or the Child Poverty Action Group in Great Britain.

Job protection

In a wage economy protection against uncertainty derives mainly from employment position; for most of the economically active population sources of support other than earnings are unavailable or insufficient. Employees are therefore very concerned to establish claims to their jobs in the face of competition (Freedman, 1976). But it is only by organized, collective action that otherwise isolated workers whose skills are not in special demand can achieve any degree of job protection.

Eliminating the unstable features of casual employment requires the development of considerable organizational resources, as the history of industrial relations reveals. Employers concede to workers' attempts to limit the rigours of competition either because they benefit from a stable labour force and predictable labour costs, or because they can find no other way of securing co-operation from their work-force.

Restrictions on job entry

The broadest form of exclusion applies to entire social groups, which may be eliminated from competition for jobs by direct or indirect means. Legislation may be instituted which has this effect, for example, immigration control or tax incentives encouraging married women to withdraw from the labour force. Exclusion may also take the form of the regulation of entry into an occupation, a practice which goes back to very early times (cf. guilds and 'combinations in restraint of trade'). (The sociological implications of exclusion or social closure are discussed by Parkin, 1979.)

Restrictions on entry into categories of jobs are usually based on educational requirements or vocational qualifications. As average levels of education rise, requirements for entry to a given occupation tend to be raised. Qualifications do not guarantee entry, especially during periods of job shortage, but they control eligibility for jobs. Indeed limits on eligibility mean that there is regulation of entry. Frequently members of occupational groups organize to set up bodies which register entry for those completing formal or informal training (e.g., chartered accountants). In some occupations entry requirements can be met by the purchase of a licence without any training requirements being enforced, though training may be recommended (e.g., hoteliers). In the case of other jobs very little formal training is provided but a minimum period of experience is required, as under certain apprenticeship arrangements. Licensing and credential requirements are justified as providing protection for the public by maintaining standards of practice. However, they also promote the interest of occupational groups which are often able to gain government recognition. The role of 'policing' members of an occupation is delegated to these bodies, which can also control entry and hence to some extent terms of employment. How successful such occupational bodies are depends in part on the market for their members' services and the position of their membership in the class structure. The most successful occupational groups are the professions which exert control over the market for their services across all industries (e.g., the medical and legal professions). The less able an occupational group is to confine special expertise for which there is demand to its own members, the more open the group is to competition. Closed shops attempt to limit competition from outside (non-unionized) labour. Unions were first effective where members had special individual skills, as in the case of craftworkers. These skills may be acquired either through formal training or on-the-job experience, and continue to provide a basis for collective action. Where special experience is required, and especially if promotion ladders further differentiate between employees, there is less possibility of substituting labour from outside.

Competition is reduced not only by restrictions on entry to an occupation but by limiting entry into employing organizations. This may be especially necessary to secure claims to jobs where the work has no traditional occupational content, either because skills have been eroded and new forms of job design applied to production work, or because job content is based on generally available skills such as literacy and numeracy, for example, in the case of administrative workers. Not only entry but progress within the firm may be subject to control, within 'internal job structures'. In some cases a set of nominal job hierarchies are established in which adjacent levels are distinguished by wage differentials rather than by greater responsibility (Freedman, 1976, p. 57).

The introduction of nominal hierarchies has been attributed to a 'divide and rule' policy pursued by employers who benefit from a diversity of interests among their work-force and can create artificial distinctions even when real skill differences have been eroded (K. Stone, 1975). In contrast with this line of argument Rubery points out that:

> The existence of a structured labour force where jobs are strictly defined and workers are not interchangeable, provides a bargaining base for labour against management's attempts to increase productivity and introduce new technology. Changes in job ladders, skill demarcations and the pace of work become areas for bargaining whereas a . . . homogenous labour force, interchangeable in function, would lay itself open not only to competition from the external labour market but also to further declines in worker's control of production and a continuous undermining of bargaining power. Divisions of custom, rule and status are essential parts of any union's bargaining strategy (Rubery, 1978, in Amsden, p. 260).

Employment conditions in the same industry vary as between countries depending on the effectiveness of collective action by the workers (see Rubery, 1978). Evidence of the success of worker organizations in maintaining some control over job structure despite the destruction of the craft system is to be found in countries where primary employment conditions obtain in sectors which are relatively illpaid elsewhere (e.g., workers in the US construction industry enjoy relatively more favourable employment conditions than in most other countries).

Personal and social costs of segmentation

The need for job security is a basic factor underlying activities which promote segmentation. The personal costs involved in staking a claim to a job can be illustrated by an example from Blackburn and Mann's study of unqualified male workers.

> Fred was a machine operator. His work cycle was less than 10 seconds, his movements within that time were simple, undemanding, repetitive (unless the machine proved faulty). Managers were concerned that any-one in their firm should be asked to perform such sub-human tasks, and they had apparently proposed to Fred various schemes of job enlarge-ment and job rotation. Fred had rejected these, saying that this was his job, he didn't want to move and he didn't want to share it with anyone. 'How can you reform industry with workers like that?' reasonably asked one manager. What he and the other managers correctly per-ceived was that Fred was giving about as much of himself (i.e. virtually nil) to this firm as he wanted to. Nobody was going to persuade him into higher levels of commitment and co-operation. What was not fully realised, however, was Fred's reasoning. For Fred's machine was a very tangible sign of his job security and his job property rights. As long as that machine was needed, so would he be. Making him interchangeable with other workers in a more interesting, even participatory structure would reduce his security. He felt himself protected and given a work identity to some degree by an internal labour market which marks out specific job titles with wholly artificial lines of demarcation from other jobs. (Blackburn and Mann, 1979, p. 29)

The personal costs of this kind of compromise are high, but may be felt to be unavoidable to achieve some degree of job protection. The economic costs in terms of barriers to the introduction of new technology which job demarcations produce are also likely to be high. The question arises as to whether a greater degree of job security, as provided to the industrial élite of 'life-time workers' in Japan (Dore, 1974) can ease the introduction of new forms of work organization, a topic which cannot here be explored.

Despite the operation of severe constraints workers can sometimes col-lectively influence the terms of employment even under unfavourable bargaining situations. Wilkinson and Tarling (1982) cite the Webbs' analysis of the expectations on the supply of craft labour:

> Over a large part of the industrial field, the wage-earners cling with stubborn obstinacy to certain customary standards of expenditure. However overpowering may be the strategic strength of the employer, however unorganized and resourceless may be the wage-earners, it is found to be impossible to reduce the wages and other conditions of par-ticular grades of workmen below a certain vaguely defined standard. In the years of worst trade, when thousands of engineers or boilermakers, masons or plumbers, are walking the streets in search of work, the most grasping employer knows that it is useless for him to offer them work in their respective trades at ten or fifteen shillings a week. Sooner than suffer such violence to their feelings of what is fit and becoming to their social position, they will work as unskilled laborers, or pick up odd

jobs, for the same, or even lower earnings than they refuse as craftsmen. (Webb, 1926, p. 693)

The capacity to influence outcomes in difficult circumstances depends on employers' reliance on the craftsman's skills. In other cases deliberate collective action is used to control the supply of labour through strikes or work stoppages. As Parkin has pointed out:

> Workers in a number of key industries now enjoy a form of social lever-age arising from their 'disruptive potential' which is quite distinct from the social facts of organizational unity. . . . It is not merely the potential for collective action that governs the effectiveness of solidaristic forms of closure but also the purely contingent feature of production. (F. Parkin, 1974, p. 104)

In the UK dock-workers provide an example of an occupational group who have created stable employment conditions through collective action under favourable economic conditions. Their position is now threatened by changes in market and political conditions which have altered the balance of power in favour of employers. The ultimate sanction which employers can and do use is to close down a work site altogether. But it is clear that workers sometimes benefit from the market for the product of the industry in which they work; where the employing organization has market power as a sole supplier, or provides a product or service in heavy demand, employees' bargaining position may be enhanced. In this way economic and social factors combine in the determination of the employment conditions of workers, indicating that demand and supply side influences are not separate, but interactive forces structuring employment.

4. The mutual conditioning of supply and demand

So far we have discussed the demand for and supply of labour of various kinds as though they were relatively independent of each other. But in the analysis of labour market segmentation the main focus should be on the extent to which demand is structured by supply conditions and the supply of labour shaped by features of demand in ways which are mutually reinforcing, but which can also create conflicting interests.

We now examine aspects of the mutual conditioning of supply and demand looking at the position of individual job seekers faced with structured demand, and that of individual employers faced with a differentiated labour supply.

The individual on the labour market

The range of work open to job seekers is objectively limited by the structure of job openings. The vacancies for which job seekers are in practice eligible are further limited by their age, health, gender, qualifications and work experience. There are also differences in *perceived* alternatives depending on the information available to job seekers. Awareness of alternatives is limited for job seekers by their network of social contacts and the information at their disposal on job openings and conditions. The resources of employer and job seeker are not equivalent in this respect. Employers are in frequent consultation with each other on prevailing rates and conditions while unqualified workers depend on casual information obtained from friends and relatives or terse job descriptions in vacancy notices. Where members of the occupation are not well organized it is less likely that professional or trade journals will be available to provide job information. Manual workers, in particular, can find it very difficult to obtain a clear picture of the range and relative rewards of available jobs (see, for example, Blackburn and Mann, 1979). Job seekers' ability to classify, much less select jobs according to their 'net advantages', as assumed in neo-classical economic theory, is very limited. Position in a social network is likely to determine the segment in which workers seek jobs in the first place and to influence their outlook and the rewards they expect from work.

Orientation to work and employment options

Job aspirations and expectations for rewards from work are shaped initially by the individual's experience in the family, community and educational system, and so have their basis in social structure. Some writers have emphasized the extent to which outlook and rewards expected from work are brought to the job 'from outside the factory gates' (see Goldthorpe *et al., The Affluent Worker*). We use the term 'orientation to work' to refer not only to the influence of factors outside work on outlook and expectations but also to the further influence of experience in working life on personal outlook. Workers do have certain personal preferences, for example, for outdoor work or caring work (Blackburn and Mann, 1979) but their expectations are modified and further shaped by their experience of working life and of the alternatives open to them.

Job alternatives become increasingly limited with age, and expectations are lowered accordingly. Manual workers come to assess a job on its own merits often adopting a very narrow frame of reference. Although expectations are influenced by education and training, an individual's experience of job seeking in a limited labour market will lower expectations among those who find themselves over-qualified for available jobs. Many employees are resigned to doing work for which they have low expectations as regards job content and pay. This has been found to apply especially in the case of women workers (e.g., Beynon and Blackburn, 1972). Awareness of their weak position in a competitive labour market is an important influence. A self-reinforcing process occurs in which knowledge of pay rates in comparable jobs shapes expectations while at the same time pay rates are indirectly influenced by the limited expectations of those accepting poorly paid jobs; often the jobs are such that workers with higher expectations would not accept them. The low expectations of vulnerable workers as regards job content, pay and conditions can be compared with the higher aspirations of groups of craftsworkers. (Further discussion of work orientation and satisfaction can be found in Alan Fox, 'The Meaning of Work' in *The Politics of Work and Occupations*, 1980.)

Options are not only limited for those who lack skills; workers can also acquire skills of a job-specific kind which in effect tie them to their present type of work. Employment experience does not always increase job possibilities; it can also have the effect of narrowing options and confining workers within limited job segments.

Workers are prepared to remain in low paying jobs because access to outside opportunities is limited, for example, by age, where entry jobs are restricted to specific age-groups. They are also motivated by the need for security. Long service is the best insurance against redundancy. This 'locking-in' of workers to specific job categories and industries is to some extent unaffected by relative wages. This has important implications for differential employment conditions and wages as between firms and industries. Employees are not free to transfer to jobs in other firms and sectors without sacrificing the relative advantages which they acquire from seniority and experience. Employers do not therefore need to provide comparable pay and conditions for jobs requiring comparable but non-transferable skills in different firms and industries. Even jobs for school-leavers or young people can provide different pay and conditions for recruits of comparable standard if there is an excess of young applicants. All these factors reduce labour mobility and operate against the equalization of wages paid to workers whose labour is of equivalent quality as assumed in neo-classical theory.

Worker performance and co-operation; skills and status

Early writers on labour market segmentation assumed that a process occurred which was similar to the 'equalization of wages for labour of equivalent quality,' as postulated in neo-classical theory. This process was the allocation of high productivity workers to well paid and secure jobs and the use of workers characterized by instability and lesser efficiency in jobs with secondary employment conditions. But there are reasons for questioning this assumption. We have seen that individual productivity is difficult to assess. Productivity is a function of interaction between co-operating individuals. Measures of productivity are influenced by economic performance which depends in turn on competitive conditions, effective marketing, etc., while productivity depends on equipment used by workers. Individual performance of workers assigned to high productivity equipment is not necessarily greater than that of workers having similar educational levels who are taken on by firms using low productivity equipment. Indeed the level of skill required of individuals may be greater on the equipment which is less mechanized. Higher wages may be due to a greater ability to tolerate wage costs by the employer and/or the collective bargaining position of the work-force, rather than to greater productivity of individual workers.

High wages are only one method of obtaining co-operation from the work-force and good levels of performance. Various types of labour control system are used, and are further discussed in Chapter 4 on the Labour Process. We can note that secondary employment conditions predominate in small firms, and that employers in this sector often do not have the resources to control and supervise their work-force closely. Administrative systems like payment by results are costly for some firms to operate. These firms may rely on the self-discipline, loyalty and co-operation of their employees, especially from the experienced workers.

An important form of external control is exerted by labour market conditions and the market position of workers; where job options are severely limited workers need to co-operate to remain in employment.

The assumption that workers in secondary sector employment conditions are less skilled is not confined to the academic literature; witness the popular conception of jobs performed mainly by women in the service sector (cleaning, catering, providing assistance to the old, young or sick) as unskilled. In practice such jobs make more extensive and varied demands on workers than do many manufacturing and office jobs. This suggests that the low social status of those doing these jobs has an influence on the way in which their skills are classified. The labelling of jobs as skilled or otherwise depends not only on the demands made by the job (job content and worker's knowledge and abilities) but also on the bargaining power and status of those employed (Craig *et al.*, 1984).

Industrial competition and job quality

One of the main ways in which demand and supply side structures interact to create segmented employment structures is through the relationship between low wage employment and competitive industrial conditions. We have just seen that pay levels are not systematically related to skill but reflect labour market status, alternative employment openings and the bargaining power of the employees. Some industries (e.g., clothing) base their operations around the employment of disadvantaged workers paid low wages; the kinds of jobs carried out may require as much skill as jobs in higher paid industries. But firms may not be able, even if managers wished to do so, to reward their workers more adequately because they face competition from firms making similar use of low-wage labour. Competitive market conditions are not necessarily an independent explanation of low pay; the employment practices of the firm have a major influence on the nature and extent of competition. Historically, firms in a given industry have sought through employers' associations to establish minimum terms and conditions of employment and to establish 'rates for the job' to 'take wages out of competition'. This tends to be in the general interest of employers as a group, though individual employers have incentives to pay low wages to undercut their competitors. In the current recession firms in many industries with well-established collective bargaining systems and primary employment conditions now face the threat of low-wage competition either from within the UK or from imports. Some argue that this kind of competition increases efficiency, but others argue that it destabilizes product markets, undermines the position of efficient firms using modern technologies and provides advantages to inefficient firms using obsolete technologies; the most serious potential effect is the discouragement of product and technological development necessary for long-term competitive survival in the industry (Craig *et al.*, 1982). There are close links between labour market forces and broader economic conditions as this issue reveals. The area is beyond the scope of the present unit but once again press reports relevant to competitiveness of industry and wage costs are very relevant.

Making segmentation acceptable

In the first section of this chapter we saw that the supply of good jobs in the economy is shaped by the development of the industrial and technological structure. We have also examined factors which differentiate the labour force and create segmented sources of supply, that is, job seekers divided into non-competing groups. Class and ethnic differences in expected working conditions and living standards serve to provide alternative sources of labour. This process is reinforced by the educational system to which there is differential access. Training arrangements and the provision of qualifications function as rationing devices, controlling access to good jobs. In the current recession, the authorities emphasize the need for training and qualifications as a means of obtaining employment. By implication the uneducated unemployed are held partly responsible for their plight and may themselves accept this viewpoint.

The family plays a central role providing both access to educational institutions and a differentiation of male and female labour, as we have seen. Employers are not indifferent to these sources of labour- force segmentation. They draw on different labour market groups both in allocating work and also in designing jobs. Existing differences in the population make the process of allocation and differences in rewards attached to jobs more acceptable. Because job demarcations and allocations conform to wider social divisions, conflict is reduced and co-operation promoted despite inequalities at work.

We have examined technical and economic constraints on the kind of jobs employers can offer, of which industry-specific job structures provide evidence. Custom and practice further limit alternatives. But there is also scope for discretion to be exercised by employers in features of job design, work organization, job grading and payment arrangements. Discretion is widest in relatively new industries where job structures have not been institutionalized. Even in established firms and industries tasks assigned to jobs can be combined in various ways, for example, by excluding or including heavy tasks, travel requirements, on-the-job maintenance tasks, etc. Working arrangements can also be varied to attract recruits from certain social groups (nights shifts for male immigrants, twilight shifts for married women). For example, some heavy tasks may be included in a job which then is considered unsuitable for women, or overtime work may be required of all staff, with similar effects. In this and other ways jobs come to be designed as appropriate for men and women respectively in view of their conventionally accepted capacities and family responsibilities. The jobs to which women are allocated are usually low paid, a process which is facilitated by the different qualifications held by men and women, but which is partly independent of educational attainment. Girls' educational qualifications are, however, improving in relation to boys (*Social Trends*, 1984). The demarcations which result in occupational segregation (Hakim, 1979) are deeply ingrained; they draw on and reinforce the culturally accepted division of labour between men and women. Moreover, the wages earned on jobs in which men predominate are required to maintain living standards for many families. These rates of pay may be threatened if a supply of workers who are prepared or forced to accept rates of pay below family subsistence requirements compete successfully for jobs currently paying a 'family wage'. The prospect of this situation presents trade unions with a dilemma. Trade unions have a commitment to social justice, to equal access to jobs and the protection of vulnerable workers; however, they are also required to promote and protect the interests of the majority of their members. For this reason certain unions representing mainly male employees may not oppose and may even reinforce management strategies to reserve better paid jobs for male nationals. This may be seen as the only way of preserving wage levels which are high enough to support a family as opposed to wages which will at best support one adult.

Practices which create *de facto* demarcations between men's and women's jobs and reinforce earnings differentials are basic to labour market segmentation. They are not in most cases illegal, since they are based on informal job segregation; in current legislation the equal pay requirement applies to similar work carried out by men and women (see

Craig *et al.*, 1983). These practices provide a means of legitimizing pay differentials and promoting employee co-operation. But they also entail heavy social costs. They confine most women to low-paying jobs regardless of income needs. There are many households with a woman as the main wage earner. Like other members of the female labour force most of these women earn low wages, in many cases insufficient to support a family (Dept. of Employment, *Women in Employment Survey*). Low wages paid to women may also contribute to inefficient production and the continued use of obsolete technology (Craig *et al.*, 1982). The use of immigrant labour, crowded into relatively few low-paid industries and occupations because of discrimination and their weak bargaining position, may have similar effects.

Internal labour markets and employment strategies

In the literature on internal labour markets for primary sector jobs great emphasis is sometimes placed on the need for employers to provide good pay and prospects in order to reduce labour turnover and minimize the costs of recruitment and training. We have already modified this explanation by acknowledging the importance of workers' bargaining capacity in making it necessary for certain employers to introduce primary employment conditions to secure co-operation from the work-force. In our research we have found that 'internal labour markets' providing work-force stability can also be based on low pay and vulnerable workers. The firms involved provide secondary employment conditions but rely on employees' attachment to the firm arising from the firm-specific nature of the skills and experience they have acquired, for example, experience in assembling circuits for particular kinds of prototypes in electronics firms. Often there is a 'captive' labour force of married women seeking short working hours in a residential district with limited transport facilities. These workers are often unable to seek jobs elsewhere. The weak position of such workers on the open market makes it unnecessary for secondary sector firms to pay a premium to retain skilled workers, often women, even where experience and efficiency is recognized to be crucial to the success of the firm. Lack of formal qualifications is especially likely to prevent workers from transferring to equivalent jobs in better paying firms or industries.

But even where workers acquire qualifications such as from clerical or semi-professional training, a break in employment, especially in the early stages of a career, will result in the loss of position within internal labour markets. Age requirements normally prevent access to a 'port of entry' job on a promotion ladder. Under-utilization of skills is especially common among women re-entering the labour force after a period of family formation (National Training Survey evidence; Elias and Main, 1982, p. 4). Re-entrants not only have to start again at the bottom of the job hierarchy, but often cannot fulfil job requirements demanding the absence of domestic obligations. Part-time jobs are mainly held by women re-entering the labour market.

Employers usually accord part-time jobs secondary employment status whatever the content of the work, and exclude these jobs from promotion ladders. In many cases part-time workers perform special functions within the organization, such as night nursing, specialist teaching, skilled manufacturing tasks. Here married women form a source of ready trained labour and employers can adopt the strategy of providing part-time work for this group rather than training internal employees or offering higher wages to attract trained male staff. Married women workers lack the resources to organize to obtain better employment conditions and the mobility to seek more favourable openings elsewhere. In excluding part-time workers from the 'internal labour market' employers usually have the tacit consent of more favoured workers who may feel the need to restrict access to the more desirable jobs in the firm in order to protect their own position. The same arguments may apply to workers on temporary, seasonal or fixed-term contracts, who provide a buffer against uncertainty.

Different employment contracts are drawn up for certain workers, those to whom employers minimize their commitments, from those applying to internal employees. Often collective bargaining arrangements apply only to the latter. Legislation protecting employees has become more comprehensive (unfair dismissal procedures, maternity leave, etc.)[1] although, as we have seen, employers can bypass these provisions. They can use firms providing contract services (e.g., for cleaning and catering), use home workers or self-employed professionals on a non-salaried basis, or even pass on certain manufacturing processes to satellite or independent firms through subcontract arrangements. These strategies segment the labour market, concentrating relatively stable well-paid employment in certain sectors. But even here security is only relative, since shut-downs and wholesale redundancy still looms large. In recession conditions, the struggle to obtain labour 'shelters' is even more likely to involve exclusion of certain groups than when job prospects are more favourable.

5. Contributions to theories of labour market segmentation

In this final section we discuss how various contributions have modified theories of labour market segmentation and provided further evidence on labour market structure.

---

[1] Although in Britain this legislation has been restricted again under the 1980 and 1982 Employment Acts.

Segmentation theory arose as a critique of orthodox theories of the labour market. We have not attempted a full discussion of neo-classical economic theory of the labour market. Standard textbooks (e.g., Hunter and Mulvey, 1981; Samuelson, 1980, ed.; Lipsey, 1979) provide an elementary exposition and suggest further reading. (For a more detailed critique see Appelbaum, 1978.) However, our discussion has called into question three features of the orthodox theory of the labour market. The first is the notion that workers can exercise choice in such a way as to 'equalise net advantage' in selecting jobs. Secondly, we questioned whether wages are or can be directly based on individual contributions to output. Thirdly, it is open to question whether effective performance on many jobs requires or depends directly upon 'investments in human capital', i.e., on an individual's educational attainments and formal qualifications; these may be used to ration access to desirable jobs, regardless of practical requirements. Segmentation analysis calls into question on theoretical grounds the notion that jobs and wages reflect the quality of the available labour force. Unemployment among the well qualified during recessionary conditions supports the contention that good jobs are scarce because of inadequacy in the demand for labour rather than because of deficiencies in the quality of labour.

Neo-classical theory views labour as a scarce commodity; in a properly functioning economy job availability is not inherently limited (see, for example, Samuelson's critique of the notion of a limited quantity of remunerative work in *Economics,* 1980, p. 541). Neo-classical economists adopt a long 'time perspective' as regards the growth of employment opportunities, pointing out that in the long term redundancies may improve productivity and create jobs. They adopt a short 'time perspective' as regards labour scarcities, assuming that these will before long result in wage increases in a given set of jobs. While recognizing the importance of short-term labour shortages, LMS theorists emphasize the alternative sources of labour available to employers. They point to historical evidence which shows that as labour shortages develop, new sources of labour supply become available whether through immigration, internal migration or the use of hitherto untapped reserves (e.g., married women). The relocation of industry to Third World countries is a further example of the search for new supplies of low-wage labour.

In contrast with neo-classical theorists, writers concerned with labour market segmentation take as their problem the structure of jobs and the factors which in practice insulate labour markets from each other. Some writers on labour market structure have considered dualism or segmentation to be a relatively recent development, i.e., associated with advanced capitalism (Edwards, Gordon and Reich, 1973). This view is based on the argument discussed earlier according to which technologically advanced firms having power over their products develop internal labour markets and provide favourable employment conditions because they need to protect firm-specific skills. However, this argument suggests that labour markets were previously unified and competitive, whereas the historical evidence indicates that labour markets have always been segmented. This was recognized in the nineteenth century, notably by J. S. Mill in his analysis of non-competing groups and by Cairnes, writing before neo-classical theory on labour markets became accepted orthodoxy. More recently writers on labour market segmentation have rejected the notion that employers' aims and needs fully account for the growth of primary sector employment conditions, as argued initially by Edwards, Gordon and Reich (1973). On the workers' side many of the activities which contribute to segmentation arise from organized attempts to secure their position on the job in the face of competition (Freedman, 1976). Employers go along with these attempts in so far as they benefit from employee stability and when they operate within a cost structure which makes it possible to provide primary employment conditions for sections of the work-force. The evolution of job structures is not the result of pressure from the workers' side or management side alone but is the outcome of compromises and accommodation as well as fixed positions taken in the face of unyielding constraints facing employers and workers respectively. Historical case studies show that there is 'a continual process of conflict, compromise and even co-operation between capitalists and workers over the form and content of the components of technical change' (Lazonick, 1979). This issue is explored further in Chapter Four on the Labour Process.

Human capital endowment (i.e., education and training) are among the factors which explain the allocation of workers to primary and secondary sector jobs. Jobs can be ranked by pay and productivity levels; in principle, workers can also be ranked according to their education, skill and potential productivity; and under perfectly functioning markets they would be allocated to jobs accordingly. According to orthodox theory, those having higher human capital endowments would be allocated to the most productive and best paid jobs. However, in practice age, race and sex are often treated as indicators of a worker's productivity, without reference to education. Moreover, there is evidence on the disparity between formal educational requirements and what is actually needed in the way of training in order to perform many primary sector jobs. There is often an inflation in the level of educational requirements when jobs become scarce and applicants are numerous. Human capital differences cannot explain the extent of pay disparities, nor their structure.

Criticizing the 'human' capital explanations of the allocation of individuals to primary and secondary sector jobs, Barry Bluestone wrote:

> Given the opportunity to escape to the high wage sector, many low-wage workers would perform admirably. Without years of extra education, without massive doses of institutional and on-the-job training, without learning a new 'industrial discipline' many low-wage workers

could fit into a unionised, profitable, capital-intensive industry and begin to earn a living wage. (Bluestone, cited in Hunter and Mulvey, 1981, p. 273)

Evidence on women drawn into male craft jobs during the War, and who performed well without full qualifications can be cited in support of this argument. (See the film *Rosie the Riveter* about women workers in the US during and after the Second World War.) In contrast, Doeringer and Priore described a 'feedback' influence by which workers acquired poor working habits from secondary sector jobs, which rendered them unsuitable for employment in the primary sector (P. Doeringer and M. Piore, 1971, p. 65). In his recent book (with Berger, 1980), Piore modifies this position by emphasizing that the institutions and culture within segments determine behaviour at work, so that unchangeable worker characteristics cannot be deduced from behaviour within any given segment. Nevertheless, Piore retains the neo-classical assumption that higher paid jobs are found in segments requiring a more skilled workforce. He recognizes that the tasks required by firms providing secondary employment conditions are more varied in many cases than in primary sector firms, but argues that these tasks are carried out under closer supervision. This argument is not backed by systematic analysis of the labour process of secondary sector firms. Evidence obtained by the Labour Studies Group of the Department of Applied Economics, Cambridge (Craig *et al.*, 1982, 1984), indicates that while many secondary type jobs are classified as semi-skilled or unskilled, this reflects relative wages paid rather than the actual learning time, range of tasks or system of labour control associated with the job. Industries using advanced technology *may* generate professional and technical jobs requiring advanced skills. However, the overall effects of technical advance on skill structures depends on the relative balance between a tendency to deskill traditional jobs and the growth of new products and technologies in which skilled jobs are essential to new forms of production.

Writers on labour market segmentation are sometimes accused of failing to provide a consistent theory because they are divided among themselves (e.g., by Hunter and Mulvey, 1981). But a new framework of analysis must undergo continual modification until a mature and coherent theory emerges which is capable of making sense of evidence which is not adequately accounted for by conventional theory. In this case, for example, evidence on the skill and effort requirements of certain poorly paid jobs in specific industries has been assembled in order to provide a more accurate analysis of the characteristics of secondary sector jobs and workers than was produced by early LMS writers (Craig *et al.*, 1982, 1984). Cross-national studies have shown the need for historical analysis to assess cultural and national influences on labour market structure. The search for evidence is now under way, through comparative national studies (for example, articles in Wilkinson, 1981, and Piore and Berger, 1980), through national case studies of firms and surveys of industries (Craig *et al.*, 1982, 1984) and national statistical evidence (Freedman, 1972; Edwards, Gordon and Reich, 1982). Greater weight is now attached to the influence of organized labour on job structures, as we have seen. New areas of inquiry are being opened as evidence is analysed from a different perspective and new theoretical contributions are made.

The subject matter of labour market analysis is of pressing importance, confronting as it does issues of poverty, relative wages and social exclusion, insecurity and job protection, productivity and industrial performance. As more evidence is analysed in relation to the emerging theoretical framework, policy implications will become increasingly relevant and extensive public debate on the issues raised by the new perspectives will be required.

In the eighteenth century Adam Smith criticized the restrictive practices of 'corporations', that is, of occupational bodies representing special interests. The role of the state was to ensure free play for the forces of supply and demand under the influence of which labour would be rewared according to its proper price (A. Smith, 1976). Throughout the nineteenth century this doctrine was accepted by successive governments. But in practice, both those supplying and those requiring labour have continued to take action and preserve institutions which operate to diminish the unpredictability and instability in earnings and labour costs which would be entailed by unregulated market forces. In a wage economy the prospect of marked fluctuations in earnings over a person's life-time under the influence of unpredictable changes in the supply of and demand for given types of labour remains unwelcome and especially so under unfavourable economic circumstances. Employers too, we have seen, seek to render both labour costs and labour supply more predictable, and some have provided primary employment conditions in doing so, to ensure employee co-operation and performance.

These issues invite speculation. It is arguable that the attachment to stability and predictability shown by employees under prevailing circumstances would be less intense if the well-being of households depended less on wages and salaries, if non-wage income based on personal and family need were provided to all citizens through public transfers or grants and if income based on earnings and benefits from employment made up a smaller proportion of personal income than is now the case.

In part at least 'labour market imperfections' denote social practices designed to reduce uncertainty and promote stability of household income, benefits which are not accorded to those excluded from job shelters. Governments seeking to remove obstacles to the 'free play of supply and demand in the labour market' might find it necessary to offer the voting public some alternative means of achieving the desired ends which are attained now through job shelters. One way in which reliance on earnings could be reduced would be through income maintenance policies capable of meeting genuine household needs, not simply basic subsistence costs such as are provided by current social security payments. Would a more extensive role for state action be entailed if the government were to attempt to prevent restrictive practices in the labour market? These issues are contentious and possible policy outcomes unclear. What is certain is that the system of wages and structure of labour markets could be significantly changed by public policies.

CHAPTER FOUR

Work organization

STEPHEN WOOD

Introduction

Discussion in British sociology of work organizations have in the past ten years been dominated by the labour process debate. The expression, the labour process, refers simultaneously to a conception of the nature and origins of work within capitalism, and a theoretical tradition which explains this sort of work. Both derive, ultimately, from Marx and, more recently, Braverman.

The emphasis in Marx was on the development of manufacturing; with the increasing use of machines, capitalism developed from handicraft production to what he called machinofacture. Braverman's *Labor and Monopoly Capital* (1974) has followed this development; he stresses that, especially with the advent of monopoly capitalism and large-scale industrial organization, capitalism involves a complete subordination of labour to capital. In this process all possibilities of initiative, direction and control are wrested from the worker. Whereas the old style artisans/craftsmen were responsible for a large part of their work, including at least some part in the design of the product and the production process, capitalists scientifically regulate all production through increasingly hierarchical management control.

As Brown (1984, p. 269) says, 'What was important about his [Braverman's] approach . . . is that within a coherent theoretical framework it directed attention to a variety of issues and topics which had previously been seen as largely unrelated'; and central to this, he continues, 'are the processes of production and reproduction of labour itself'. For example, there is a need to ask, 'where does the labour force come from? . . . How are workers socialized?' The broader issues are dealt with in Chapter Three. The emphasis in this chapter will be primarily on the questions of skill and control.

The four issues which will *not* be explored in great depth here are: worker resistance; the question of the similarity between capitalist and socialist labour processes; the location of changes within the labour process and the intensification of work within the context of other forms of rationalization and internationalization of the economy; and finally, the relationship between employment and domestic labour.

This chapter is concerned with the design and nature of jobs. With the development of mass production methods and systematic managerial control in the twentieth century, have jobs increasingly become devoid of skill and intrinsic meaning? If so, why? Does this reflect changing technology, or is it, as Braverman suggests, more a reflection of a scientific management inherent to the capitalist enterprise? If there is a trend towards deskilled jobs, is it inevitable? What of counter tendencies, or attempts to reverse the trend through the use of humanistic methods largely derived from social sciences?

Section one introduces Braverman's deskilling thesis, in which emphasis is placed on the specificity of the capitalist labour process and the importance of Taylorism in it. This is followed by a section on skill, which ends with a brief discussion of the problems involved in assessing the changing trend in jobs. Section three discusses the role of technology and the extent to which jobs reflect it. Section four looks at the question of alternatives to scientific management and attempts to 'humanize' work.

A major concern of this chapter is to introduce the readers to some of the methodological and empirical complexities involved in the development of work organization. Attention will focus mainly on factory work, partly because as we saw in Chapter One it is treated as the stereotype of all work, but also because of its centrality in both economy and past writings about it and in the labour process.

1. The deskilling thesis

We have seen in previous chapters the centrality accorded, in much recent discussion on work organization, to the domination of capital and the need for control. There has been what P. Thompson (1984) calls a rediscovery of the labour process and Garnsey (1984), a rediscovery of the division of labour. Central to these rediscoveries, as both authors note, is Braverman's work which is an attempt to *renew* Marx's theory of the labour process and apply it to subsequent historical development, taking a fresh look at skills, technology and work organization. The argument is that it is the logic of capitalist accumulation, and not the imperatives of technology, which dictate work organization. There is, within this Marxist perspective, a fundamental conflict between workers and capitalists, and this, coupled with the economic efficiency of specialization, dictates that capital, through the process of management, eliminates the scope for workers' control or discretion for the individual worker.

The importance of the notion of a labour process is, as Garnsey (1984, p. 38) says, that it provides a more direct focus on the division of labour itself in contrast with analyses which treats the 'prevailing state of technology' as given. As Garnsey also stresses, Braverman directs attention away from a technological determinist interpretation of Marx, arguing 'that the capital intensive deskilling and labour displacing features of modern industrial technology are to be accounted for with reference to the structure of constraints and incentives created by the property relations of capitalism'. As such Braverman, and other recent followers of Marx, 'analyze division of labour as the outcome of a given distribution of power, they reject the premise that technology is neutral, and inquire into the ways in which the direction of technological development has served specific interests' (Garnsey, 1984 pp. 38–40).

Deskilling and Taylor's scientific management

Central to Braverman's thesis is the importance of managerial control – the merciless directions from the control room (Kamata, 1982, p. 200) – rather than technology. On the deskilling process F. W. Taylor's famous work *Scientific Management,* first published in 1912, emphasized the need for systematic study and the planning of work. His central concept was the distinction between conception and execution, between designing tasks and carrying them out. Taylor argued that professional managers should take full responsibility for conception, thus: 'The art of management is knowing exactly what you want men to do, and then seeing that they do it in the best and cheapest way' (see 1947 edn., p. 21).

Taylor's proposal for scientific management involved three important tasks:

  (i) the development of a science for each element of a man's work, which replaces the old rule-of-thumb method;
 (ii) the scientific selection and training and development of workmen;
(iii) the co-operation with the men so as to ensure that all of the work is being done in accordance with the principles of the science which has been developed.

Taylor contrasted this proposal with existing styles of management which were either highly authoritarian (the workers being driven or coerced by their bosses) or *laissez-faire* (the worker being 'left to his own devices'). He argued that most experienced and enlightened managers were adopting the *laissez-faire* approach and, by so doing, were leaving the task of management to the workers. They were thus placing 'before their workmen the problem of doing the work in the best and most economical way'. Under this system success depends almost entirely upon getting the 'initiative of the workmen', and this is attempted by incentives. It was management by incentive in as much as management was through the payment system; to Taylor it was management by neglect. As Taylor says (1947, p. 62), 'Under the management of "initiative and incentive" practically the whole problem is "up to the workman".' By contrast, under scientific management, management takes on new, and previously neglected duties such that 'fully one-half of the problem is up to the management' (Taylor, 1947, p. 38).

> The management must take over and perform much of the work which is now left to the men; almost every act of the workman should be preceded by one or more preparatory acts of the management which enable him to do his work better and quicker than he otherwise could. And each man should daily be taught by and receive the most friendly help from those who are over him, instead of being, at the one extreme driven or coerced by his bosses, and at the other left to his own unaided devices. (Taylor, 1947, p. 26)

The significance of Taylor for Braverman is that he was the first management theorist to acknowledge the necessity of management control. Taylor outlined the theoretical justification and the practical means whereby this process could be set in motion: as such, according to Braverman, Taylorism is 'the explicit verbalization of the capitalist mode of production'. Braverman takes the core of Taylorism to be his usage of the distinction between conception and execution. Applying this in practice would divorce mental from manual work and would reduce the jobs of the mass of workers, including what are termed white-collar workers, to degrading tasks lacking any responsibility, knowledge or interest. The degradation to which Braverman refers can be seen to encompass a number of processes:

(i) a process whereby the shop-floor worker loses the right to design and plan work;
(ii) the fragmentation of work into meaningless segments;
(iii) the redistribution of tasks amongst unskilled and semi-skilled labour, associated with labour cheapening;
(iv) the transformation of work organization from the craft system to modern, Taylorite forms of labour control.

Technology, for Braverman, is less important than the growth of managerial control: for mechanization goes hand in hand with the advance in Taylorism, which is concerned with and appropriate to any level of technology. As P. Thompson (1984) implies, this is seen by Braverman as one of Taylorism's great strengths. It has increasingly pervaded work organization in the twentieth century, and attempts to introduce alternatives to it – for example, through the application of social science such as the human relations theory developed since the 1930s (to be discussed in section four) – are significant, in Braverman's thesis, only in so far as they 'habituate' workers to the dictates of Taylorist systems. There is thus a big gulf between the rhetoric and the reality of modern 'human relations' whose significance is essentially ideological: 'Taylorism dominates the world of production; the practitioners of "human relations" . . . are the maintenance crew for the human machinery' (Braverman, 1974, p. 87).

The deskilling debate

Braverman's work has been subjected to a great deal of examination, much of it critical (for full details of this, see Thompson, 1984; Wood, 1982). Central to it is Braverman's self-imposed limitation to what he terms the objective aspects of capitalist development. This, as Thompson (1984) notes, amounts to a 'deliberate exclusion of the dimension of class struggle and consciousness', or as Braverman puts it, 'the modern working class on the level of its consciousness, organization and activities'. Accordingly, Braverman (1974, pp. 26–7) claims that his argument is 'about the working class as a class *in itself*, not as class *for itself*'. This has attracted the criticism that in so following this procedure he neglected the role of class struggle in history, and its manifestation in industrial conflict. There are at least three possible implications one can draw from this:

(i) Braverman's work needs to be extended to take account of the consciousness of the working class and its struggle against the dictates of capitalism;
(ii) when developing their control strategies, especially with the increasing unionization of workers in the twentieth century, managements have to take account of potential worker resistance;
(iii) work organization is partly the outcome of struggle between capital and labour, and subjective and ideological assumptions, for example about gender, also influence it.

Whilst it may be misleading in certain cases to identify an author too rigidly with a particular one of the above arguments, it is possible to suggest authors to illustrate each type. Zimbalest (1979), introducing a set of interesting cases on the labour process, is illustrative of the first. He defends Braverman on two counts: first, that where workers have resisted they have not been able effectively to limit managerial control, and second, that Braverman is talking about a long-term tendency.

Both Friedman (1977) and Edwards (1979), who emphasize the importance of resistance by workers, for example to Taylorism, in relation to *managerial* behaviour illustrate the second of the arguments. In the twentieth century, managements have had to come to terms with resistance, especially in times of full employment. As a result, they have had to adopt more liberal methods than Taylorism: what Friedman terms 'responsible autonomy' strategies. Methods such as the gang system, human relations, job re-design, are all treated by Friedman as genuine alternatives to Taylorist methods, or 'direct control' strategies, as he prefers to call them. In certain circumstances management has to come to terms with human needs and potential recalcitrance of workers, by building real autonomy and discretion into jobs or by allowing groups of workers to run themselves. This contrasts with Braverman's position, according to which such methods merely represent an alternative *style* of management rather than a genuine change in the position of the worker. For Friedman, the collective organized strength of work groups can force management to adopt strategies other than direct control, or Taylorism.

The third of the three implications listed above points to the omniscient, almostly overtly conspiratorial, model of management in Braverman's work, in which he presents the reorganization of the labour process as the outcome of a conscious design rather than as the product of the struggle of contending groups (Zeitlin, 1979; Cressey and McInnes, 1980; Littler, 1982; Wood, 1982). While it may be necessary to have hierarchical modes of management and specialized divisions of labour, strategic groups of workers often play a crucial role in the determination of the structure of these hierarchies and in the division of labour. Moreover, the struggle is not simply a battle between autonomous and free-floating policies of management and workers, for these policies themselves are forged out of the changing technological and market opportunities available to enterprises.

Any solutions to management's problem of control are, in this view, temporary and precarious. Management is not onniscient, nor does it have an absolute prerogative over the design and conception of work. A minimum of consent and co-operation has to be gained for management's plans and rights, and this need is rooted in the collective nature of the labour process. Even consent based on the 'dull compulsion' of the labour market and the coercion of economic necessity is necessarily precarious and has to be supported by ideologies concerning the importance of employment and economic efficiency. Furthermore, management may not accord absolute primacy to the problem of control. Even within Braverman's terms, control is for profit, and not necessarily for its own sake. This latter point goes beyond Friedman's argument that employers may seek to avoid conflict with highly organized work-forces, and cede control over task performance, provided the work group attains a minimum level of productive efficiency. The maximization of productive efficiency cannot be reduced to labour intensification. Goods are produced for sale on the market, and profitable production presupposes past investment decisions that secure the 'right mix' of production processes. Very often the labour process debate takes place in the vacuum of the shop floor, and can fall prey to a kind of thinking which values above all else production for production's sake. But the structure of the market can limit the kind of labour process used, and, on the other hand, the market itself is not totally independent of managerial initiatives. For example, in the early 1980s British car components manufacturers attempted to lift this market constraint by reducing their product range and securing access to foreign markets, thereby creating the conditions for volume production.

In appraising Braverman we should focus not so much on what he neglects, as on his treatment of what he does deal with; as P. Thompson shows, Braverman acknowledges opposition to Taylorism, but treats it as having little or no significance or effect. Furthermore, Braverman makes certain assumptions about working-class consciousness and organization that can be questioned: essentially, that workers' aims are purely to secure economistic objectives such as high wages and job security, aims which mirror the dominant profit motive of capitalists.

We might also question Braverman's particular use of Taylorism. At the fundamental level his treatment of it as expressing the logic of capitalism and as providing an adequate language with which to describe the objective side of the development of the capitalist enterprise can be challenged. Certainly Braverman relies very heavily on Taylor's own account of scientific management when outlining the development of the capitalist labour process: he does not examine in sufficient depth actual work situations or conscious applications of Taylorite principles, and consequently relies excessively on the theorization offered by management theorists of organizations. At least four consequences follow from this. First, Braverman does not pay sufficient attention to the problems attached to the implementation of Taylorism. Second, he ignores the resistance that some workers and managers have offered to inhibit its introduction or transform its effects. Third, he does not examine empirically the effects of Taylorism in practice. Fourth, human relations and other forms of management cannot, by definition and not by analysis, be genuine options – for Taylorism is *the* labour process of capitalism.

There is also the problem of Braverman's conception of Taylorism. For example, Taylor (1947) was conscious, and increasingly so, of the problem of co-operation and gaining consent, legitimacy and shared understandings: 'Without cooperation there is no scientific management', he wrote. He struggled to arrive at an answer, and to convince managers of the need for a change in their attitude. This 'mental revolution', as he called it, would involve treating workers with care and consideration as opposed to the more normal tyrannical approach. Ultimately Taylor fell back on the authority of science to legitimize his ideas and management's role.

Rather than assuming the supremacy of Taylorism, it is more useful to start from an appreciation of the limits of, constraints upon, and contradictions within scientific management. For example, an individualized work organization may not always be feasible. It is perhaps not surprising that the Tavistock Institute's attempt to develop an alternative to Taylorism's socio-technical theory (to be discussed later) – with an emphasis on autonomous groups without supervisors and flexible working arrangements – began in coal mining (Trist and Bamford, 1951) and not manufacturing. More generally, we should be aware of the variety of labour processes which exist. In some cases, it may not be technically or economically possible to specify closely all the tasks to be performed, especially in small batch production.

As was stated at the beginning of the chapter, a full treatment of all issues is beyond the scope of the present context. Having concentrated on Braverman's highlighting of Taylorism at the expense of technology, we shall now concentrate on three problematic features of the deskilling thesis: the content of skill, the role of technology and the nature of work humanization.

2. Skill

For Braverman, Marx's assertion that the capitalist must both provide the right materials for the worker, *and* exert control over the conditions within which the speed, skill and dexterity of the worker operate, means that all jobs will be increasingly fragmented and devoid of skill. There are many social science studies (see, for example, Beynon (1974), Linhart (1984) and Cavendish (1984), which describe work which accords with Braverman's characterization. Assembly line work which is machine-paced, repetitive and devoid of skill, is commonly treated as prototypical of modern work, its character linked as it is to the mass-production methods assumed to be intrinsic to modern industry. The implications for work motivation are well expressed by one of the car workers Beynon (1974, p. 114) wrote about in *Working for Fords*:

> You don't achieve anything here. A robot could do it. The line here is made for morons. It doesn't need any thought. They tell you that. 'We don't pay you for thinking', they say. Everyone comes to realise that they're not doing a worthwhile job. They're just on the line. For the money. Nobody likes to think that they're a failure. It's bad when you know that you're just a little cog. You just look at your pay packet – you look at what it does for your wife and kids. That's the only answer.

Pollert (1981, p. 98) reports similar boredom on the part of the women workers she studied who talked about the routine nature of their jobs:

> Jackie: 'You're stuck up there on the machine and honestly all you've got to do is wait for the red light to go on, and then you've got it over and over again.'
> Jenny: 'When I first worked in here, I went home and I see these packets coming down the line.'

Such accounts, it may be argued, are hardly surprising since by definition the jobs to which the quotations referred are either unskilled or, like routine automobile assembly work, are classified as semi-skilled. But the very use of the term semi-skilled does raise questions about the official categorization of jobs, and as Braverman (1974, pp. 424–47) suggests this is perhaps somewhat arbitrary. This suggests skill might best be treated relatively and not as an absolute: that is, not simply as something that either exists, as in skilled work, or does not exist, as in unskilled work. There is thus a question as to how skill is to be defined, which must be posed prior to any consideration of whether modern work is deskilled.

For many, including Braverman, the exercise of skill is assumed to involve the creative use of initiative and brain power. Skilled manual work is assumed to combine skills of the hand and brain and to resemble the traditional artisan's craftsmanship. It is this kind of creative work which Braverman assumes will disappear as capitalism develops. The picture gained from Blackburn and Mann's (1979) study of one locality in Britain, is one of widespread absence of skill in the jobs available to a large proportion of the working class. It is important, though, to bear in mind that this study excludes skilled jobs; so that it cannot be used by itself to support a simple deskilling thesis. But it does describe the content of a large number of the jobs in the labour market, and what its authors term 'the objective situation of the majority of the manual working class'. The only feasible choice available to such workers is between working indoors, in a factory or warehouse, or outdoors, for example as park keeper or on a building site. One of Blackburn and Mann's overall conclusions is that most workers use more skill and mental effort if they drive a car to work than they do in their work itself. This comparison is important precisely because driving is a complex activity which may involve a variety of skills, albeit perhaps of a tacit kind.

It is not only academics who use the analogy of the car. Kusterer (1978, p. 50) remarks, 'Over and over again, operators use the analogy between operating one of their machines and driving a car.' Kusterer (1978, pp. 50–1) goes on to argue:

> The main point that they were all trying to make is that it is not enough just to know how to start, stop, clean and maintain their machines. That level of knowledge . . . knowing the 'rules about driving' . . . is about the level that the women reach by the end of their three-day training period. The next higher level of knowledgeability, which is the real *sine qua non* of successful machine operation, requires that the operators learn the idiosyncracies of their individual machines.

Manwaring and Wood (1984) use the term 'tacit skills' to describe the kind of knowledgeability referred to in this example. They use this concept to question the assumption that capitalism inevitably reduces workers to automators and to point to the dangers of associating skill with conscious thought and of treating consciousness as an absolute. They make a number of points. First, the performance of 'routine' tasks involves a process of learning whereby skills are acquired through experience. The example of driving shows the way in which routines are developed through the interaction of both conscious and unconscious processes. At the early stages of learning such skills, too much conscious thought may be counter-productive, leading to poor judgement and co-ordination. The transformation of learning into successful routine performance is a process of internalizing patterned movements and reduced awareness. The learning of dance routines, typing, operating presses, for example, all involve a relation between the mind and body, enabling the actions to be successfully repeated without full awareness.

In addition, different degrees of awareness are required when performing different activities. The tacit routine skill of which the worker has little awareness can be contrasted with the problem of coping with unfamiliar situations for which existing routines are inadequate. To return to the motoring example, driving on a familiar road may require little direct awareness, overtaking on a motorway may become a kind of semi-aware routine, while overtaking in a dangerous situation requires much fuller awareness. In industry, the use of 'tricks of the trade', such as workers using cigarette papers as wedges in machines whose parts have been worn down, are one example of this heightened awareness.

A further aspect of tacit skills relates to the collective nature of the labour process and the necessity for workers to develop co-operative skills. There are many such skills required in the production process, including congeniality, 'mucking in' and elements of obedience. Of special significance, given the integrated nature of production, is workers' awareness of the way their jobs relate to the production process. The example of working in a sausage plant illustrates this well; a former meat-chopper told Manwaring and Wood (1984, p. 173) how he had to learn to 'read' the line ahead of him in order to set an appropriate pace for his work so that the flow of the whole line was synchronized. Such skill involves an ability to spot the problems that can arise in jobs which are related to one another, problems which are rooted in transfer systems, differential capacity levels and variable production rates.

The existence of tacit skills underlies many of the characteristics of workers valued by the managers as discussed, for example, in the studies of recruitment (Blackburn and Mann, 1979; Manwaring, 1984; Wood, 1985). The importance of experience and tacit skills in proficient production is reflected in the quest for workers who can 'fit in', even if they only need short training times. This rationale makes sense in the light of one manager's emphasis (as reported in Manwaring and Wood, 1984, p. 173) on the importance of the distinction between 'making widgets, making widgets *efficiently* as part of a production system, and making widgets efficiently as part of an *ongoing* production system'.

Both workers and personnel managers can describe jobs as 'lousy' or as 'monkey jobs', while at the same time being aware that these descriptions do not do full justice to the range of skills required. It is probably correct to argue that 'most workers are objectively capable of acquiring the skills necessary for most jobs; we estimate that 85 per cent of workers can do 95 per cent of jobs' (Blackburn and Mann, 1979, p. 280). But it does not follow that non-skilled manual jobs differ only in the different levels of human debasement they involve' (ibid.). The problem with such conclusions is that tacit skills are often taken for granted. Basic working motions are learned which have, however infrequently, to be supplemented by new motions required to deal with unexpected situations.

That some jobs, or aspects of them, require a good deal of knowledge and experience has a number of implications. The most obvious is that we cannot judge a job simply by its title or even by its superficial characteristics. Formal training times, whilst important, will not tell the whole picture, since much of the acquisition of knowledge is done on the job. There is a wide variety of jobs, even within one production system and just as there may be different academic evaluations of the extent or importance of such skills, so those in organizations who are responsible for evaluating and defining jobs may make differing assessments. Certainly, there can be no simple, straightforward relationship between skill and reward. Craig *et al.* (1982) show how in small firms in specialized product markets, which often pay relatively poorly, the demands made on supposedly 'unskilled' workers are significantly higher than those made on similar workers in large firms, with probably higher paid jobs.

It is often the case that much of what is conventionally defined as women's work may require high degrees of skill, often at least comparable with that which is usually associated with the skilled worker. This has prompted Phillips and Taylor (quoted in Wood, 1982; see also Phillips and Taylor, 1980) to ask, 'Are jobs female because they are unskilled, or unskilled because they are female?' This raises in a stark way the whole question of the relationship between job titles and skill levels.

The high degree of segregation between males and females is revealed in a government survey in which 63 per cent of women were found to be working in women only jobs (Martin and Roberts, 1984 p. 27). Cockburn (1983) shows how in the printing industry jobs were defined in such a way as to exclude women. In industries such as clothing and engineering, female and male jobs are found side by side in the same plant, but significantly are classified as unskilled and skilled respectively and may, in many cases, not differ substantially in content.

The common valuation of women's work as lower than men's is often held by both union officials and management (Charles, 1983) and women are paid less than men for doing what are often very similar jobs. There are also certain tasks which currently women can perform at higher rates of productivity than men. The most obvious examples are the fiddly, repetitive monotonous tasks requiring dexterity of assembly operators in the electronic industries or the machinists in the garment trade (Elson and Pearson, 1981). Even though many people feel that women are 'naturally' more suited to this sort of work, it is continually undervalued and universally defined as unskilled or semi-skilled. Part of the explanation for this lies in the fact that differences in the ability to do this type of work may reflect the way women trained for it at home from their earliest years: for work which is often highly skilled is not recognized as such, precisely because training does not take place within the workplace and is therefore conceived of as a natural ability possessed by women and not men.

So, as Cockburn (1983) and others suggest, gender differences play a crucial role in job definitions. This kind of discussion of job definitions further indicates problems of a simple, unilinear deskilling model and the assumed homogenization of the working class. The categories of 'women's work' and 'men's work' which are continually introduced and reinforced in the restructuring of production, ensure a differentiation of the working class on a basis which is relatively independent of the skill content of the various tasks concerned, whereas they may be based on an association of physical strength with men and other qualities (such as dexterity) with women. Because Braverman is attacking the job definitions imposed by capital on the working class, he can readily dismiss other categories as false ones which disguise the real process of deskilling. But if it is accepted that job definitions are determined, at least partly, through the struggles of a working class divided by sexual hierarchy, then their social importance must be recognized. In a smaller way, it is possible to accept that there are important ideological dimensions to the question of skill and that some groups of workers have been able to maintain their skilled definitions through processes of exclusion, while still maintaining that many jobs and competences, including the tacit skills discussed earlier, require considerable training and aptitudes.

The need to get beneath the broad classification of jobs, and the issue of exclusion, has been central to the discussion of male skilled work, as well as women's work. As P. Thompson (1984) says, by idealizing craft work it is possible to overestimate the extent of its destruction. There is too much emphasis on a particular model of crafts when skilled work is being discussed. For Braverman the continued use of the term 'skilled worker' reflects a labelling process which his deskilling thesis is concerned to de-mystify. This is an extreme form of what has been known as the 'social construction of skills' thesis. This thesis – that jobs are labelled skilled even though their content is largely unskilled – is linked especially to the question of the extent to which workers in modern industry, who are recognized as skilled (through the serving of an apprenticeship or some other accepted route to skilled work such as seniority), actually use or need their skills, and indeed of the extent to which they have acquired skills at all.

Two versions of the argument that skill is socially constructed are possible. One might stress the way in which labels attached to certain jobs are created or maintained by managements as a way of coping with worker resistance; that is, they are used to segment and reduce the power and cohesion of the workers. This is the way in which some radical writers have chosen to use the notion of internal labour markets; that is, to assume that the creation of a ladder of jobs is not founded on any significant differences in the skill content of jobs, but rather is an attempt to divide and rule work-forces. At the other extreme is the argument that job labels are the direct result of workers' resistance or initiatives; in particular, strongly organized groups of workers may secure for themselves a level of wages normally or previously associated with apprentice. Trained workers may even create and control their own apprenticeship system, perhaps designed to reinforce exclusive unionism rather than to provide a necessary and comprehensive training.

Both these views are extreme and can be attacked with the same evidence and argument. For example, Penn (1982), drawing on empirical material from the British engineering and textile industries, shows how workers were able to defend their jobs from managements' attempts to deskill them, by strategies of exclusion which maintained the privileges of skill and even in some cases created skill. This does not necessarily mean that there was an underlying deskilling process, for successful exclusion took place before mechanization, and was linked to the strategic importance of the skill in the industry's overall production process. More (1982), drawing on historical material on the apprenticeship system in the nineteenth century, suggests that those who possessed the label of skill exercised (and exercise) functions necessary for efficient industry. The implications are that skill demands are, at least partly, related to technological developments and that there will be variations between industries, and countries, in the effects of changes in the craft system.

Strictly speaking, in sociological terms, all skills are socially constructed, since even 'genuinely' skilled jobs are not simply derivatives of a god-given technology. The issue hinges on the basis on which jobs and skills are constructd, and whether the criteria by which jobs are defined and workers differentiated are relatively independent of the 'technical' skill content of jobs. It is necessary, as Beechey (1982, pp. 63–4) suggests, to distinguish between three elements when discussing skill:

  (i) objectively defined complex competences;
 (ii) control over conception and execution; and
(iii) 'socially defined occupational status', which may be largely independent of the level of objectively defined competencies.

The importance of these distinctions is that they point to the problems of making general conclusions about the changing nature of work and occupations. First, there is the question of evidence. If we rely on government statistics we must work with relatively broad categories: this, albeit to a lesser extent, is also a problem with the sociological studies of occupational structure. Secondly, there is the problem of generalizing: is it meaningful to talk of an average level of skill in society, and hence to attempt to monitor changes in it? Thirdly, there is the question of the role of technology. Many of the attempts to paint broad, historical pictures tend to read off job contents from the historical development of technology, since it is tempting to link modern industrial organization with the quickening pace of mechanization in the last decades of nineteenth century. We shall now look more closely at the issue of technology.

3. Technology and the labour process

In the 1950s and 1960s, with the advent of the computer and an increasing optimism about technology, as well as a technocratic ideology, the latest technologies were being heralded by some as a means of enhancing work. Just as the car worker was seen as prototypical of mass-production assembly work, so the chemical worker was viewed as prototypical of the modern process industries. He or she would not be doing boring, routine, dirty work but exercising judgement, sitting in a clean environment, monitoring the controls of a highly complex technology. Blauner (1964), in his study of *Alienation and the Worker*, gave sociological credence to this line of argument. He suggested that there was a U-shaped relationship between alienation and technology and that the worker in modern industries would be less alienated than his or her predecessors. Mass production, assembly line work did indeed represent the low point in the development of the labour process, but it should not be regarded as its final state, or as prototypical. This approach is consistent with the studies of Kerr *et al.* (1964), which see the process of economic development and large-scale production as having a given logic, a *logic of industrialization*. Because of its emphasis both on the increasing diffusion and development of modern technology and on given consequences, this approach is often labelled technological determinism. In assessing such thinking there is a danger of creating a strawman by imputing an excessive technicism to authors – certainly Kerr *et al.* (1964) in emphasizing technology as the primary motor of modern industry, do not rule out other factors and particularly the role of ideology or culture. There is also a danger of over-reacting against this approach and denying any independent role to technology. All too often in such discussions it is the model of technology itself that is inadequate or insufficiently developed – although a weakness of Blauner's work is also his failure to really explore the content of the jobs to which he refers. Blauner's approach and the weaknesses underlying it have been succinctly put by Hill (1981, p. 97): 'The stages and evolution of technology are based on a description of previous events, which are then extrapolated into the future without a full explanation of the underlying tendency of change or with insufficient consideration of the consequences of such a tendency.'

At least two types of sociological study have been used to refute technological determinism. First are the international comparative studies, three of which stand out, because similar plants in different countries are compared, and hence technology held constant. Dore's (1978) comparison of two plants in the electrical engineering sector points to differences, at least in the conditions of employment, between Japanese and British workers, explicable largely in terms of cultural differences. Similarly Gallie (1978) points to similar differences through comparison of a British with a French oil refinery, and Maurice *et al.* (1980) through a comparison of British, French and German plants. Although none of these studies go into the details of the content of jobs, they imply that there are differences in the allocation of tasks to jobs, as well as in the qualifications of job holders. Thus, in the study by Maurice *et al.*, the proportion of skilled to unskilled workers and educational qualifications were higher in France and West Germany than in Britain.

Second, there are studies which concentrate on the introduction of 'new' technology. Child (1984), for example, shows the variety of contexts in which new technology is introduced and the resulting variety in its consequences. The study by Bryn Jones (1982) also stresses this variety, and concludes by making an important general methodological point, that the effects of new technology are contingent on the product and labour markets of the firm, as well as the overall managerial strategy and on the balance of power between the management and trade unions.

The study by Wilkinson (1983) of the introduction of new technology emphasizes the political nature of the process of introducing it. Although Wilkinson ends up supporting a Braverman-type argument that management's introduction of technology is largely motivated by a desire for control, he does admit that its effects may be ameliorated by resistance from existing job holders. Cockburn's study of print workers also illustrates the uneven and unpredictable effect of new technology. Cockburn suggests how jobs are created as masculine and feminine, with their skill contents continually redrawn so as to assert male exclusivity. From its beginning in the fifteenth century, printing has kept women out, establishing a lengthy and ritualistic apprenticeship that prohibited female entry. Cockburn shows how printers have created definitions of the appropriate worker as tough and competitive, and able to survive in the heat, dirt and clamour of the composing room. To secure the male identity of their jobs, printers even accepted a degree of heavy manual work which they could well have off-loaded on to lower paid workers. So, as employers attempted to divide work further, compositors insisted on redefining their job to include a range of different skills. Their appeal to the ideal of an all-round worker established their work as strictly men's work. The new technology, with its keyboards like that of a standard typewriter, creates a paradox: after years of fostering an association of such work with female labour, they find themselves fighting to secure jobs which increasingly look like those done by women. Men have continually attempted to maintain their position and create a politically defined skill: to claim that 'they are skilled, even if the job is not'. Consequently, collective struggles over new technology may focus on skill, even when they are not simply about skill, but about employment, or the basic issue of the value and control of labour power. So, Cockburn concludes, new technologies do have an impact on both skill and employment levels, but not in a deterministic way.

Taken together, the above studies may refute a straightforward technological determinism. But in so far as they will develop differently away from it, and since their authors interpret their results within a different perspective – Dore, Gallie, Maurice *et al.*, for example, highlighting the importance of national cultures and education; B. Jones, market and strategic contingencies; Cockburn, Marxist feminism; and Wilkinson, a Marxism similar to Braverman's – they suggest that there is perhaps no simple alternative.

The importance of technology

In reacting to 'technological determinism' it is useful to distinguish:

(i) questions concerning technological development;
(ii) questions concerning the linkage between technological changes and work organization.

The first question involves a more detailed examination of the sociology of technology than can be given here. But it is important to stress that in much organization theory, including that which accords primacy to it, technology tends to be treated as an autonomous force. This has been well exposed as a myth by Melman (1974, pp. 56–8):

> A mystique of technology has been developed by many writers which holds that society is not only powerfully affected by technology, but that man and society have become the creatures of the machine. Technology is understood as having its own internal dynamics and direction: man's inventing only makes concrete what is predetermined by the inherent scheme of the machine process itself. The resulting view is that men, individually and as society, are significantly shaped by the self-initiated technology . . . [But] man's social – especially economic – relations are imprinted upon technology. It cannot be otherwise because there is no way to make technology that is abstracted from society. Thereby, technology has built into it characteristics of the given

> social relational system, especially the decison-making process on pro-
> duction. In that way criteria for decision making (relations of produc-
> tion) are built into the means of production. There is no way of having
> a means of production without that being the case. . . . There is no
> socially abstracted means of production, or other technology.

Without the myth of autonomous technology, it becomes less easy to
see the course of human history as a simple reflection of scientific and
technological progress. The extreme form of technological determinism
marries with a common tendency to associate the development of science
with serendipity and individual genius, each new step being made possible by the historically prior one. The counter-interpretation is that scientific advance is neither as orderly or individualistic as this, nor as free of
choices, particularly choices as to where investment in research should be
made. Emphasis here is placed on the way in which such choices reflect
the needs of the military and industry, and on the fact that the technological application of science is not simply triggered by advances in human
knowledge, but is stimulated with the powerful sense of the possibility of
profiting from it.

As far as the second question is concerned, a simple example can be
used to show that the linkage between technology and work organization
is not a simple deterministic one: the example of the multi-purpose, man-
ually controlled turret lathe, which at all times and places represents the
same level of technological development, if it is defined in terms of the
mechanization of the production activities carried out on it. Yet,
operator jobs on the traditional lathe can be very different. Operators
may, for example, be engaged in single unit production; they do not then
manufacture two identical pieces, but their tasks change from product to
product and they have to work from technical drawings and often change
the setting of the machine often several times a day. In contrast, operators
on identical machines can be engaged in short cycle, repeated work tasks
on a single product that does not vary from month to month. In the
former case, the work is varied, interesting and autonomous, and
operators are unlikely to be pressured or to be on piece work. In the latter
case, however, the piece to be machined comes to the operators directly
from the machine doing the previous operation, and the machine is set
for them. Consequently, the speed of their activities is to a great extent
fixed, and they are classified as semi-skilled; they are working on a piece-
rate system and their job is of a routine, monotonous nature. These differences in the content of work clearly cannot be attributed to differences
in the technological level of machinery; in the two cases the person-
machine relationship is the same. There are, however, very significant
differences in the person-production system relationship. In the first case
the machine and person are part of a workshop doing a single-unit production, that is a workshop producing prototypes or a repair shop; in the
second they belong to a unit where large batch production and perhaps

even mass production is carried out.

It is the potentiality for such differences in work organization within the same technology that led social scientists to coin the term mentioned earlier, socio-technical systems, to draw attention to the totality of the production system and not simply the person-machine interface. This notion emerged from the famous Tavistock studies of, for example, mining, in which alternative forms of organizing the newly mechanizing systems of production were discussed (Trist and Bamford, 1951). It is at this point that arguments about developments in technology and work organization intersect. For there is an argument that it is precisely because technology is not inherently deterministic that technologies may be designed with the human in mind.

There are two versions of this. There is the socio-technical systems argument which, having established the success of different types of work organization within a given technology, argues for a role for the social scientist in the design of technology. Most recently this argument has been applied to computer installations, with a view to ensuring that allowance is made for the human operator and the users of the system. At the other extreme is the argument that implies that capitalists have little choice but to build the – or to be more accurate its – human problem into the design equation by developing technologies which increase managerial control and reduce the discretion of the operator. This would be the view consistent with Braverman's emphasis on Taylorism, and it is supported by Noble (1978) and Wilkinson (1983), who have suggested that it is management's motivation for control that dictates the introduction of new technology, since such control is increasingly being built into machines. This kind of argument, however, may imply a highly conscious engineering process. The more typical case is that implied by Rosenbrock (1984, p. 167) who suggests that though the human element is not totally ignored by engineers, it is treated within a perspective which considers people as though they were robots, a perspective which is firmly ingrained in the ideology of engineers and others responsible for job design.

For such an argument to have force in relation to job design, note that the implication must be that technology at least sets limits to the types of work organizations which can be achieved. Indeed, it would appear to constrain the nature of tasks. There may, for example, be a varietyof types of assembly line, and control systems surrounding them, but the routine nature of tasks (even with job rotation), and the speed of the line, are ever present. Thus it may be that, in many of the instances he cites, Blauner's account of work tasks and their direct linkage to the technology is accurate, as one of his critics Hill (1981, p. 94) admits. But a further problem arises, as Walker and Guest (1952) highlighted in their classification of the car assembly worker, because of the variety of jobs involved even within a given plant or technology: Nichols and

Armstrong (1978) have also highlighted this problem very well, for in the case of the process industries, Blauner's theory focuses on the new style white-collar operators concerned with monitoring the plant, at the expense of the majority of production workers in such plants, who are in effect labourers, just humping bags of materials around. Similar mistakes are often made in connection with the recent new technology. The optimistic view about the effects on jobs – the elimination of boring jobs and the development of a service orientation amongst workers – focuses on specific tasks, and forgets that the production of the parts for the new technology are being produced on very conventional routine assembly lines. There are plants in south-east Asia, for example, producing billions of microchips a month through a highly fragmented labour process. The pessimistic view of the new technology, likewise, concentrates on one type of job, jobs which are deskilled or eliminated, again at the expense of the new, often highly skilled jobs created by it. As Cockburn (1983, p. 218) says in the conclusions to her book: 'Management cannot reduce all of us to the identity of robots because someone has to design and maintain its labour process.'

4. Taylorism and work humanization

The practice of Taylorism

Having pointed to some of the problems involved in discussing deskilling, we shall now look more closely at the attempt, inspired primarily by social scientists, to consciously modify the effects of an increasing division of labour. Until Braverman's thesis, there was a tendency amongst social scientists to present industrial sociology as consisting of a progression from human relations to more modern theories built on, for example, socio-technical or action concepts. The implication, intended or otherwise, was that Taylorism could be relegated to a matter of historical curiosity or, at best, as something not applicable to the modern technologies which were being developed: it had been superseded by alternative, more humanistic and richer approaches, which could be treated as being totally distinct from, or as overcoming, the weaknesses of Taylorism.

The precise relationship between Taylorism and subsequent theories is complex and a matter of debate. Certainly, it is not necessary to treat the latter as totally distinct from Taylorism; that is, different on all dimensions. Mayo (1949), one of the forefathers of the human relations movement, took the increasing utilization of Taylorism as his starting point, almost as if his intention was to compensate for its effects, rather than modify them or point to forms of work organization different from a Taylorist system. One of the strengths of Braverman's approach is that he questions the extent to which Taylorism has been superseded, at least in practice; for whilst its theoretical underpinnings may seem outmoded to academic social scientists, it may remain relevant to industrialists and therefore continue to dominate the way they structure both their thinking and the work systems they manage. Nor need they be applying Taylorist principles consciously; either because – as Armstrong (1984) implies may be the case for many engineers – such principles are an integral part of their ideology or taken for granted, or because, as Braverman's analysis implies, in order to survive in the capitalist market place they must adopt what amounts to the most efficient labour process.

One of the criticisms made of Braverman was that he does not pay sufficient attention to the practice of Taylorism and certainly not to the more humanistic approaches. Although he recognizes that there are both theories and practices of management, he relies too much on accounts of management theory, given either by Taylor himself or by supporters and commentators on his work. The question of the extent and success of its implementation, as we have seen, is largely side-stepped.

Clearly, any conclusion about the implementation and efficiency of Taylorism depends in part on how broadly the notion is defined. A broad definition which equates it (*à la* Braverman) with all forms of managerial control will lead one to see it as all pervasive; whilst a narrower definition is likely to point to a lesser degree of influence. Writers such as Palmer (1975), who wish to limit its definition, question whether it can be taken to characterize all labour processes in modern society. But, as Littler and Salaman (1984) note, the direct and indirect influence of Taylorism on factory jobs has been extensive. Regardless of one's definition, it is necessary, as Wood and Kelly (1982) stress, to take account of the different contexts in which it has been implemented and the variety of forms it has taken. The implication of Braverman's broader definition is that the so-called alternatives to Taylorism are, as we have seen, simply adjuncts to it, and certainly not genuine options; they are part of the process of managerial control over labour, fragmentation of work and degradation of the labourer which constitute Taylorism.

Work humanization

Given the assumed motivation of managements for introducing alternatives to Taylorism, it is argued by Braverman and others (1978) that many of the changes have been trivial, minimal and 'cosmetic', and that there is a gulf between the rhetoric and reality of job design, 'a certain air of hollow unreality'. Above all else, Braverman (1974, p. 39) concludes, such modern methods 'represent a style of management rather than a genuine change in the position of the worker'. Such changes can be compared 'with the marketing strategy followed by those who, having discovered that housewives resent prepared baking mixes and feel guilty when using them, arrange for the removal of the powdered eggs and restore to the customer the thrill of breaking a fresh egg into the mix, thereby creating an "image" of skilled baking'.

Similar views, that job enrichment programmes are essentially a cheat, have been argued; for example, by Blackler and Brown (1978) who claim:

> Attempts to improve the quality of working life by job redesign alone are likely to amount to little more than a modern version of 'human relations' management. On this view, notwithstanding the language of self-fulfilment and personal development characteristic of job redesign writings, the use of such ideas may serve as little more than an unobtrusive device to control others' behaviour. (p. 12)

The important point, the answer to which is not always clear, is whether the new human relations approach has any real impact on work systems. The argument that it 'is totally cosmetic' implies that it really causes no such changes, and that its significance is solely, though perhaps importantly, ideological. The associated assumption that workers will be deceived by it implies that the recipients of such schemes are passive and totally acquiescent. Such assumptions discourage any further analysis of the phenomenon of redesign. It also leads to assumptions being built into the analysis, particularly about the negative effects of job redesign, as well as the atomization of the work-force.

Bosquet (1980) is one writer who does attempt an answer to the question: what are the actual effects of work humanization? He recognizes that its introduction by management is aimed at increasing morale and inducing a cheerful obedience on the part of the worker. Yet job enrichment, according to Bosquet, 'spells the end of authority and despotic power for bosses great and small. . . . It replaces the order and discipline of the barracks with the voluntary co-operation of workers whose autonomy and power extends to his (or her) work.' It will lead workers to question the whole nature of the production system, and they will question the necessity of particular products, alleged technical and scientific necessities, and the whole basis of subordinate–superordinate relations. Job redesign contains an inherent dynamic towards increased autonomy and participation, and management's attempt to increase the meaning that people find in their work will thus almost inevitably 'boomerang against capital', as questions about the nature of domination and control will spring from it.

Whilst perhaps a useful corrective to the incorporation theory, according to which managerial techniques will manipulate workers into an acceptance of managerial goals and prerogatives implied by Braverman and others, this argument nevertheless appears to go too far in the other direction. Bosquet's excessively positive evaluation arises partly from his starting point, which involves an unnecessarily negative description of the factory prior to the arrival of the new human relations as a prison or barracks, based on despotic power. Furthermore, Bosquet works with a unilinear view of participation: he equates the notion of autonomy with an embryonic form of workers' control, and does not adequately distinguish participation from job redesign, where the latter is concerned simply with granting workers some autonomy as regards certain decisions about their immediate work.

Despite these weaknesses, Bosquet's work does serve to point to the need of considering, in any overall and complete evaluation of managerial initiatives, workers' reactions to them. How workers react to human relations methods is important, both because they may turn them to their own advantage, as Bosquet implies, and because work methods are, ultimately, jointly determined (Cressey and MacInnes, 1980). Even the most instrumental and economic workers, with no overt concern for the so-called intrinsic aspects of the job, can and do decisively influence the way in which production is actually achieved.

The key question, then is not whether work humanization schemes deceive workers, but how they react to them. As Roberts and Wood (1982) have shown, different work-forces, even within the same company, may react differently to what is essentially the same management initiative: some are able to resist parts of the programmes, turn others to their advantage and, in certain situations, to go on the offensive. It is important not to neglect the economic motivations of both managements and workers. For, as Kelly (1982a, 1982b, 1984) has shown, many reorganizations of work are largely introduced to overcome production problems in the context of particular product and labour markets. Furthermore, any increases in productivity which follow them are explicable not primarily in terms of higher levels of work humanization, but rather in terms of both the changes in pay levels and systems and the improved co-ordination of the production system.

In conclusion, the quotation of a worker commenting on a job enrichment scheme at the back of Nichols and Beynon's book (1977), 'you move from one boring, dirty monotonous job – and somehow you're supposed to come out of work enhanced', should be taken as the starting point. For it is misleading to infer from their minimal psychological impact that such schemes are essentially artificial. First, the danger in dismissing them as trivial is that we are applying an absolute standard, rather than measuring their significance against the past and current economic structures and issues which form the relevant reference point for the workers concerned. Secondly, we cannot assume a passive worker who is totally gullible in the face of the human relations marketing strategy. There is nothing in the above quotation from one of Nichols and Beynon's respondents to suggest that the writer concerned was duped by it. Thirdly, we must not lose sight of the significant role that work restructuring plays in attempts by management to solve production problems or economic crises through increases in efficiency and productivity. This last danger is especially prevalent in Friedman's (1977a, 1977b) work in which non-Taylorist methods are seen as attempts during periods of labour scarcity to come to terms with the associated increase in the political power of labour. In the early 1980s, as the recession in Britain deepened, firms continued to introduce flexible working groups, to reduce the demarcations between craft and production workers and redesign and combine jobs. There is no evidence (certainly in Britain or the USA) that such job redesign which managements have tackled in the recession has only been along strictly Taylorist lines.

Many of the changes in working practices, at least in Britain, have been made without recourse to notions such as job enrichment or explicit reference to intrinsic job satisfaction. According to Kelly's argument, it is doubtful if such notions ever dominated the bulk of job redesign programmes even before the recession. Such schemes have always been concerned with labour flexibility, control of quality and the introduction of new technology, albeit perhaps not in such an explicit manner as they were in the early 1980s. Yet, work humanization has been given a fresh impetus and dimension by attempts to import quality circles from Japan – that is, to introduce small groups usually of between five and ten employees who work together and meet regularly to discuss and solve job related problems. Such experiments are perhaps best seen not as developing out of an opposition to Taylorism, but rather in relation to it with all its limits, constraints and contradictions (Wood and Kelly, 1982; Kelly, 1982). Certainly this latest technique, Quality Circles, is not a complete rupture with Taylorism. Their development may very well reflect the fact that Taylorist methods have never succeeded in reducing workers to automata, and hence show the importance of the collective nature of production and need to harness the tacit skills of workers (Manwaring and Wood, 1984). As such, they are not necessarily cosmetic or necessarily manipulative. Nevertheless, they are minimal joint creations within the context of capital's domination and it is this issue which deserves exploration. Workers have an interest in the success of their enterprises and this explains, at least in the British context, the way in which managements have been able to harness workers' skills to successfully improve productive efficiency (Bradley and Hill, 1983). Equally the contradictions surrounding this interest helps to explain their failure in many situations where management have tried to introduce them, and also to explain the conflict which undoubtedly surrounds them in many plants and the way they may not have altered the degree of trust between management and workers.

Conclusions

We began this chapter by noting the centrality of Braverman's work to the recent rediscovery of the labour process and the division of labour system; the first section of this chapter dealt more directly with Braverman's thesis. Because of the importance of Taylorism, to both Braverman and the reality of work organization, the section included a brief outline of some of the major aspects of Taylor's account of scientific management. Part of the thrust of the argument was to point to the features of Taylorism which can get ignored and, as a particular example, to Taylor's emphasis on the need for management to obtain co-operation from workers and on the differentiation of his own methods from authoritarianism. Such aspects of Taylorism, and the need to get away from treating it as a given technique, is a central element in some of the debate on *Labour and Monopoly Capitalism*. In section two, aspects of this debate were presented: attention was paid particularly to Braverman's self-imposed limitation to the objective, and directed to the three ways of proceeding beyond this limitation.

A full debate about deskilling must be a debate about the labour process and its relationship to the mechanisms – such as the location of plant – which mediate between the development of the modern economy and job contents. Furthermore, no discussion of work can be complete without a reappraisal of all the types of relationship involved, such as that between domestic labour and paid work. The remainder of the chapter has, however, been limited to three issues: in section two we discussed skill; section three encouraged a reappraisal of technology in the light of Braverman's attempt to underplay its role – in particular the need to treat it as a relative concept, and to distinguish between the issues of objective competencies, of the divorce of conception from execution and socially defined occupational status. Section four looked at the attempts, conscious or otherwise, to either humanize work or overcome the problems of Taylorism. The implication is that, while Braverman is right to be sceptical of job enrichment and other techniques which constitute the 'quality of working life' movement, and to point to the importance of the economic and political context in which they are embedded, this context cannot be reduced to a simple matter of managerial control. It must include the role of co-operation and the element of subjectivism in the labour process.

Any discussion of the changing nature of jobs in the twentieth century must address itself both to the changes and to the stability within the hierarchy which exists between managerial and professional positions and the lowest unskilled level. This hierarchy, as defined and labelled in firms or occupational classifications, takes in the manual/non-manual distinction as well as the skilled/unskilled divide. The very fact that such vague terms as white-collar and blue-collar jobs are used by academics, managers and workers alike testifies to the problems involved in assessing and describing skills, some of which we have already discussed. Apart from the issue of the extent to which there is mental work of some kind involved in even the most unskilled jobs, three questions stand out as of crucial importance in the light of changes of work in the twentieth century: First, what of the growth of education and the rise of middle-level, white-collar and senior jobs? Secondly, what of the continued importance of skilled jobs? For there is a higher number of craft jobs than the deskilling thesis would appear to indicate, and in some plants with the new technology the ratio of skilled to unskilled workers has increased. Thirdly, what of the occupational segregation between men and women?

Some of the issues involved in these questions are, as we have seen, of a fundamental methodological and sociological nature. Some may simply concern the quest for generality, for the value of Braverman's thesis may be its highlighting of a major tendency within capitalism. There are authors (including P. Thompson) who, despite many criticisms of Braverman, accept deskilling as representative of the twentieth century. Without detailed historical and national studies it is very difficult to ascertain the validity of this. Yet from the limited studies we have discussed, a polarization of skill – that is, the upgrading of certain jobs and the deskilling of others – seems the more probable.

CHAPTER FIVE

Work outside the capitalist framework: the case of China

CRAIG LITTLER

Preliminaries

China is a vast, varied and complex society with a long history stretching back to at least 1600 BC, when the first dynasty, that of the Shang, started. Given this complexity it is not possible to provide a comprehensive introduction to China which does the country and its one thousand million people justice. The content of this chapter is, therefore, inevitably selective. In particular, I shall not attempt to deal with the regional variations within China. Similarly, the focus of the chapter is specifically orientated. Roughly 870 million people live in the countryside and are dependent on agriculture, whilst 130 million lives in cities. It is the latter group, and especially those employed in industry, with which we shall be concerned. To some degree this selectivity is arbitrary: it so happens that the research which I have done in China has been concentrated in industry. But there is a sound theoretical reason for this selection, which is that the debates over Chinese work organization have been focused on Chinese factories: it is here that the Chinese experience seems to provide the most interesting comparison with that of the West.

There is another dimension of selectivity. Research on China has become much easier over the past five years, and access to organizations and people is remarkably easy in comparison with the Soviet Union. Having been through the tumultuous years of the Cultural Revolution and the political conflicts afterwards (1966–76), the Chinese are willing to speak more openly about their mistakes and policy dilemmas. Nevertheless, any Western researcher is presented with a selective picture of China and is subject to a certain amount of stage-managing. In my

own research on twenty-nine factories in four areas of China, I have tried
to maintain a scepticism, but not a cynicism, about some of the material
presented to me. Even so, some of the material is open to various
interpretations and the reader should be alive to this problem.

It should be noted that the Romanization system for spelling Chinese
words has changed in recent years. For example, 'Mao Zedong' replaces
'Mao Tse-Tung', and 'Beijing' replaces 'Peking'.

Introduction

Many studies of work organization and work experience are located
within a capitalist framework. This chapter specifically aims to move
beyond the limits of that perspective and examine some of the realities of
work experience in a non-capitalist society. Such realities are not static,
but have been changing, and changing rapidly, in China. It is therefore
impossible to present a simple, one-dimensional picture, and later I provide a broad historical picture, so that the swings and shifts of Chinese
industrialization can be understood.

The capitalist/non-capitalist comparison is important because there is
a long-standing debate within sociology and economics about the nature
of industrial societies. This debate centres on the so-called convergence
thesis, which asserts that all industrial societies display common structural features which become increasingly dominant over time, replacing
the political and cultural distinctions which initially mark off societies
one from the other. It is argued that common solutions to problems of
social and industrial organization come to prevail in all industrial
societies. The motor for these changes is thought to be imperatives
associated with the complex technological organization (levels of education, occupational structure and mobility, increasing scale of markets,
etc.) characteristic of societies achieving high levels of economic development. The convergence thesis is bedevilled by confusions over the level of
analysis. What characteristics are crucial? In the comparison of any two
societies, differences are always discernible, but are such differences
peripheral or central? I shall not attempt to deal with the broad patterns
of stratification and so on, but shall focus on the organization of work.
This will enable us to side-step some of the difficulties in interpreting the
convergence thesis, because there is a relatively clearly-defined form of
that thesis at the level of work organization: *do modern methods of production, especially mass production, result in common, inescapable
forms of work organization and division of labour?* This question and
the following questions should be borne in mind throughout the chapter:
Why is the Chinese case important? Why does it represent a better test
case of alternative forms of work organization than the Soviet Union?

Some of the reasons why the USSR is a less suitable test case are as follows:

(1) The pattern of industrialization followed in the Soviet Union was clearly different from that in Britain, and work organization has also some marked divergencies from that in the West. As far as the division of labour is concerned, modern technology tends to be more heavily manned in the USSR and to function with labour-intensive auxiliary processes. With regard to the structure of control, the practice of dual control – Party hierarchy and managerial hierarchy side by side – is a significant component, indicating the political penetration of economic organizations. Most important, the majority of Soviet workers possess a degree of job security which removes the continual threat of unemployment common in the West.

2 Despite the above points, the USSR has demonstrated a ready acceptance of Western mass-production methods, such as Taylorism and Fordism, and has shown no systematic efforts to organize labour processes in a way fundamentally different from those of capitalism.

3 In contrast, Chinese developments in the 1960s and 1970s did appear to constitute serious efforts to re-think patterns of division of labour and hierarchy in order to organize work in radically different forms. It is these developments and their outcome which make the Chinese example a significant test case.

China's pattern of industrialization

In this section two key concerns are:

(i) To what extent does the pattern of industrialization in developing countries differ from the patterns of the early industrializing countries, such as Britain and France?
(ii) Why did the Chinese turn away from the Russian pattern of industrial and economic development?

Many of the early transformations to industrialism could not have taken place without the active role of the state. In this pespect the British case stands out as peculiar. Nevertheless, all of the early transformations took place in societies where the greater share of resources remained privately owned, and where much of the allocation of resources was achieved through the operation of markets – markets in which workers sold their labour, the rich sold their capital and populations purchased the commodities they laboured to produce. These capitalist industrializations, however, were the product of particular historical circumstances. With the important exception of Japan they all occurred either in Europe – where skilled labour was available, living standards were high prior to industrialization and, initially, population growth was low – or in the United States and other former colonies, where a supply of skilled European labour was obtainable and land and other resources were abundant (Howe, 1979, p. 126).

The industrialization of the Soviet Union presents a different starting-point. A poor, backward country, it had few of the advantages of the early industrializers and was desperate to catch up. The traumas of its emergence as a modern industrial state resulted in a different pattern of development. The crucial characteristics of the Soviet model of industrialization are as follows:

  (i) Ownership of land and industrial capital is public, rather than private.
 (ii) The rate of growth, the pattern and mix of output and other key economic targets are decided by central planners, rather than left to the operations of markets.
(iii) A primitive, peasant-based agriculture was violently collectivized and provided the surplus for a programme of industrialization.
(iv) The overall direction of the economy was one of rapid growth in the heavy industries with, for many years, high rates of forced savings and consequent small increases in living standards, since all the growth in productivity was ploughed back into further industrial output (Howe, 1979, p. 126).

It is against a framework of this kind that the story of Chinese development needs to be explored.

China, of course, has not pursued a single linear path of development. Broadly, Chinese economic and industrial policy divides into seven periods after the success of the revolution in 1949. These seven periods can be identified in terms of the ups and downs of Chinese industrial production shown in Figure 2.

After 1949 and the devastation of the anti-Japanese war and the civil war, there was a period of reconstruction, during which the Party leaders committed themselves to a Soviet-type policy of development. The Chinese Communist Party (CCP) was faced in 1949 with unifying at least two industrial economies. Because of the long period of foreign domination, the bulk of industrial capital was concentrated in light and especially consumer industries. Many of these industrial units were in the treaty ports along the coast. Shanghai alone accounted for 54 per cent of the factories and a similar proportion of the industrial labour force (Chen and Galenson, 1969, p. 21). As Rawski points out: 'Features shared by most of these plants included moderate size, a lengthy and varied industrial history that often included repair work as well as manufacturing, and a substantial proportion of equipment that was old, self-manufactured, or both' (Rawski, 1979, p. 58). Such plants were skill-intensive rather than capital-intensive. The accuracy of the final product depended on the

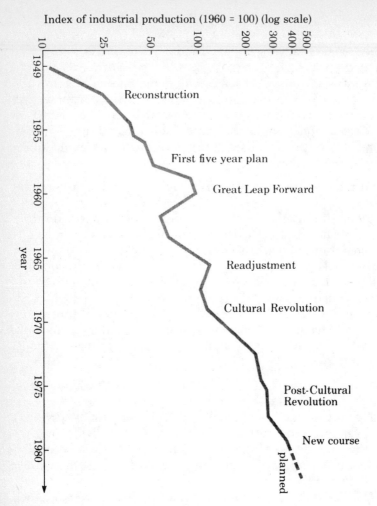

Index of industrial production (1960 = 100) (log scale)

Figure 2. Chinese industrial production, 1949-81
(Source: Lockett and Littler, 1985)

skill and experience of each individual operator. In contrast to these industrial enterprises, the north-east was a heavy-industrial base created largely by the Japanese in what had been an underdeveloped area. This area, however, had suffered most from war damage, as well as from the fact that the Soviet occupation had removed more than half of the capital equipment.

Because of the war damage and the unbalanced nature of the republican economy it is understandable that the investment programme of the First Five Year Plan (1953–7) emphasized heavy industry. In the event, 154 Soviet-aided projects were built. These were massive and capital-intensive (e.g. the Wuhan steel works, which now employs 100,000 people), often located on greenfield inland sites. They represented a discontinuous leap in technology for the Chinese economy, requiring new skills and new technical training schemes. They had, at least in the 1950s, complete State support and a high priority in China's investment strategy. The outcome, however, of the First Five Year Plan's policy of creating and supporting large industrial units to realize rapid economic growth was a large gap in management and capital intensity at the end of the 1950s: a dualism described by Andors as the 'Shanghai system of management', as opposed to the Soviet model of 'one-man management'. The Shanghai system involved a major role for the collective leadership of the Party Committee, and significant *de facto* shop-floor worker participation arising from the residues of the traditional work teams led by gang-bosses; the Soviet model, on the other hand, was essentially bureaucratic and entailed clear job definitions, job hierarchies and the widespread use of piece work and incentive schemes (Andors, 1977, pp. 50–62).

The Soviet model of management aroused growing resistance in China from both Party cadres and workers. Apart from the tension between one-man management and the principle of the Communist Party's right of control, which had also been experienced in the USSR (see Littler in K. Thompson, 1984), there was the particular circumstance that the Soviet system relied upon a substantial, technically-trained body of managers, which did not exist in China in the 1950s. More generally, during the mid-1950s Mao Zedong and other leaders within the CCP were re-assessing the relevance of the Soviet model of development for China. Concern was focused on such problems as the failure to solve the problem of unemployment, given that the new modern plants created relatively few jobs, and the lack of emphasis on developing agriculture. Another aspect of this reassessment was the issue of the relationships between 'leaders' and 'led' – cadres and masses. Partly, these problems arose from the lack of adequate resources in China to follow the Soviet path, but there was also a questioning of the priorities and implications of policies based on control and motivation of the work-force through pay and bonuses. It was argued that if the potential of the 'masses' could be tapped, this was likely to be a stronger force for rapid economic and social advance. The division of labour, in particular the division of mental and manual labour, was seen to lead to the emergence of a bureaucratic management style, a lack of awareness of shop-floor problems and, as a result, conflict between workers and managers. As Mao said a few years later:

> From our experience, if the cadres do not get rid of their arrogant attitude and are not integrated with the workers, the latter do not generally think that the factory belongs to them, but as belonging to the cadres. It is the arrogant attitude of cadres which is responsible for the

refusal of the workers to observe work discipline of their own free will.
One must not think that, in the socialist system, no effort is needed and
that a creative collaboration between the workers and the leading
cadres of enterprises will be established by itself. . . . (Mao, 1975,
p. 130)

Rhetoric is one thing, however. What of practice? At the level of practice, these views led to the policy of the 'two participants': that is, the participation of managers in manual work, paralleled by the participation of
workers in management. There was a tendency for management functions to devolve to the workgroup. The Chinese consciously revived the
traditional gang-boss system, except that the work teams were led by
politically-motivated team leaders instead of by petty-capitalist gang-
bosses. These leaders were supposed to assign particular functions
(accounting, maintenance, quality control, etc.) to individual workers,
who also carried out their usual production work. The Chinese leadership also argued that during the period of the First Five Year Plan there
had been too much emphasis on training specialists rather than
generalists. The ideal worker was now seen as a 'jack-of-all-trades', who
should have a thorough understanding of various operational
techniques. There is little evidence, however, that this new principle was
followed in practice.

The limitations of the Stalin model of industrialization, and the political tensions with Moscow, led to the Great Leap Forward of 1958–62,
when the emphasis was on mass mobilization and labour-intensive
development utilizing the resources of the under-employed peasantry.
The Great Leap Forward was a disaster. As can be seen from Figure 2,
industrial production plummeted and did not recover until 1965. Partly
this was the result of very severe weather and the withdrawal of Soviet
aid and technicians in 1960, but it was also the result of the policies pursued. A major outcome was to shatter Mao Zedong's political authority.
He was treated as a 'death-bed father', someone who was respected but
not asked for advice or guidance.

The Great Leap Forward was followed by a period of readjustment
and cautious modernization during 1962–6, associated with self-suffi-
ciency in relation to the world market, because of the simultaneous bloc-
kades by the Soviet Union and the West. Technologically speaking, this
was a period when machine tools were imported via Hong Kong and subject to 'reverse engineering', with the imported items being used as prototypes to be copied.

The years 1966–71/2 were the tumultuous years of the Cultural
Revolution, when mass mobilization and labour-intensive investment,
associated with radical political changes, were tried. Many previous
managers and leaders were removed from positions and sent to the countryside. In some cities there was a state of civil war. The impact of the

Cultural Revolution on industry is dealt with in more detail later in the chapter.

Amongst China analysts there is as yet no firm agreement on how to characterize and summarize the essence of the years 1971/2–6. Crudely, it was a period of oscillation and political struggle between the policies of the Cultural Revolution, identified with the Gang of Four, and those of Deng Xiaoping, who stressed 'modernization' through less radical policies.

On the 9 September 1976 Mao Zedong died. On October 7th the so-called Gang of Four were arrested. This marked the beginning of a new period, a new course, in Chinese affairs. The new leadership committed itself more clearly to the Four Modernizations (of industry; agriculture; education, science and technology; and defence) and speeded up the re-integration of the economy with the world market. There was a surge of imports of foreign technology: in 1978 contracts for seventy or more complete plants were signed. Moreover, in a search for new models of development the new leadership seemed to be heading in the direction of market socialism on Yugoslav lines.

Employment, unemployment and job allocation

(i) The 'unit'

In China the work organization is more than an economic organization; it is also a social and political collectivity. The day-to-day social realities of this fact are expressed in the concept of *danwei*, or 'unit'. The experience of living in a unit is well caught by Kahn-Ackermann, who spent two years studying in China:

> What is the 'unit', and what does it do? 'Units' – the Chinese word is *danwei* – are the political, economic and administrative building blocks which together compose Chinese society like pieces in a mosaic. The 'unit' that I belonged to as a student was Beijing university. For a worker it is his or her factory, for a peasant his or her agricultural brigade, for the housewife or pensioner it is their residential district. Everything that can be embraced in functional terms from the standpoint of collective life and collective work forms a 'unit'. Just as with a factory or school in our own society, so the first task of a factory or school 'unit' is the organisation and execution of production or education. But this does not give the essence of the 'unit'. It is not only a form of organisation for social activity, it is also a form of life. Wherever a Chinese person is, even if he or she is staying abroad, they remain part of their 'unit', their 'unit' remains responsible for them, they belong to their 'unit' and feel responsible to it. They can be allotted to a new 'unit', and sometimes they can change their 'unit' at their own request. It is so much part of their identity that it is customary to ask someone whom

you have just got to know: *Ni shi nage danweide de? – which 'unit' are you from? – before you ask their name.*

> *Danwei:* always translated by the Chinese interpreters as organisa-
> tion, or work unit.
> The *danwei* gathers together within the control of a single body all
> the threads of the individual's life, it measures according to its own
> standards the tastes, habits and behaviour of every person, it is the
> unit and norm of work, of life and of thought, it is the sole leadership
> of the Party in the context of daily life, it is the Party in flesh and
> blood. (C. and J. Broyelle, *China: A Second Look,* 1980, p. 22)

This definition explains something of the complex and all-embracing character of the 'unit'. Yet it is still incorrect in some respects. Here the 'unit' appears simply as an instrument with which the Communist Party carries out its goals at the rank-and-file level and in everyday life. It is this, and very much more. It is responsible for the political control and political education of its members, and for the local executive of national political campaigns. It sees to it that a struggle decreed from above, for example against pests such as rats or flies, is efficiently organised.

The leadership of the 'unit' is exclusively in the hands of the appropriate Party committee. The 'revolutionary committees' established during the Cultural Revolution, through which non-Party people could also participate in the leadership of a 'unit', only filled a temporary power vacuum which had arisen with the destruction of the Party organisation in the confusion of the Cultural Revolution. When the Party was reconstructed in 1969, these 'revolutionary committees' declined into administrative organs without any real power. Today they have disappeared at the 'unit level.

The automatic way in which Chinese identify the rule of the Party with the 'unit' is shown by the fact that they do not necessarily mean the whole collective when they speak of the 'unit', but often only the Party committee or the administration. Thus you ask the 'unit' for home leave, meaning the appropriate Party committee. And it is the 'unit' that provides the tickets required, meaning the department for social welfare.

This can give the impression that the 'unit' is simply a system imposed on the Chinese people from above with the object of control and mobilisation in the interest of the current Party leadership. Yet this still gives only an incomplete picture of the nature of the 'unit'.

The 'unit' has taken over many social functions that in old China were performed by the kinship group. It is responsible for the social welfare of old people and children, for the political education and specialist training of its members. Many 'units' maintain their own kindergartens, schools, even colleges. Just as the extended family insists on the right to have a say in all important decisions faced by its members, so the 'unit' today has a fundamental influence on the personal and professional destiny of those who belong to it. It decides on their choice of work, the allocating of jobs and housing. When the leadership of our school gave in to our requests and permitted foreign and Chinese students to live together, I asked a Chinese friend to move in with me. He replied that this was a matter for the 'unit'. He was not prepared to make a move on his own initiative. When I was allotted another roommate, I was angry. He accepted it with a sympathetic shrug of the shoulders; we would still have sufficient occasion to see one another.

Applications for further education need the backing of the 'unit', and it can forbid marriage if there are strong political or medical reasons against this. And just as the clan in earlier times saw to it that members' lives were morally unobjectionable, so today the 'unit' supervises behaviour in accordance with political and moral norms. Sexual relations before or outside of marriage are forbidden in China. This did not apply so strictly to us foreigners, who were tolerated in this respect so long as we kept ourselves to ourselves, behaved discreetly and gave the 'unit' no cause to take notice. In one case this limit was clearly crossed. The woman, though only she, was reported to the Party committee of our 'unit' and severely reproached. She was forcefully requested to dedicate herself more to her studies in future, so as 'not to disappoint the hopes that her family and her country had placed in her.' As a foreigner she could afford to pay no attention to this warning and continue the relationship in question. For a Chinese woman this would have had serious consequences. In the extreme case, if reprimand and criticism had not been sufficient, she could have ended up in a labour camp.

The 'unit' organises the entire spectrum of material care: sickness insurance, provision for old age. It has its own clinics or medical stations, clubs and cinemas. If one of its members has financial difficulties, the 'unit' will lend to him at little or no interest. It builds homes for its members and distributes the coupons for rationed goods such as cotton and sugar. In bureaucratised China, an ordinary person has few occasions to visit a public office. Direct contact with the anonymous and impenetrable apparatuses, which always provokes in me a diffuse terror, is something they hardly experience. When my bicycle was stolen, I did not apply to the police, but like any Chinese person would, to the appropriate department of my 'unit'. It was finally found and returned to me, together with a long lecture not to leave it standing around in the district in future. I was also partly to blame for the theft. Both things were part of the 'unit's' duty: the return of the bicycle and the lecture.

The 'unit' provides its members with a certain material security and tranquillity, releasing them from the countless vexations and insecurities that sour our lives. I scarcely had occasion to cross the walls that surrounded our 'unit'. I took my dirty clothes to the 'unit's' laundry, where they were washed for a few pence. If I needed a new shirt, I had it made in the 'unit's' tailoring shop, not very elegant, but practical and cheap. If the electric plug in my room wasn't working, I informed the caretaker and the 'unit's' electrician appeared and mended it. I obtained the reading matter I needed in the 'unit's' bookstore and in summer I swam a few lengths each day in the not too clean water of the 'unit's' own swimming pool. When I returned from China via Moscow and had to change stations, I stood for a while on the platform and waited for a representative from the 'unit' to appear to take my trunk and lead me to a hotel, until I realised that in future I would have to do all these things for myself once more. (Kahn-Ackermann, 1982, pp. 76–80)

The diffuse, clinging paternalism described by Kahn-Ackermann is a daily reality which makes Chinese work organizations very different from those in the West. At this level – the level of the employment relationship – there are clearly marked and obvious differences. There is no labour market; labour is not a commodity in China. For many urban Chinese, the first job is often the last: a lifelong occupation that ends only with retirement or death. But how do people get into units; how does one get a job in the cities and towns of China today? This question is explored in detail later.

(ii) Unemployment and job allocation

What are the levels of unemployment in China? The Great Leap Forward was officially credited with having achieved full employment, and this question could not even be raised in the People's Republic of China. Even now (1984) there is no official category of unemployment, only one of 'waiting for allocation'. Nevertheless, unemployment is now recognized as a major economic and social problem, and has again become a topic of analysis.

Chinese estimates of unemployment vary greatly, from 10 to 25 million for the urban population. The accurate figure is probably near the lower end of this range, which means that the unemployment rate is around 10 per cent, higher than might be expected. Ten per cent unemployment means that on average there will be one jobless person in every five urban households, assuming that each household has two of its members in the labour force. Hence unemployment has become a major political issue in recent years.

What are the sources of unemployment? As in Britain, most of those seeking work recent school-leavers looking for their first jobs. In addition there are older youths who have returned from the countryside since 1978. They had been dispatched to rural areas during the Cultural Revolution and in the early 1970s to break down the urban/rural divisions and to 'solve' the employment problems of that period. But after 1978 city after city was flooded with thousands of conspicuously idle youths who roamed the streets or camped in front of Party or municipal headquarters demanding jobs, ration cards and housing. In Shanghai there were street riots.

The government response under the new economic policies has been to widen the structure of employment opportunities. Until the Great Leap Forward, outside the State sector people were still able to look for jobs in private and co-operative enterprises, and employers in these enterprises were free to hire whom they pleased. But in 1956–7 the socialization of all enterprises destroyed all but a few traces of a labour market; instead, State labour bureaux alone had the power to make job assignments. Since 1977, however, there has been considerable reform of hiring practices in urban areas, leading to the expansion of self-employment and collective employment. Between 1977 and 1980, thirteen million new jobs were created: of these, collective enterprises provided twelve million or 92 per cent, while the number of self-employed grew by just under one million. During these years, state-sector plants reached saturation level and most job openings in these plants resulted from labour turnover, i.e. the replacement of older workers as they retired.

The problems of unemployment and finding a job have led to enormous pressure on factory leaders to hire the children and relatives of existing workers. In some factories this has led to an official 'replacement policy'; that is, guaranteeing a job to one child of every retiring employee. For example, at the Chongqing Iron and Steel Company over 90 per cent of the 8,000 or more new workers recruited in 1979 were the children of their own employees.

Increasingly, then, employment positions are being inherited across generations, creating a closed status system. The nature of this system is explored in the following section.

(iii) Segmentation of employment

In many ways the basic divide in the Chinese industrial economy is between the State sector and the collective sector: between two systems of formal ownership. The origins of the collective sector lie in the handicraft workshops inherited from the pre-revolutionary period. According to Xue Muqiao, 'handicraft workshops and household handicrafts accounted for about 20% of the country's gross industrial output' in 1949 (Xue, 1981, p. 39). During the 1950s the handicrafts sector was reorganized into co-operatives, until by the late 1950s the socialist transformation of this sector was complete. During the Great Leap Forward the existing producer co-operatives were reorganized and placed more under State control, but at the same time many new co-operatives and collectives sprang up as neighbourhood workshops, often utilizing unemployed or under-employed women (Lockett, 1981, p. 20). This pattern – the rise of a great number of neighbourhood enterprises in the cities – was repeated in the 1970s (Xue, 1981, p. 62).

There are sharp differences between the State and collective sectors with regard to capital equipment, productivity, size, wages and working conditions. If we take the last point first, a visit by a British trade union delegation to China provides a more blunt Western reaction to the conditions in one part of this industrial sector than the over-polite responses of academics. In 1980 a National Union of Mineworkers delegation visited a small neighbourhood factory in Hangchow employing thirty people. It had been set up a few years before by ten women who had sought technical advice about extruding copper wire in order to make electronic components for a state factory. The group reports that 'Our first reaction to the most unsafe practices, high-speed unguarded belts on all machines, "Heath Robinson" design of all equipment, was that the place should be closed down'. Having made this point to their Chinese hosts, they were partly persuaded that 'economic reality and job provision were paramount'. The trade unionists have on record that a certain dilemma occurred when, at the next house they visited, they were received by a woman with her arm in a sling: she had been injured when her hand was trapped in a machine (NUM, 1980, pp. 10–11)!

The variations in average size of enterprises according to the system of ownership are set out in Table 1.

Table 1. The structure of Chinese industry, 1978

	State-owned	Collective/ co-operative ownership	Total
No. of enterprises	84,000	264,000	348,000
No. of employees	74.51m	20.48m	94.9m
Total wage bill (in Yuan)	46.9 billion	10.0 billion	56.9 billion
Mean size of enterprises (employees)	887	78	

Source: Lockett and Littler, 1985

There are no reliable figures on differences in capital intensity between the two sectors, but most indications are that the capital employed in the collective sector is a small fraction of that used in the State-owned plants. For example, 1975 figures show that gross output per collective worker was only 28 per cent of that of the State worker (Rawski, 1979, p. 43, Table 3.1). Finally, as far as wage differentials are concerned, in 1980 the average earnings in the State sector were Yuan 803, compared with Yuan 624 in the collective sector (Lockett, 1981, Table 8). These wage differentials are not, of course, the product of unmediated market forces. Thus Xue records: 'In some cities it was stipulated that members of neighbourhood enterprises under collective ownership should get lower pay and fewer benefits than the workers and staff of the enterprises under ownership by the whole people' (Xue, 1981, p. 62; also p. 41). The differences in the wage and non-wage benefits between the two industrial sectors of China's economy is given a vague, but nevertheless real, justification in terms of the notion that ownership by the whole people is a higher form of socialist ownership, whereas collective ownership is a less mature form of ownership (Xue, 1981, pp. 45–6). It used to be a widely promulgated precept that lower forms of ownership would be transformed into higher forms. This view, however, is now under question in China. At a policy level, the State has begun to promote the collective sector as an important supplier of consumer goods and as a means of job creation.

The difference between the State and collective sectors is a critical aspect of a Chinese worker's labour status, given that urban enterprises have become focal points for the provision of welfare and social services. What, however, of labour segmentation within State enterprises? The use of temporary, casual or contract labour in industry seems to be a common response in many developing economies to the problem of an oversupply of unskilled labour. In Japan, for example, these labour statuses have become institutionalized. In China, on the other hand, they have run up against a spasmodic policy of egalitarianism. Before the Cultural Revolution most State factories were run on the basis of two groups of workers. There was a core of permanent workers who were members of trade unions and were a privileged section of society, entitled to insurance benefits, medical treatment and almost complete job security and able, when they retired, to nominate one of their children to succeed them. In contrast, there was a periphery of temporary and contract workers who constituted up to 27 per cent of the total urban labour force in the late 1950s (Unger, 1975, p. 70). These temporary workers were not union members, were paid less than permanent workers and were ineligible for many welfare benefits.

The divisions of the Chinese working class according to job status were a major source of conflict during the Cultural Revolution. New organizations of temporary and contract workers emerged and came into sharp conflict with the existing trade unions. There were systematic attempts to end the split between permanent and temporary workers and also to erode urban/rural inequalities; indeed, these two aspects overlapped, because many temporary workers came from rural communes. The so-called 'worker-peasant' schemes, however, which involved bringing in temporary workers from the countryside to replace permanent workers in urban industries whilst the industrial workers were sent to the countryside for a period, created enormous opposition and furore.

The hostility aroused by the egalitarian policies attempted during the Cultural Revolution seems evident enough, but what is not clear is the outcome of the struggles of that period. Has there been a widespread re-emergence of temporary and contract labour in recent years? The answer is that we lack any aggregate evidence on this point. At the level of the enterprise, the topic seems to be a difficult one to investigate, and, during a recent research trip, only one factory director seemed willing to provide detailed information. At the Beijing Television Factory there was a labour force of 1,600 permanent workers, with 400 temporary workers. The majority of temporary workers were youngsters, usually the children of existing workers, who were 'waiting for employment'; a few were retired workers who did not want to give up work completely. The factory director suggested that this division in labour status had arisen because of the serious unemployment problem and asserted that when the youngsters had been allocated work or 'passed their exams' they left the factory for good. Nevertheless – and it is a significant nevertheless – they were replaced when this occurred, so that a force of temporary workers was maintained. Of the other factories at which research was conducted, the majority admitted to the existence of temporary workers, but quickly went on to add that they were only a few or a 'handful'.

This is only part of the recent story, however. In order to create more labour flexibility and to increase labour productivity, it has been official policy since February 1983 to promote widespread experiments in labour contracts. Newly recruited State-sector workers can now be employed on the basis of long-term contracts or of short-term contracts of one to five years. There has been considerable resistance to breaking the 'iron rice bowl' (i.e. job security) and replacing it with a 'mud rice bowl', and it is not yet clear what the outcome will be. In order to allay workers' fears, Chinese official statements have stressed that contract workers should enjoy the same welfare benefits as permanent workers and be eligible to join trade unions. If these promises are honoured in practice, then there could be a major rupture in the system of labour statuses.

The division of labour

In recent years in the social sciences there has been a continuing and widening debate about the labour process. This debate has focused on the division of labour, on job design and on the dynamics and directions of change in work organizations. One group of writers (the Brighton Labour Process Group) has set out three basic 'laws' of the division of labour under capitalism:

(i)   The increasing division of intellectual and manual work.
(ii) The elaboration and maintenance of work hierarchies.
(iii) The continual tendency towards job fragmentation, or deskilling.
      (BLPG, 1977, pp. 16–20)

The assertion of these general tendencies has been challenged, but many writers nevertheless accept them in a qualified fashion as the main trend of the evolution of work under capitalism (e.g. Braverman, 1974; P. Thompson, 1983). Ignoring for the purposes of the present argument the variations of work design within capitalist societies, we may ask: do the tendencies outlined by the Brighton Labour Process Group exist in societies which are theoretically non-capitalist?

As we have already seen, the experience of the Soviet Union does not suggest that the dynamics of capitalist industry are unique. But it has been argued that the USSR is not a good test case and that China provides more substantial fuel for the division of labour debate, because of the reported attempts during the Cultural Revolution to bridge the mental/manual divide and re-shape the patterns of industrial work. The rest of this section accordingly examines the Cultural Revolution in industry and the more recent changes since 1976.

1. The Cultural Revolution in industry

Starting in the field of education in 1966, the Cultural Revolution was the culmination of the efforts of Mao and those who supported him to change the direction of Chinese development. In a sense, the Cultural Revolution was a kind of second Great Leap Forward, in response to a Maoist need to vindicate the first one. The catastrophic failures of the Great Leap Forward (1958–62), however, had stiffened many Chinese leaders to resist any repetition, and many cadres had to be removed. (For example, the entire Party Committee of Beijing was charged with revisionism and replaced.) As a result, the Cultural Revolution was marked by a political and social viciousness which is still remembered with bitterness in China today. Starting from a position of weakness, Mao and his followers promoted a gigantic mass campaign run by a new type of organization, the Red Guards, composed of zealous young people and students, behind which Mao had the support of large segments of the People's Liberation Army (PLA).

The Cultural Revolution spread into industry, and the mass mobilization of workers resulted in serious industrial conflicts, not just between workers and managers but between groups of workers. For example, at the Kiangsi tractor factory in Nanchang production was disrupted for thirty-one months and was at a complete standtill for eight months. Factory managers faced a seemingly endless series of 'struggle sessions', i.e. sessions of collective criticism. The longest such session lasted for four days and three nights and was one of fifty sessions during a six-month period. There were also serious fights between workers. After criticism, many factory cadres were sent down to the shop floor (or to the countryside), and factory management was taken over by Revolutionary Committees, which typically consisted of cadres who had supported the Great Leap Forward, workers' representatives and PLA personnel (sent into the factories to restore order after 1967). The factory Party committees were to disappear until around 1970, an indication of the general disorganization of the Chinese Communist Party in the immediate aftermath of the mass movements of the Cultural Revolution.

There are serious problems of evidence in assessing what actually happened on the shop floor during the Cultural Revolution – a question to which we shall return. Within industrial enterprises, it was reported that there were major changes not only amongst managerial personnel but also in work organization and the technical division of labour. The main effects were as follows:

(i) Cadre participation in manual work. This again became a major political concern. The ideal was that cadres would do one or two days of manual work per week, as well as a concentrated period of one or two months at some point in the year. This was not always strictly enforced, however, and was resisted by some cadres, besides coming into conflict with production priorities.

(ii) Worker participation in management. This is the complementary aspect of the 'Two Participations'. In 1967 the so-called 'power seizures' began, which involved the apparent replacement of traditional management hierarchies by the Revolutionary Committees. The latter were elected, though with an uncertain degree of vetting and guidance from higher-level bodies. A varying proportion of workers (as opposed to engineers or cadres) was elected to them – between one-third and two-thirds – although the Committees appear not to have been regularly, if ever, re-elected. The relative importance of Revolutionary Committees was, however, reduced in the early 1970s with the re-emergence of enterprise-level Party Committees, which involved a smaller proportion of workers. The Revolutionary Committees maintained a formal, but increasingly meaningless, existence up to 1978, when they were finally abolished.

(iii) Changes within work groups. The key change here was that small work groups would take on additional administrative tasks, thereby lessening the importance of administrative departments and, by extension, of purely administrative cadres. The intended result was a reduction of administrative and technical staff and the elimination or simplification of paperwork. The nature of the decentralization of managerial work to work groups varied, both between sectors and between enterprises. In general, work groups assumed a degree of autonomy in their internal organization and in relation to the division of labour. Typically, some workers would be assigned a particular responsibility for such things as inspection, maintenance, safety or production planning.

(iv) Job rotation. Apart from changes within work groups, there were reports of attempts to introduce job rotation, involving the circulation of workers between groups and workshops. An example from the Beijing Knitwear Factory is given by Berger (1972), who says:

To avoid problems, both mental and physical, due to continuous work on one operation, the mill has a system of transferring workers from one job to another. Besides helping to diversify skills, so that the workers can be deployed to assist in any sector which may be lagging behind, this also helps them to develop as all-round human beings. Workers take their turns in the hosiery, knitting, dyeing and bleaching, and tailoring shops and can thus make a more effective contribution to the output of the factory as a whole. This change-round of labour includes work in the kitchen. Every six months some of the workers take a turn as cooks since, in the words of the Deputy Chairman, 'all work is in the service of the people'. In the past, he said, cooks were treated as menials. The switching round of jobs helped to break down any such prejudices.

We shall return to this example below.

(v) De-bureaucratization. The Maoist ideology of the Cultural Revolution involved a struggle against bureaucracy and bureaucratism. Virtually all industrial enterprises reduced the size and power of their staff departments. People who 'moved their mouth and not their hands' became suspect, and redundant cadres were sent to production shops or to the countryside for 'remoulding'. At the same time, the complex system of paperwork, whereby requisitioning a screw required ten forms, was cut back severely.

The radical policies of the Cultural Revolution were often implemented in a non-radical social environment, with the result that they were degraded at the level of the workplace through unprincipled factionalism, personal hostilities and jealousies, and manoeuvring for sectional advantage (White, 1982, p. 6). Nobody felt safe. For a long period the Chinese leadership was able to restrict the scope of mass campaigns and limit the number of groups alienated by them. The failure of the Cultural Revolution occurred precisely because these limits were violated. The number of people threatened and under attack was too great. Social order was destroyed, and a conservative backlash developed.

2. *The present position*

As a political movement the Cultural Revolution was a failure, but has the wheel turned full circle? Have the radical industrial policies collapsed into the past? In order to answer this question, let us take another look at one factory – the Beijing Knitwear Factory – described by Berger during the Cultural Revolution. I visited this plant in 1981 and there was no system of job rotation either between or within workshops. (There would have been some value in workshop rotation because the Bleaching Shop, for example, provided wet, steamy and unpleasant working conditions.) This type of evidence, however, provides no clear answer to our question, because the factory cadres denied that there had ever been systematic job rotation, except for a brief and limited experiment. Managers in other factories made similar statements, and several Chinese academics, during interviews, denied that the Cultural Revolution had produced new forms of management: 'it was all Gang of Four propaganda'.

The best interpretation of this type of evidence involves two lines of argument. First, the Western reports of the Cultural Revolution were probably exaggerated and highly selective in relation to shop-floor events, though some experiments did take place. Secondly, it was noticeable in most Chinese factories (such as the Beijing Knitwear Factory) how little specification of job boundaries there was – people helped each other and wandered around the workshops. In other words, the traditional patterns of group working in China make discussions of job fragmentation and its corollary, job rotation, misleading.

So far we have looked at the present realities of job rotation, but what about the 'Two Participations' and the reported attempts to undercut the mental/manual division? Generally, there has been a reassertion of managerial hierarchies, and Revolutionary Committees have given way to Party Committees and to powerful factory directors. Many factory directors have been reinstated, often after having spent ten years on the shop floor or in the countryside. Some lip service is still paid to managerial participation in manual work (though this is not true for scientific and technical personnel) and managers are supposed to spend one day per month doing manual work, but questions to factory directors about what they did last month are frequently met with a slight smile and an explanation that they were too busy.

In general, the changes since the Cultural Revolution represent a significant shift away from the concerns of those such as Mao who saw the division of labour as a major policy issue, particularly with regard to the potential emergence of a new bureaucratic ruling 'class'. The organization of work is now seen as more of a technical and long-term problem than a political one. In this vein, it is the future development of the productive forces that is seen as crucial, and all attention is thrown on to the Four Modernizations. Thus in many respects the technical division of labour still resembles that of the capitalist West and the Soviet Union, though modified by traditional patterns of working.

The structure of control in Chinese work organizations

Many Western writers have argued that democracy should not stop at the factory gates, but should extend into the factory itself. Indeed, the view that workers should participate in the management of the factories in which they labour has been a persistent theme in Western radical thought for over a century. There are, of course, an enormous number of divergent standards of democracy and, consequently, various systems of democratic and elective relations between managers and workers have been advocated.

During the Cultural Revolution many Western analysts found support for their ideas in the reports of the development of new management structures in China. Since 1976 and the overthrow of the Gang of Four, writers such as Bettelheim have argued that there has been a great leap backwards: 'This step backwards favours the managers of enterprises and the technicians: it tends to strengthen the state bourgeoisie, those who occupy leading positions in the economic administrative machinery and in the party' (1978, p. 52). Equally, it is argued, the step backwards withdraws technological initiative and management from the workers and concentrates decision-making powers in the hands of the factory directors and Party leaders (ibid., p. 50).

Such a dramatic view is misleading, however. It fails to take into account the pattern of control in Chinese industry before the Cultural Revolution, the realities of the Cultural Revolution and the present policies of the new regime. The rest of this section briefly examines these questions.

Since 1949 there have been three main centres of power in large Chinese work organizations: the Party structure, the management structure and the trade union. Whilst there have been many variations in factory organizations over time, as well as between industries and regions, the basic picture before the Cultural Revolution is outlined in Figure 3. The details of the factory management structure need not concern us here, except for the major differences from Western structures. We have already noted that Chinese factories are part of an administrative and planning system responsible to a State bureau. At the opposite end of the hierarchy, the Chinese reliance on work teams led by team leaders represents a cultural continuity rather than a conscious act of social reorganization. Figure 3 portrays the parallel management and Party hierarchies. The Party Committee was elected by all the Party members in the plant, and in smaller factories they sometimes constituted all the Party members in that factory. (Membership of the Party, however, has never been more than 20 per cent of the work-force and usually much less (say 5 per cent): nationally, the Party is considered a vanguard, an élite organization consisting of 3 to 4 per cent of the population.) The Party secretary and the factory director usually developed a similarity in function and daily routine. The director was generally a member of the enterprise Party Committee, and where this was not the case, the Party secretary became the major source of influence in the plant and *de facto* director.

The third source of influence in a large Chinese factory was the trade union. Unions, however, have always been weak organizations in China, not helped by the fact that, despite formal statements about elections,

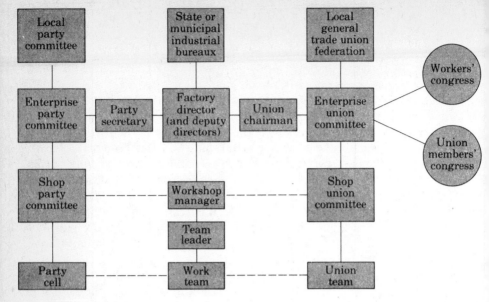

*Figure 3. Simplified diagram of a large plant organizational structure
before the Cultural Revolution*
(Source: Littler and Lockett, 1983)

most union officials have been appointed from the top down rather than
elected. One factor strengthening collective control was the role of the
Workers' and Staff Congresses, a role set out in 1949 regulations. The
congress was to be organized by the labour union, but to remain outside
the union structure – hence the specific role of Trade Union Members'
Congresses in determining union affairs. According to one writer, 'The
congress was not authorized to make authoritative decisions and its
resolutions had to be ratified by the factory management committee and
promulgated by the factory general manager before they took effect. Its
main function was to expose the general manager to a fairly large representative body which would listen to his report and offer criticisms and
suggestions concerning his management of the factory. Factory general
managers were frequently required to make a public "self-examination",
the importance of which should not be underestimated. Managers were
considered as "intellectuals", preoccupied with questions of "face", and
the management-worker gap was, to a far greater extent than in the
West, reinforced by class and cultural distinctions' (Brugger, 1976, p.
221).

This, then, was the picture (with many variations and complications)
of the pattern of control in large Chinese factories before the Cultural
Revolution. Management did not derive authority from an elected collective, despite the existence of workers' congresses, but from the Party,
which enjoyed a solid position within the factory as well as outside it.

The Cultural Revolution disrupted much of the in-plant structure depicted in Figure 3. Unions were abolished, so that one side of the bureaucratic trinity was swept away. With them went workers' congresses, which ceased to function. Moreover, as the Cultural Revolution became a mass movement and spread, the Party itself was attacked, and the pace of the movement in many places began to outstrip the Party's capacity to resist or to set up alternative leadership to that of the Party Committees. This disruption of Party control during the Cultural Revolution years is historically unique to China – there are few parallels in Soviet-type societies. The turbulence of the period also meant that disputes over technical authority and technical decision-making became overt conflicts, and, as we have seen, factory management was taken over by the 'Revolutionary Committees'.

The interpretation of the degree of democracy during the Cultural Revolution centres on the Revolutionary Committees: were they in any sense democratic? Many of the Revolutionary Committees were initially elected, and many factories did elevate workers who had no former management experience. In addition, many Revolutionary Committees contained older cadres who had supported radical policies in the past, as well as younger factory managers (Andors, 1977, p. 203). After 1967, up to one-third of the members of the Revolutionary Committees were People's Liberation Army (PLA) cadres, who had been brought in with the crumbling of Party authority. Moreover, apart from the question of the position of the PLA, the Revolutionary Committees, once set up, were not subject to re-election and became as authoritarian as any management structure, particularly with the persistence of fractional disputes. However, the picture is not one-sided: the Cultural Revolution did create a popular spirit of criticism and a widespread desire for participation, but by the early 1970s this had dissipated into cynicism. For example, one Chinese writer describes a political meeting in a factory in Hunan where he worked:

> I was astounded at the workers' open indifference to the workshop and to the factory leaders' attempts to pull them into line. We had political study meetings on Tuesday and Friday afternoons, and spent at least one morning listening to reports on the general political situation. At school, the more rebellious of us had sometimes whispered to one another, but here the workers openly ignored whatever was going on at the podium, talking in groups about their own affairs, the women knitting long underwear and sweaters, the men smoking and spitting sunflower seed hulls. (Liang and Shapiro, 1983, p. 220)

The reasons for this cynicism were twofold: the Maoist leaders of the Cultural Revolution failed to convert the ideals of democracy, participation and greater equality into sustainable social institutions, and to link them to the concrete issues of material improvement and economic efficiency. People's lives were filled with slogans, theories, struggles and political movements, instead of oil, salt, fuel and rice for their daily needs (Hua, 1983). After 1976 the new regime promised more bread and fewer circuses.

Given the priority of modernization under the new regime of Deng Xiaoping, what of industrial democracy? Has an emphasis on material development and consumerism resulted in a political 'great leap backwards', as Bettelheim claims? The new Chinese leadership has sought to re-introduce some of the pre-Cultural Revolution forms of industrial democracy, particularly workers' congresses. Indeed, since 1978 workers' congresses have been promoted much more systematically than in the past and their powers extended. A national framework for their operation was set out in June 1981, which made it clear that the congresses are not to be seen as simply consultative or advisory bodies, but are the 'organs of power' through which workers and staff are to take part in decision-making to supervise cadres. The main powers of the workers' congresses are:

(i)   To scrutinize the director's production plans and budgets.
(ii) To decide on the use of the enterprise's funds for safety measures, welfare (including housing allocation) and bonuses.
(iii) To decide about any proposed changes in the structure of management, the payment system or training.
(iv) To supervise leading cadres, to the extent of making reports to the higher authorities.
(v)   To arrange the elections of leading cadres.

The paper power of workers congresses is, therefore, wide-ranging; but what of the realities? In the rest of this section I shall focus on one critical element – the formal power of the congresses to arrange the elections of managerial cadres.

At a national congress of trade unions in 1978, Deng Xiaoping announced that 'workshop directors, section chiefs, and group heads in every enterprise must in the future be elected by the workers in the unit' (*Beijing Review*, 20 October 1978). Thus from 1978 official Party policy was to start a process of election of managers, a new development of industrial democracy in China. To what extent has the policy of electing managers been implemented? The available data are summarized in Table 2.

Table 2 makes it clear that though the system of elections does not cover the majority of enterprises (even in the State sector), nevertheless, on the face of it, the shift towards the election of shop-floor managers had proceeded remarkably quickly in less than four years. Even so, there has been a significant degree of managerial opposition to elections and a variety of objections to control from below, disguised in terms of the supposed need for secrecy in management work and the possibility that the work-force will not make the 'right' choice. Moreover, the spread of elections has not been uniform. In Guangdong Province it proved unusual during a research trip in 1982 to find a factory which had had *any* form of elections. For example, at the Guangzhou No. 2 Cigarette Factory there were no elections of any kind, and the factory director said quite decisively that there were no plans for any in the future (interview, 29 September 1982).

Table 2. Election of Managers

	June 1982	% of State industrial enterprises
Workgroup and section leaders	29,400	35
Workshop directors and deputy directors	14,800	18
Factory directors and deputy directors	8,900	11

Sources: *Summary of World Broadcasts*, 14 March and 12 June 1981; interview with All-China Trade Union Federation, 8 September 1981; *Beijing Review*, 28 June 1982. The base for the percentages is 84,000; see Table 1. Percentages are rounded.

Table 2 also indicates that the extension of election to senior managers and especially factory directors has been a far more limited process. This was certainly our impression in Sichuan Province, where it was stated in 1981 that only one of 400 advanced enterprises had an elected factory director. In Guangdong Province, representatives of the Economic Commission said that they knew of only a handful of enterprises (out of 5,280 State enterprises) where the factory director was elected (interview, 5 October 1982). In contrast, at the end of September 1982, 447 enterprises in Beijing had elected their directors.

Despite the obvious slowness of some provinces in changing over to the election of factory directors, the views of the top Party leadership were clarified by the 'Provisional Regulations on the Work of State Factory Directors' issued in 1982. These stipulate that in all State enterprises workers' congresses should elect their directors, who are then approved by higher authorities (Summary of World Broadcasts, FE 7204/BII/16). Presumably it is such high-level support which has resulted in a particularly rapid advance of elections of factory directors from 1981, when a figure of around 1,000 was still being quoted, to the 1982 total of 8,900.

Apart from the diffusion of factory elections, there is the question of methods. In general, the method of election has not been standardized, partly because there seems to be a good deal of confusion and ignorance about representative democracy. Some of the elections have involved secret ballots, whilst others have involved votes at public meetings. As far as factory directors are concerned, some of the elections have been direct, whilst most have been limited to the representatives of the workers' congress. Perhaps crucially, the pattern of nomination has varied from factory to factory. Generally, most of the argument goes on *before* the election, so that the process of nomination is crucial. In some cases the trade union collects opinions amongst the workers and produces a list of names; in other cases standing committees of the workers' congress perform this task, whilst at other enterprises the Party plays a significant role.

The Beijing Leather Products Factorty provides an interesting indication of the development of factory elections. It was stated that most of the top factory management, including the director himself, were 'elected'. Detailed questioning made it clear that the present factory director had taken up his post in 1978 and was elected by the workers' congress in 1981; there were no other candidates. Having been elected, the factory director submitted a list of five other deputy directors to the congress for discussion and approval. These nominations were then accepted by congress and the managers duly 'elected' (interview, 5 September 1981). This example illustrates some of the problems in talking about democratic elections in China: the potential for manipulation is considerable, and even where it does not occur, high administrative levels and the Party may still exert considerable influence. Candidates may not be nominated or voted for if it is known that their election would not be approved.

In sum, since 1978 there have been extensive moves towards the election of lower-level managers and surprisingly large steps taken towards the election of factory directors. Elections, however, have faced obstinate opposition from middle-level cadres, who see their power and privileges being challenged if they are subject to control from below. Moreover, even if elections do occur, industrial democracy in China remains subject to a higher-level veto on the outcomes.

Has there thus been a 'great leap backwards' in industrial democracy?

Such a view makes a number of assumptions which are difficult to sustain:

(i) There are different and varying ideas about industrial democracy, and Western notions of elections and representative democracy are not well understood in China. Since the Liberation in 1949, there have been important elements of worker participation, but these have usually taken place within a framework of Party influence.

(ii) The Cultural Revolution began with ideals about extended democracy and participation and did help to break down some of the traditional social barriers in China. It quickly degenerated, however, into factionalism and authoritarianism, leading to widespread cynicism. Indeed, the Party itself destroyed much of its own moral authority during the Cultural Revolution, with young workers being particularly disillusioned.

(iii) The new regime of Deng Xiaoping has sought to re-introduce older forms of worker participation (the workers' congresses) and combine them with Western ideas (election of managers). These forms of democracy, however, are subject to the usual problems in the Chinese context: lack of understanding, resistance by entrenched cadres, manipulation and control of electoral outcomes. The present policies are limited experiments in participation, but little more can be claimed for earlier policies.

Conclusions

Has China succeeded in establishing a new, more advanced mode of production? Has she succeeded in establishing a new pattern of manager/worker relationship? Has she successfully adapted Western and Japanese technology? The answers to these questions are important beyond any concern with China herself, because, as we said at the beginning of this chapter, they raise the question whether modern forms of large-scale production entail inescapable forms of work organization and division of labour, so that working in a car factory in Shanghai is the same as working in a car factory in Birmingham.

These questions are not easy to answer, because China is in a state of rapid change and has been since 1949. Indeed, 1976–8 particularly has been a watershed: the coup of 1976 and the overthrow of the Gang of Four appeared to re-channel all the economic and social policies of China. This has led to a great deal of questioning by China scholars: were the views of yesteryear all an illusion? As one analyst puts it:

> One is struck, in looking at this period, by the extent to which so many of these changes were unplanned, piecemeal, in reaction to vilified abuses rather than as part of a well-articulated conception of an alternative form of organization. One is arrested by the gnawing realization that the only 'Maoist experiment' that ever existed was to be found in the intellectual reconstructions of Western observers. (Walder, 1981, p. 37)

This view is, I think, an exaggeration. There clearly were consistent threads to Maoist forms of work organization: the concept of the 'Two Participations' was widespread (at least at the level of rhetoric) and was intended to break down the mental/manual divide. At the same time, the Western reports of the Cultural Revolution were, as has been said, probably exaggerated and highly selective.

The Cultural Revolution, then, was not a complete illusion, and even the crimes of that period (though totally reprehensible) do not make the Maoist vision empty of content. But the Cultural Revolution did clearly fail: what conclusions can we draw from this? The first difficulty is to assess the nature of that failure. The failure may have been for political and/or economic reasons, so leaving the question of work organization indeterminate. The evidence, however, points to the opposite conclusion: in so far as experiments in work organization were implemented, they failed in their own terms. The division of labour was not radically altered, and worker participation, leading to a new system of worker control, was not extensively introduced. The barriers proved too great. And the outcome proved to be factionalism, authoritarianism, cynicism and worker alienation; 'eating socialism' (looking after number one) became commonplace on factory floors.

Might such experiments, though, succeed under more favourable conditions? The labour process, it should be noted, is the interface between the social relations of production and the *means of production* (technology, techniques, etc.). What the Cultural Revolution, and the trends of development since then, demonstrate is that achieving new forms of work organization is an immensely difficult task. The basic means of providing mass-produced goods in a competitive world system are more or less fixed, not by inescapable laws, but by the costs or re-developing technology. There is no technological determinism; instead, technology permits a choice and variety in relation to work organization and job design. Some writers have labelled the potentiality of choice a 'design space' – a variable area of manoeuvre in relation to any new technology. At present, the West seems to be in a phase of development where the new technology is genuinely new: that is, it appears to be malleable and to offer a range of options. But developing societies are faced not just with new technologies but with older technologies, in which the form of the technology has been closed off by a series of decisions and technical developments which, in combination, constitute sunk costs – so that unwinding them, making a series of different choices, becomes an impossible cost burden. The failure of the Cultural Revolution was in part the failure to recognize the immense costs involved in developing technology that fitted the political ambitions of the movement.

In more developed economies, with larger surpluses and less immediate pressures of population explosion and potential starvation, it may be possible to re-think technologies (this is the argument pursued by Rosenbrock, 1985). But without this re-thinking, societies like China are condemned either to be importers of Western and Japanese technology or to become, eventually, like Burma or Albania, economically backward and isolated on the fringes of history.

In addition, the structuring of Chinese domestic policy choices has been partly determined by international forces. It should not be forgotten that the Chinese leadership considered itself to be facing the threat of nuclear strikes from *both* the Soviet Union and the USA. (There were serious border clashes with the Soviet Union in 1969.) At another level, the impressive economic performance of China's Asian neighbours – the so-called 'four tigers' of South Korea, Taiwan, Hong Kong and Singapore – has also exerted pressure on Chinese economic policy-makers. Thus, from both military and economic viewpoints there were compelling fears that China might be left behind in the world race.

None of this means that there are not divergences between Chinese forms of work organization and those in the West. We have indicated some of these in the text. Chinese work collectives are fusions of economic, social and political organizations. This reality – the factory as community – can be seen as influenced both by the cultural traditions of China and by the political form of Chinese society. Equally, labour is not a commodity in China. There is little semblance of a labour market. Instead there is guaranteed job security for many (not all) factory workers, a situation which is paralleled in the other Soviet-type societies. Some Chinese economists and bureaucrats wish to change the labour system and introduce more contract workers, but up to the present this has been resisted at all levels in the society. Such a change requires a number of pre-conditions which have not yet been established, such as a new system of social insurance and of housing allocation. At present, welfare entitlement and housing are linked to the enterprise as part of the concept of the factory as a community.

These divergences *do* affect the nature of working China, but they leave untouched the (for Western analysts) burning issues of the range of variation in work design and the pattern of control within modern, large-scale industries. we have seen in Chapter Four the difficulties in constructing a general model of capitalist work organization; the divergences are more than would be expected in terms of a simple economic model or a model based on labour-process dynamics. But, in contrast, the Chinese experience up to the present, combined with that of the Soviet Union, suggests that the range of variation in work organization is more limited than might be expected across the capitalist/non-capitalist divide.

CHAPTER SIX

Houseworkers and their work

MARY MAYNARD

Whether women are engaged in paid employment outside the home or not, many additional hours of work are spent in unpaid domestic labour. This activity is not formally rewarded with a wage and may be largely hidden to family members, who take for granted the services which are provided. Nevertheless, housework is an important and necessary element in the maintenance of daily life for husbands and children, whilst also contributing indirect benefits to the economy and wider society. For many women it constitutes their major work role and occupation.

The focus in this chapter will be on the nature of housework in our society, who performs it, what it entails and how it is experienced. These issues will be explored via examination of the changes that have taken place in domestic work as a consequence of industrialization, consideration of the contemporary housewife role and an analysis of the wider theoretical significance of housework. The aim is to establish that housework is a form of 'work', with a significance which extends beyond the confines of individual family units.

Historical changes in domestic work

1. The impact of industrialization

Social scientists and historians commonly accept that industrialization has dramatically changed the nature of work. For women, it has been claimed, the processes accompanying industrialization totally transformed their economic role. The model typically used to describe these changes is based on the analysis of two interrelated processes (Zaretsky, 1976). The first is the transfer of production away from the family to separate economic institutions of work. Prior to capitalism, and in its early stages, the family household as a whole was the basic economic unit for the production of goods and services. All family members contributed to the maintenance of the household by working at various productive tasks which helped to feed the family. By the nineteenth century, however, the family had been stripped of many of its productive functions and the development of the factory system and increasing industrialization had established the economy as an autonomous sphere. The logic of capitalist development removed labour and the basic processes of commodity production from the private efforts of individual families to centralized large-scale units.

The second transformation is the emergence of a sphere of life located in the home and independent of the economy and production. Alongside the development of the factory system occurred the creation of the family as a separate area of personal fulfilment, where women had particular responsibility for love, personal happiness and domestic well-being. Whereas men entered the harsh public sphere of work as the family breadwinner, women remained privatized in the home as housewives and mothers.

As Zaretsky puts it, 'The housewife emerged, alongside the proletarian – the two characteristic labourers of developed capitalist society' (Zaretsky, 1976, p. 64).

Thus the separation of home from work is a fairly recent historical phenomenon. The family is now regarded not as productive but as a unit of consumption for goods produced elsewhere. This helps to explain the reason for the apparent devaluation and low status of the work performed by housewives and mothers. As the family lost its core identity as a productive unit, their work was no longer seen to be integral to the production of commodities: it was not valued as being economically productive. Despite its general utility, however, there are a number of problems with this rather simplistic and mechanistic model of the effects of industrialization on women's economic role. A consideration of these problems highlights several points of significance for a sociological understanding of housework.

Although it is acknowledged that industrialism and its attendant processes occurred gradually over a long period of time, the model is essentially linear and evolutionary. More specifically, it overlooks the fact that the pace of industrialization differed from region to region, industry to industry and in different sectors of the economy. Thus the picture of the single and inexorable growth of industry precipitating men into wage labour and retaining women as housewives in the home is not borne out by a close analysis of specific historical processes (Tilly and Scott, 1978). Although it is true, for example, that many women from the 1770s onwards found paid employment away from home in cotton textile mills, the garment industry mechanized very slowly. Garment factories appeared in England only after 1850, and even then manufacturers found that supplies of cheap labour justified the continuation of the put-ting-out system organized in sweatshops or as home production. Alongside this system, yet other women busied themselves in the home, making clothes not for wages but for use by family members. Women therefore made similar goods under different circumstances. Some were unpaid domestic labourers, others produced the same commodities in the home for wages, the rest made clothes under factory conditions. Further-more, as some women were drawn into wage labour in the cotton mills, one of the results was to prevent women from spinning cotton at home – an age-old female domestic occupation (Pinchbeck, 1930). All this points to a complex interrelationship between the various types of work women have done, both in and out of the home. Industrialization was not a simple process rendering all married women housewives.

The accepted model of the changing circumstances of domestic activity also under-emphasizes the different experiences of different class group-ings. Documentation of the lives of women employed in the cotton mills of industrial Lancashire shows that they frequently worked such long hours that it was necessary either to delegate domestic duties to a daugh-ter or pay other women to wash, sew, clean or mind children (Hewitt, 1958). Women doing piece-work at home, on the other hand, had to fit such activities as best they could into a lengthy working day and often around cumbersome machinery. While many women were employed as domestic servants doing other women's housework, others undertook casual jobs, such as street hawking, which left rather more time for domestic chores. The point to be emphasized is that the lives of working-class women exhibited a complex and variable pattern. Women con-tinued to perform, or to be responsible for, domestic tasks which mainly comprised the most basic maintenance of family members. The buying, preparation and cooking of food was by far the most important element, together with other activities such as making, washing and mending clothes and nursing the sick. The amount of effort women were able to put into these household tasks, however, depended on the nature of the other, paid, obligations they had to fulfil. Industrialization did not diminish the working-class woman's domestic responsibilities while for those involved with paid work it became rather more difficult to combine the two activities (Tilly and Scott, 1978).

For women of other classes, of course, the picture is very different. The upper-middle-class woman, as portrayed by commentators of the time, lived a life of leisured gentility, cocooned in a large house and serviced by a retinue of domestic servants. Recently, however, it has been argued that such an image is not typical of the vast majority of middle-class house-holds and is far too stereotyped (Branca, 1975). Most of these women, for example, employed only one general servant rather than a number of maids who each had their own specific tasks. Moreover, the possession of servants did not necessarily relieve the women of the house from domestic responsibilities, to live in idleness. Rather, it altered the nature of her duties from actual housework to the supervision and management of the household. This became increasingly time-consuming as emphasis was placed on the importance of the preparation of household budgets and accounts, and running the home to predictable schedules and routines (Branca, 1975; Davidoff, 1976). Housework itself was made more difficult by the design of Victorian clothes and of the furniture and ephemera. These, not noted for their simplicity, efficiency or convenience, made housework a continual routine of tidying, dusting and polishing.

The nineteenth century also heralded a growing concern for motherhood and infant care. Such issues were no longer left to take their own course but became matters of drawing room debate and of detailed pronouncements from clerics, doctors and fashionable philanthropists. The care, nurture and moral development of the future generation were thus made the specific and spiritual duty of the Victorian mother (Branca, 1975).

Given these extensions in the nature of domestic obligations and the increasing need to combat the dirt and unpleasantness of urban life, it is scarcely surprising that the nineteenth century saw a significant expansion of domestic service as a paid occupation for women (Horn, 1975; McBride, 1976). Not only was there a ready source of female labour in the new industrial towns, but it became a status symbol and a sign of respectability for the middle classes to employ live-in domestic help.

'For any nineteenth century family with social pretensions at least one domestic servant was essential, even if at its lowest level this merely meant that recruitment of a thirteen year old "skivvy" from the local workhouse at a wage of a shilling a week' (Horn, 1975).

Domestic service for lower-class women was emphasized as a safe, honourable and edifying employment. It was, after all, training for future marriage. The irony, of course, is that while servants were paid, many women performed domestic work in their own homes for nothing.

The rise of servanthood as a significant urban activity accompanied the acceleration of urbanization from the late eighteenth to mid-nineteenth centuries and the growth in the numbers of urban middle classes. An important aspect of this is the feminization of domestic service as an occupation involving single and, overwhelmingly, young females. Domestic service played a significant role in modernization since it formed an important channel for urban migration from rural areas and was a major employer of female labour until the 1920s. From the 1880s onwards, however, numbers fell as a result of declining prosperity, alternative sources of employment for women and dissatisfaction with the loss of privacy imposed by live-in helps (McBride, 1976). After this date domestic work increasingly became the province of older charwomen employed on a daily or occasional basis.

Industrialization thus had a diverse effect on the domestic role of women. Some were involved in waged employment, others in unpaid domestic labour. Many were paid to perform domestic tasks in others' homes. Although some middle-class women undoubtedly lived a life of leisure, for the majority, the growth of responsibilities in the personal and private space of the home brought new and enlarged obligations of home management and mothercraft.

2. *The ideology of domesticity*

The expansion and elaboration of the female domestic role cannot be understood solely in terms of the physical separation of home from work and the changing nature of production. The gradual articulation of an ideology of domesticity is also important (Davidoff, 1976; Davidoff *et al.*, 1976; Hall, 1979). Although the roots of this can be traced back to the seventeenth century, it is particularly associated with the nineteenth century when its influence became more widespread. This ideology is important not because it accurately reflected the material circumstances of women (it clearly did not), but because it provided a moral benchmark against which the middle classes judged themselves and measured their superiority over others. It also provided the goal to which all should aspire. The ideas involved signify the beginning of a dominant ideology of domesticity for women that was developed and extended throughout the nineteenth and into the twentieth centuries.

The two major elements of this ideology are a specific image of womanhood and an image of what should constitute the ideal home. The first of these focused on the cultural differences between men and women and treated them as absolute and natural. Women were regarded as cleaner and purer than men and therefore more suitable as the guardians of conscience and morality. Women, it was argued, should be protected from the taint of worldly forces and remain unsullied in the privacy of their homes. Here their job was to maintain domestic order and harmony – to create an environment within which men could be protected from their baser selves. According to such views, if the husband looked for excitement and amusement outside the home, the domestic atmosphere was at fault and should be improved 'to counteract the weaknesses of male human nature' (Davidoff *et al.*, 1976). At the beginning of the nineteenth century such moral redemption was described in religious terms. However, the basic concepts of peace and salvation remained a general part of secular morality well into the twentieth century. The wife was the linchpin of the domestic idyll supposedly created in the home (Davidoff *et al.*, 1976).

The second ideological aspect emphasized the home and the family as the citadel of moral righteousness in a changing society (Davidoff, 1976). Morality was regarded as beginning at home and to be signified by cleanliness and order. Women were exhorted to maintain high standards of housework and housekeeping, as the plethora of manuals, advice books and magazines of the period show. Their special task was the creation of cleanliness and order in their own households; everything was to be spick and span, and smoothly running.

The combination of the two images of domestic ideology symbolized both a moral treatise and a social commentary on the home life of others. Firstly, they served to maintain a physical and social boundary between the respectable home and family life of the middle classes and 'The Great Unwashed'. Cleanliness and order were equated with a certain status and class position. 'The middle and upper class house . . . was the clean, tidy haven in the midst of public squalor and disorder. It was the housemistresses' responsibility to make it so' (Davidoff, 1976). Secondly, and paradoxically, although the mistress of the house was responsible for the overall domestic order she was also pictured as increasingly withdrawing from specific active involvement in this task, since even housework came to be associated with dirty, manual work and therefore with the unseemly side of life. It was certainly not the proper endeavour of a feminine lady. The mistress of the house might be involved in domestic management but, as has already been seen, other females, servants, increasingly did the actual work.

These images of domesticity had become part of the dominant culture by the 1840s. In the government reports of the period, working wives and mothers were presented as unnatural and immoral. Working-class women were continually castigated for being poor housewives and inadequate mothers, and by the 1870s a domestic economy movement was attempting to train girls to improve their standards of domestic care (Davidoff, 1976; Hall, 1979). The middle-class ideal of the family came to be regarded as the proper way of living, and this meant that married women should not work. According to the ideology, the laws of nature decreed that all women should be regarded first and foremost as wives and mothers (Hall, 1979).

3. Housework as a form of 'work'

The historical development of domestic activity then was a complex and varied process. Industrialization did not affect it uniformly but instigated changes which differed depending on region, occupation and class. A domestic ideology was generated to which many aspired, but which fitted the material circumstances of only a few. Moreover, it is now clear that although some sort of division was created between home and work, the public and the private spheres, this division was not as clear-cut or absolute as some writers have implied. Although industrialization did deprive the household of production, the family continued to influence the productive activities of its members.

Most commentators overlook the fact that the family is (and always has been) a unit within which members make economic decisions. These decisions implicitly assign economic value to all household tasks. Depending on factors such as historical period and class position, households allocate the time of different members differently. This is determined by opportunities available outside the home and by the activities of the various members. For example, the amount of time a mother spends with her children depends on the value assigned to children and the meaning ascribed to childhood at a particular point in time. This is then weighed against the benefits that would be brought to the family by the woman doing paid work outside the home (Tilly and Scott, 1978). It is therefore inaccurate to make a sharp division between work and home, the economic and the familial.

Once the relationship between the family and the economy is acknowledged, it becomes possible to display the grounds for treating housework as work. A distinction can be made between three sorts of female activity: domestic (unpaid household labour); productive (wage-earning labour); reproductive (bearing and raising children) (Tilly and Scott, 1978). These activities have always been the major components of women's contribution to the family economy, although their meaning, value, location and nature have changed over time and the three forms have become increasingly distinct during industrialization. If work is defined as 'productive activity for household use or exchange', then it is clear that women's domestic, productive and reproductive labour is 'work', since it has economic value both to the family and to society. Before industrialization, activities such as keeping animals, making clothes, preparing food, growing vegetables had economic value since they were performed to satisfy household needs. This kind of work was indistinguishable from women's other household and productive chores. Thus, during the seventeenth and eighteenth centuries the term 'work' encompassed all of these activities. To use the term 'work' subsequently to refer only to wage earning occupations ignores 'not only the domestic and reproductive activities of women, but the implicitly economic function of those activities within the family' (Tilly and Scott, 1978). Activities previously regarded as work are now excluded by a somewhat arbitrary definition of work as concerned only with waged labour. The absurdity of this is underlined by an example: a housewife cooking a meal is not performing an economic activity, whereas she would be if hired to cook a similar meal in a restaurant. Similarly, whereas the housework performed by a housewife is considered a labour of love, the same chores carried out by a domestic servant are regarded as work. This obscures the fact that the domestic tasks women perform, and have always performed, for their families, constitute useful, economically valuable, if unpaid, work.

Contemporary housework and the houseworker role

1. *The sexual division of labour*

A review of the historical material indicates the complexity of the changes in domestic labour which accompanied industrialization. But although different authors emphasize differing aspects of these changes, there is agreement that household tasks were largely female tasks and that there continued to be a distinction between those duties and responsibilities performed by women and those carried out by men. At its most simple this is described as the sexual division of labour. This is the demarcation between male and female roles and the separation of the sexes into gender specific areas of work, family commitment and psychological identity. Women are regarded, and see themselves, as responsible for home and domestic life. Even when they are engaged in paid employment (also highly sex-segregated), their primary responsibility is for the family and its members. Men, on the other hand, are primarily breadwinners and are expected to have less involvement with their families. This division between the sexes is legitimated on the grounds that it is natural, necessary and a biological inevitability. It is taken for granted that the social world is, and should be, organized in this way.

Although the sexual division of labour was clearly a feature of nineteenth-century life and remains a central dimension in the organization of contemporary society, some sociologists have claimed that, particularly within the home, a strict segregation of duties and obligations is breaking down. It is argued that the family structure in Western society is evolving in such a way that women's and men's roles are becoming more 'symmetrical'. More women are working outside the home in addition to performing their traditional family roles, and men are increasing their investment in the family, while maintaining their work commitments. This symmetrical family form is regarded as the dominant mode of family organization for the future. It implies a movement towards a balance between the involvement of husband and wife in the two spheres of domestic and paid work (Young and Willmott, 1975).

Such a view has some resonance with the current picture of family life depicted by the mass media. This picture is based on an interpretation of two particular socio-economic trends. Firstly, it is said that, since the number of women doing paid work has increased substantially, some sharing of household tasks is now the norm. Secondly, the growth in household technology is presumed to have removed the drudgery from female domestic work, saved a substantial amount of time in its performance and rendered most tasks so simple that they can be undertaken by any household member (Bose, 1982). Such an account also appears to set the conditions for a symmetrical family form and the gradual breakdown of a domestic division of labour based on sex.

But despite the predominance of this view, a vast amount of empirical evidence suggests otherwise. This evidence is of two kinds: American time-budget surveys, and sociological surveys and studies of housework and the housewife which are mainly British in origin.

2. Time-budget studies

In recent years a number of time-budget studies have measured time spent on housework and other activities such as paid work and leisure. Such research generally involves either asking respondents to record their activities for specified time intervals over a number of days, or having them keep diaries registering the number and nature of tasks performed and the amount of time spent on each. The findings are remarkably consistent.

One study, for example, completed in the late sixties, shows that women who have no employment outside the home work an average of fifty-seven hours per week on such activities as preparing and clearing up after meals, washing, cleaning and tidying the house, taking care of children and other family members and shopping (Walker and Woods, 1976). More recent research shows women spending similar amounts of time on domestic tasks, to the extent that if it was paid employment it would certainly be regarded as full-time work (Berk and Berk, 1979).

For women employed outside the home, it appears that the more waged work they do, the fewer hours they spend on housework but the longer their overall working week. It has been reported that women who are in paid employment for more than thirty hours per week work a total of seventy-six hours in all, including an average of thirty-three hours spent on housework (Walker and Woods, 1976). Yet those husbands whose wives have the longest work weeks, have the shortest work weeks themselves. It appears that the husbands of wives in waged work do not spend any more time on housework than those with full-time housewives. This apparent lack of responsiveness by husbands to women's waged work is corroborated by other research, including a 1976 study of 3,500 couples in the United States. Wives employed outside the home worked substantially more hours every day than either their husbands or full-time housewives. They also spent about double their weekday time for housework doing domestic chores on their days off, whereas husbands, and even full-time housewives, had the weekend for increased leisure (reported in Hartmann, 1981).

This burden increases substantially when there are very young children, or many children, in the family. In either case the wife's work week expands to meet the needs of the family. Research shows that in families with a child under one year old, the typical full-time houseworker spends nearly seventy hours a week in housework (Walker and Woods, 1976);

nearly thirty hours of this is spent in child care. The typical father spends five hours a week on this task, but reduces his time spent on other work around the house, such as home repairs, decorating and cleaning the outside of windows, so that his total domestic commitment does not increase. When the wife is employed outside the home for fifteen or more hours a week, the average husband spends two hours more per week on child care, increasing his overall household labour to twenty hours. His wife spends over fifty hours on housework, indicating that the amount of time spent on housework by the employed woman increases substantially with the presence of young children.

In addition, researchers do not appear to regard the housework or childcare activities of husbands as particularly significant (Berk and Berk, 1979). They point out that men are more likely to be occupied in this way after dinner. At this time child care typically consists of playing with and talking to children, which is not particularly burdensome. Moreover, while husbands are occupied in this way, their wives are tied up with the less than exciting after dinner chores. When men are involved with other domestic tasks it is frequently because their wives have to leave for employment after dinner and so are not themselves available to perform them.

Thus the activities of husbands are a form of back-up, or reserve labour, for a series of tasks which remain primarily the women's responsibility. Most married women still spend a considerable part of every day performing the necessary and most time-consuming work in the household. It is also noteworthy that the work week of domestic labourers is longer than that of the average person in the labour-force. Thus it is clearly demonstrated that although waged women do less housework than their unwaged counterparts, this has little effect on the allocation of particular tasks within the home. Domestic labour is still very rigidly differentiated along sex lines and this division appears to be constant across localities, regions and nations (Gershuny, 1982; Robinson, 1977; Szalai, 1972). Time-budget data indicate that there has been no significant change in the sexual division of labour within the household.

3. Changes in the nature of housework

One significant finding suggests that during the last century there has been an alteration in the content, although not in the amount, of housework performed (Bose, 1982; Cowan, 1976; Vanek, 1974). Although technological changes were slower in reaching the home than the workplace, they did begin to enter the more affluent homes towards the end of the nineteenth century. However, major technological developments did not affect the households of most of the population until the early decades of the present century. The significance of these developments cannot be underestimated. As Rothschild says, 'Gas and electricity for cooking, heating, and lighting; indoor plumbing; and the washing machine dramatically reduced filthy and back-breaking labor for the housewife' (Rothschild, 1983). Labour-saving devices such as refrigerators, vacuum cleaners, freezers and convenience foods have also made activities such as cooking and cleaning easier. This has led one commentator to suggest that technological changes in the home have been on a par with, and as important as, those of the Industrial Revolution (Cowan, 1976).

Thus fifty or sixty years ago a large proportion of a housewife's time would have been spent in heavy routine and repetitive jobs such as fetching, hand-laundry and cleaning. Today, time is more likely to be spent in managerial activities, particularly child care and planning shopping expeditions. The continuing emphasis on the physical, moral and emotional stability of childhood as a significant component of mothering has obviously influenced the amount of time women spend on child-rearing. But despite the increased availability of household technology, the purchase of appliances and gadgets does not neccesarily alleviate woman's domestic role (Bose, 1982; Cowan, 1976). Rather, it is suggested that the more technology present in a household, the more time is spent in its acquisition, use and maintenance. For example, food mixers encourage the preparation of more ambitious meals, and washing machines, together with higher standards of cleanliness, mean that more washing is carried out more often. Indeed, Parkinson's Law seems to operate, keeping women's housework at a constant level despite improvements in household technology. The situation appears to have changed very little over the last fifty years, since the amount of time devoted by full-time housewives to housework has remained remarkably stable during this time (Vanek, 1974). Moreover, household technology has been developed on an individual, familial basis, thus increasing the privatized nature of the domestic work which women perform. Despite the many developments made in this area, housework remains decentralized and is performed in isolated, relatively inefficient units. For all these reasons it has been argued that instead of challenging the sexual division of labour within the home, modern technology has tended to support, and even reinforce, the traditional allocation of domestic roles (Rothschild, 1983; Thrall, 1982).

Additionally, the increase in the number and range of goods available for purchase, together with the focus of advertisers on the mother and housewife as the major consumer, have made the home the centre of consumption. Women are the major consumers in our society. They are responsible for most of the expenditure on food, clothing and footwear and for the purchase of most household and chemists' goods. They are also largely responsible for the actual decision to buy most goods in the consumer durable section (Scott, 1976). Moreover, shopping and consuming should not be regarded as synonymous. Whereas the former refers to the physical process of buying goods, the latter involves a whole set of social and psychological factors surrounding the ultimate decision to purchase a particular item. The act of buying can be performed fairly quickly; the process of consuming can be a very complex and drawn-out business (Scott, 1976).

4. *The experience of housewives*

Sociological studies and surveys of housework corroborate the findings from time-budget studies. This research has been conducted mainly via interviews aimed at eliciting the nature of the work involved, strategies of coping and the meaning that housework has for the houseworker. Despite its differing orientation, the evidence concerning the sexual division of labour within the home continues to be overwhelming.

Oakley's much quoted research (1974) indicates that only 15 per cent of husbands in her sample assisted with housework and 25 per cent with child care. Her work reveals that husbands performing such tasks were still regarded as household aids, while the woman remained responsible for ensuring that tasks were completed, and for the daily management of housework and child care. A similar study found that the husbands of both waged and unwaged wives helped around the house on a spasmodic rather than a regular basis and were more likely to be involved in jobs outside than inside the house (Hunt, 1980). Moreover, this research corroborates the time-budget findings that husbands do slightly more in the home when wives are employed, but less than when both of the couple are employed but childless. The waged wife still does a double shift and has to revert to being a full-time houseworker at the weekend, when she catches up on her chores. Even the professional wife of the dual career family retains her domestic responsibilities. A number of studies report that husband's child care is still regarded, not as part of the role of being a father, but as a favour to the wife (Gavron, 1968; Ginsberg, 1976; Hunt, 1980; Oakley, 1974). The man's involvement with children is again revealed as recreational rather than physical, involving playing and talking with children, thereby freeing the mother to perform domestic work.

The sociological evidence suggests that only a very small minority of men participate in domestic work on anything like an equal basis. This finding holds regardless of whether wives work outside the home or whether they are full-time houseworkers.

The qualitative material concerning the experience of being a housewife reveals that a series of contradictions and conflicts are involved. Firstly, the ideology surrounding domestic labour defines it as non-work and many wives report that their husbands think they 'get off lightly', with little to do all day (Hunt, 1980; Oakley, 1974). The conditions under which housework is performed, however, often resemble factory-like and assembly-line organization. This is particularly so in the morning, when the housewife's major job is organizing those of the family who have to leave the house to do so on time. Other aspects of domestic work also resemble the conditions of other forms of work. For example, housewives comment on the monotony of the activities and their repetitive nature, since many jobs have to be done daily and seem never-ending (Hunt, 1980; Oakley, 1974). Additionally, housework is experienced not as a single activity but as a collection of heterogeneous acts, which are often contradictory and demand a variety of skills and actions.

Secondly, in order to cope with a job where there are no set specifications and standards, and where it is difficult to judge how much work is adequate, housewives devise their own standards and routines (Oakley, 1974). In the absence of formal rules for procedure and obvious rewards, such as wages, the satisfactory fulfilment of one's own standards and routines can bring its own psychic recompense. This process of self-rewarding is significant in a job which, because of its nature, draws attention from other household members only when tasks have not been properly completed. However, bringing coherence and self-reward to work in this way can lead to the loss of autonomy and constraint on creativity. For some women the imposition of rigid job specifications can lead to an obsession with tidiness and cleanliness, 'the houseproud wife', and to guilt and anxiety if housework is not performed to the self-defined standards.

Thirdly, one of the aspects of their work particularly liked by housewives is the sense of autonomy and of 'being one's own boss' which it conveys. Moreover, the women in Oakley's sample chose cooking and shopping as their most favoured activities. This seems to be because cookery has an element of creativity attached to it and, of course, is closely associated with woman's self-image as nurturer and carer. Shopping, on the other hand, is a public activity, involving social contact and freedom from the more menial household tasks. Paradoxically, however, the more women set themselves schedules and routines for housework, the less autonomy they have and the less time is available for the pleasurable domestic duties. A conflict emerges between spending time on tasks which are enjoyed and working through the schedule of less agreeable jobs.

Fourthly, a similar contradiction is associated with children. Women overwhelmingly report child care as one of the most satisfying aspects of housewifery (Gavron, 1968; Oakley, 1974). However, children continually impinge upon and interrupt the household routine, extending the length of time spent in basic tasks and eroding those periods set aside for particular involvement with them. In addition, there is a conflict between the object of housework as a means of controlling dirt and tidiness, and the present 'progressive' notion of childhood, which emphasizes the importance of freedom in the early years (Davidoff, 1976). The new tolerance of disruptive behaviour is particularly incompatible with the ideal image of good household management. Often the competition between children and housework presents an obstacle to job satisfaction for the housewife (Oakley, 1974).

Fifthly, a sizeable majority of housewives openly express dissatisfaction with their work, particularly with housework, and menial chores. Nearly 70 per cent of the housewives in one study (Oakley, 1974) and nearly two-thirds in another (Ginsberg, 1976) were dissatisfied with being full-time housewives and mothers. Clearly not every woman perceives contradictions and ambivalence in her houseworker role and not every housewife is dissatisfied. But mothers continually refer to the fact that they are staying at home because of the children, whilst recognizing that this contributes significantly to their loneliness and isolation (Gavron, 1968; Ginsberg, 1976; Oakley, 1974). Women can derive considerable satisfaction and enjoyment from their children, yet still find the day to day work of child care highly frustrating. This is yet another aspect of the guilt and frustration which researchers have identified as part of the housewife role. More poignantly, it appears that those women with pre-school children are more likely to feel isolated and lonely, and to be dependent on drugs. Evidence indicates that feelings of conflict and low self-worth are related to the high consumption of psychotropic drugs (such as tranquillizers, sedatives and anti-depressants) among women with pre-school children (Ginsberg, 1976). There is also evidence that work outside the home can protect women against psychiatric disorder (Bose, 1982; Gavron, 1968; Ginsberg, 1976). But this leads to a final contradiction since the majority of females are channelled into paid work which is often limited by a sense of what would be compatible with their domestic responsibilities. A principle of 'occupational compatibility' is in operation: the job opportunities which are open or closed to women, and the beliefs held about women as paid workers are coloured by real and imaginary ideas about the limited availability and competence of women, because of their domestic work. The woman who wishes to escape from the houseworker role will inevitably find that all social relations are organized around the assumption that women are responsible for housework and child care (Berk, 1980).

5. The problems and contemporary research

The time-budget and sociological evidence describes a situation where the typical houseworker is female and where a rigid sexual division of domestic labour ensures that women retain responsibility for the completion of household tasks and child care. However, although providing a comprehensive picture of contemporary housework, this picture is rather unsatisfactory because of its essentially descriptive nature. The houseworker appears in an isolated domain of her own, cut off from the wider context of the world outside. Moreover, the use of the dichotomic concept 'sexual division of labour' as a focus for analysis underplays the possible inequalities in a relationship and makes it difficult to address questions of power and dominance. Put simply, to organize our understanding of housework in terms of the sexual division of labour is merely to redescribe empirical regularities without attempting to explain them. The 'sexual division of labour' is a descriptive, not a theoretical, concept. It helps to organize our empirical material but does no more. To move beyond mere description it is necessary to ask questions of a more general, contextual and theoretical nature. This can be demonstrated by looking at some recent socio-economic approaches to housework.

The significance of housework to society

1. *The household and consumption*

Many writers regard the household, not as a unit of economic production, but solely as a unit of consumption. The housewife's relation to the wider economy is merely that of passive consumer. This approach is suggested in the description of the elimination of women from domestic employment during industrialization as their conversion into 'a crypto-servant class' (Galbraith, 1974). The modern economy has subordinated women into this menial role for the primary economic purpose of indefinitely increasing consumption. Woman's role in this is to be responsible for those household tasks which are related to the consumption of goods. Consumption is therefore woman's supreme economic contribution to the modern economic system.

Such an account is interesting for two reasons. Firstly, it indicates that women's consumption has an economic function and that this is hidden because, conventionally, the value of household services is not added to the Gross National Product. Secondly, Galbraith argues that, because the economic unit of analysis is taken to be the household and not the individual consumer, relationships within the home are ignored. Thus the household in established economics acts as a disguise for male authority, since women normally have the power to implement decisions but not to make them. In a society which values financial achievement, authority inevitably resides with the person who earns the money.

Although he does not develop his analysis further, Galbraith's comments illustrate the focus of recent developments in the study of housework. These centre on the economic productivity of domestic work, the relationship of housework to the economic structure of capitalism and the power relations generated through a wife's servicing of her husband.

2. The New Home Economics

Recently, economics involved in what is referred to as the 'New Home Economics', have challenged the accepted wisdom that households merely consume. It is argued that the household is really a small factory combining capital goods, raw material and labour to clean, feed, procreate and otherwise produce useful commodities (Berk, 1980; Berk and Berk, 1979). Whereas traditional economics treat households as empty boxes – market goods go in one side and somehow utilities come out of the other – this new framework acknowledges the existence and importance of production in the home. In the household, it is argued, time and market goods are combined to produce commodities that in turn are immediate sources of utility. Such commodities can take various forms from a made bed and a cooked meal to a disciplined child or watching television. The major question to be asked is, 'given a set of efficient household production techniques, how might a household select the one for each kind of output that will lead to the best results?' (Berk, 1980).

There are several problems with the New Home Economics approach to housework, as Richard Berk has pointed out (Berk, 1980). Firstly, as currently applied it does not allow for more than one household commodity to result from a single production process. This rules out any psychic rewards from producing. For example, the output of cooking a meal is only a meal, whatever feelings of frustration, boredom or creativity might also be experienced. Secondly, since the household is taken as the decision-making unit this rules out the existence of tension and conflicts between family members. Thirdly, the distinction between common-sense notions of leisure and household commodity production become blurred and indistinguishable from each other. Lastly, Berk suggests that it is all too easy to take this model of household production as prescriptive. The traditional household division of labour is justified because it appears to facilitate the production of household commodities. The possibilities of inequality or exploitation are defined away. If husbands happen to do little housework, this may be explained in economic terms as due to their relatively lower marginal productivity or their higher wages. Equally important is that because the New Home Economics is essentially astructural, the household is regarded as reacting to an essentially 'neutral' outside environment (Berk, 1980).

3. The domestic labour debate

These issues are further developed by a rather different approach which also attempts to take the economic output of housework seriously. Known as the domestic labour debate, this literature is Marxist in orientation, much of the very protracted argument centring on the question:

what sort of economic value, if any, is produced for capitalism during housework? In attempting to provide an answer, the contributors to the debate site the household within the capitalist economic system and address themselves to the complicated problem of elucidating the nature of the relationship between capitalism and housework. A primary aim is to articulate how, under the socio-economic relations of capitalism, housework is a cornerstone of women's oppression.

The focus of the domestic labour debate can be illustrated by a brief consideration of an article by Margaret Benston (1980), which set the parameters of discussion for the other protagonists. As a Marxist, Benston focuses on the relationship between housework and the means of production in society, its economic organization, whereby one class controls the work and appropriates the surplus produced by another. She argues that women as a group have a definite relation to the means of production and that this relation is different from that of men. The difference is to be found in women's responsibility for domestic labour, through which they reproduce not just the next generation of workers by child-bearing but also daily reproduce the physical well-being of wage-labourers and children via their work. The vast amount of unpaid domestic labour performed by women is very profitable to the capitalist class which owns the means of production, since to pay women for doing it would mean a massive redistribution of wealth. At present the support of the family is a hidden tax on the wage earner, for his wage pays both for his work and for the invisible work of the housewife.

In line with this analysis some writers have claimed that since housework is clearly socially necessary to capitalism, it is also obviously productive work. On this basis, they have argued that women should be paid wages for working in the home which would ensure them an economic status akin to any other worker (Dalla Costa and James, 1980).

Some Marxists, however, object to the activities of housewives being described as productive labour, preferring to reserve the term for a particular aspect of Marx's theory of capitalism (Secombe, 1974). They argue that production in capitalism means the creation of surplus value and thus the exploitation of workers: workers are paid wages that are less than the value of the goods and services they produce, which generates profit for the capitalist. The housewife is not exploited because her goods, although they have use-value for a family, do not have surplus value: they do not enter the commodity market, but are consumed at home. Housework cannot be productive labour, because the domestic worker is not involved with either the means of production or the mechanisms of exchange. However, although the houseworker is not exploited, she *is* oppressed. She is oppressed by her economic dependency on her husband, by the limiting nature of her role and by her isolation from other women like herself because of her home duties.

Following this analysis, the debate has become focused on whether or not housework produces value and, if it does, how such value is to be defined. Some argue that no value is created. It is claimed, for example, that domestic labour and labour in the workplace are of a different order and cannot be analysed in the same terms (Gardiner *et al.*, 1980). It is contradictory to maintain that housework produces value, while at the same time acknowledging that it occurs outside the context in which Marx's labour theory of value operates, i.e. the market place. Others argue that housewives contribute to surplus value by performing surplus labour (Harrison, 1973). They do more housework than they would have to if they had only to maintain themselves. This surplus is appropriated by the capitalist when he buys the housewife's husband's labour power, so that it enters into the value of that labour power. Although she is an unproductive worker who has no value, the housewife contributes to surplus value through providing services for her husband and enabling him to work. Despite disagreements, however, on the exact meaning of the work of the housewife relative to capitalism, there *is* agreement that the housewife works for the maintenance of capital rather than simply for her individual family.

The problems raised by this theoretical approach to the analysis of housework can be summarized as follows. Firstly, 'housework' itself is never defined. This is a problem with all the literature on household labour that has been included here, and is usually solved by simply accepting the tasks people refer to when asked about their domestic work. Such an approach clearly leads to difficulties. For the domestic labour debate the problem is particularly acute, since the different kinds of domestic work may generate different degrees of value and productivity. It cannot be assumed that all jobs play an equal part in social reproduction.

This leads to a second issue, which is the necessity of distinguishing between three sorts of reproduction, all of which may be important for capital but again not necessarily to the same degree. It is possible to distinguish between housework that contributes to: the generational replenishment of the work-force through child-bearing; the daily maintenance of labourers and hence labour-power through feeding, clothing, sexually servicing and generally keeping men in good working order; the continuation and legitimation of the social relations of capitalist production through the socializing of children together with the general preservation of the capitalist status quo via supporting the family.

Thirdly, in focusing on women's domestic production, her role in the capitalist economy as a consumer is ignored along with the significance of her involvement in paid work. Not all women are full-time housewives. What are the theoretical implications when women do two sorts of work?

Fourthly, the debate has become so embroiled in narrow economic arguments that it has failed to acknowledge other aspects of domestic work which are of theoretical significance. For example, it would be important to analyse the ideology of domesticity, which helps to reproduce a particular form of family and places particular socio-psychological pressures on women. Similarly, particular state policies bolster women's domestic role and therefore demand specific and detailed analysis.

Finally, the different household roles of the sexes are not treated as problematic. In fact an analysis of gender relations is almost completely absent from the domestic labour debate, implying that an equal exchange takes place between the wage-working husband and the housewife. While the debate suggests that women's work appears to be for men but is really for capital, it could also be argued that women's work in the family really *is* for men, although it clearly reproduces capital as well. One alternative, for example that of Christine Delphy, postulates the existence of two modes of production, the industrial and the domestic (Delphy, 1977). The first gives rise to capitalist exploitation. The second gives rise to patriarchal exploitation. Women's position in the family is regarded as comparable to serfdom. Marrige is a labour contract. The husband appropriates the labour power of his wife, in a similar manner to the way the capitalist appropriates that of the worker. In return for being kept, the wife provides unpaid services. Moreover, women who are in paid employment are able to finance their own keep and therefore perform domestic work for husbands for no return at all. Housework is the material foundation for the system of patriarchy whereby men dominate and control women. It is the material basis of female oppression (Delphy, 1977).

Conclusion

It can be seen that the present social structure rests upon an unequal distribution of labour along gender and class lines. It is the underlying patriarchal and capitalist aspects of housework which should be the centre of our attention, since the particular forms familial relations and domestic labour take largely reflect these underlying social forces. If housework is regarded as being for the family alone, then the sociological focus must clearly be on the housewife, her tasks, problems and feelings, as a previous section on the experience of housewives describes. But this privatizes the family and housework. There is a difference between acknowledging that the conditions under which housework is performed are privatized and making the sociological judgement that this means it must be analysed in isolation from, and as if unaffected by, other social relations. Moreover, to use the term 'the sexual division of labour' in this context is to imply that the family is a complementary unit in which the man's activities and interests are to be balanced against those of his wife. But to see the household in this way is to obscure the relations of capitalism and patriarchy. It overlooks the possibility that the family is a place where people with different material activities and interests often, though not always, come into conflict with each other. An alternative analysis shifts from simply exploring the division between the sexes within the home to asking questions about the wider socio-economic context in which women are assigned to domestic labour. The sociological analysis of housework itself has to be 'deprivatized' before we can fully understand why housework is a privatized and female occupation. Only then can the real nature of housework as work be displayed and the proper relationship between domestic work and other forms of work be acknowledged. Moreover, as long as housework is regarded primarily as women's work, this will influence not just the amount of hours that women spend on domestic tasks but also the quality of life women can expect and the nature of the relationships in which they will be involved. A sociology of housework must be prepared to embrace these wider issues.

CHAPTER SEVEN

Working outside formal employment

RUTH FINNEGAN

The meaning of work

Work – it should go without saying – takes many different forms. Think, for example, of gardening, carving and fishing in South Sea islands; reindeer herding in northern Europe; agriculture and priesthood and the complex division of tasks in the Indian caste system; hunting and gathering in the Kalahari desert; co-operative work on the family farm in Ireland or France; washing, spinning and brewing by women in sixteenth-century English villages; housework, factory work and the host of service jobs and self-provisioning responsibilities in modern Britain; military service in the past and the present – the list is endless. If we start from a broad historical and comparative perspective, with some appreciation of the immense variety of work throughout the past and present, it is remarkable that the immediate reaction to the term 'work' in both conventional wisdom and academic study should be to associate it just with paid jobs. It is somehow implicitly assumed that only jobs which are remunerated through the cash nexus as part of market place transactions and are counted and taxed by government agencies are really work. This delimitation of work to 'paid employment' – or, even more narrowly, to full-time male employment - lies behind much traditional research in the sociology of work, industrial relations, economics, organization theory and industrial sociology. It is buttressed furthermore by a series of deeply-entrenched (though not necessarily now undisputed) values and classifications in our own society which associate 'work' with 'paid employment'.

The approach of this paper is to question some of these assumptions about the nature of 'work'. Our commonly held views about the 'natural' or 'right' form that work should take may be based on ethnocentric assumptions and the result of a particular phase of Western history (perhaps an idiosyncratic phase when seen in comparative perspective, and certainly one open to change) rather than possessing the quasi-universal validity that we tend to assume. Furthermore, I would contend that the central symbols of a society (not least those to do with 'work') may be so overwhelming that they sometimes mislead us about what actually happens. Because of our assumptions associating work with formal, full-time paid employment – the 'natural' pursuit of all able-bodied males in the community – other forms of working which may be of equal social and economic significance, simply get overlooked by both the academics and even (amazingly) the participants. This paper gives some account of these other 'invisible' kinds of working, those that get left out when, as so often, we focus just on formal employment.

The broader sense of the term 'work' is not a new one, unusual though it has been in traditional sociological research. Even the conventional 'folk' meaning of the term, while most overtly associated with the 'paid job', has also a wider reference in such phrases as 'working in the garden', 'housework', or 'working at' some serious amateur pursuit. Anthropologists and historians have always taken a wide view of what is to count as 'work', given their comparative coverage and perspective, so that the interest in interdisciplinary subjects which is a feature of some recent social science research has meant the drawing together of insights from these and other disciplines into a broader approach to the study of work (e.g., Pahl, 1984, Roberts *et al.*, 1984).

Several strands in academic study have also recently been coming together to query whether a concentration on paid employment is necessarily the best route to an understanding of the present social and economic realities of our society. One important impetus here comes from the feminist challenge to a number of social scientific assumptions, among them the long taken-for-granted view that 'work' is somehow quintessentially a *male* occupation, outside the home, whereas women's domestic responsibilities are merely marginal: inside the home, not really 'work', and away from the workplace and the 'real economy'. But, many would now ask, is women's productive activity within the household (or men's too far for that matter) not equally 'work'? (For further references and analysis, see Chapter Six). Again, anthropologists have always taken a broader view of work but recently have been having more direct impact on other disciplines because of their increasing focus on urban and industrial contexts. In particular anthropological and sociological studies of Third World urban areas – how people 'make do' in slums and shanty towns, and the 'informal economy' through which they somehow manage to support themselves – have linked with questions as to whether similar 'informal economic activities' may not also have some importance in our own society (e.g., Hart, 1973; Roberts, 1978; Lloyd, 1979; Bromley and Gerry, 1979). This line of thought has been further reinforced by recent historical work, especially by those using 'oral history' and other methods to tap the everyday lives of ordinary people in the past: drawing our attention to the many diverse methods people had of coping through a variety of productive activities, within local communities (e.g., Samuel, 1975; Meacham, 1977; Chaytor, 1980; Segalen, 1983; cf. Pahl, 1984, Chapters 1–3). Some sociologists too have woken up to such questions, and there is now a spate of work on 'the informal economy', 'fiddling', 'pilferage', 'the domestic economy', 'survival strategies' and 'the black economy' (see later references), some of it arising from earlier work under the head of 'deviancy'. Finally, current economic trends have added to the interest of such topics of study. When neither the 'traditional' job structure nor 'full employment' can any longer be taken for granted, questions about practical alternatives and trends become more pressing, as do the new academic approaches to analysing both 'unemployment' and the work outside employment that may now develop – or, perhaps, that has been going on all along without our having taken much notice of it (e.g., Blackaby, 1979; Kumar 1979; Gershuny, 1978; Gershuny and Miles, 1983; Sinfield, 1981, and references below).

This paper outlines some of this recent research on working outside formal employment as it applies in modern Britain, thus trying to draw together some of the diverse and exciting new work on this topic. It should be admitted, however, that partly as a result of the relatively recent development of research on such activities and partly because of the nature of 'work outside formal employment' (defined as it were in negative terms), there is still much dispute and lack of settled definition in this area. Indeed 'work outside employment' is *not,* as might be supposed, one category at all but covers a whole range of activities. These are discussed in this paper under the somewhat problematic headings of 'black', 'domestic' and 'community' work – headings taken from an earlier (but still influential) piece by Gershuny and Pahl in *New Society* (1980). As will appear, these categories are not clear-cut (and are not now necessarily favoured by the authors in the same terms as earlier), but they do have the merit of providing one convenient framework for an initial presentation. Perhaps even more importantly they lead at least to some awareness of the wide range of *different* economic processes that are involved in the simplified and homogeneous-sounding term 'informal economy'. These varied activities are of great social and economic significance and well deserve the increasing attention now being focused on them, but because they are so heterogeneous it is inappropriate to try to make generalizations that could be applied across all their manifestations.

After that general caution I would add, nevertheless, that there *is* perhaps one central and more positive theme that emerges through all the different examples and discussions that follow. This is the way in which in any society activities are *socially evaluated and labelled, and bound-*

aries drawn: some activities classified as 'work' in some full sense of the term, to be rewarded and recognized and (often) admired as socially or morally useful; some as 'work' indeed but not deserving similar rewards or prestige – labelled as, say, 'unskilled' or even 'polluting'; some, not in themselves intrinsically different or in objective terms, any less central to the functioning of society, are not to be counted as 'work' at all. This process of social labelling goes on in all societies – rendering some activities visible, valuable or legal, others as illegal or 'marginal' or invisible. In our own culture, it applies particularly to the ambiguous classification of productive activities outside the standard category of 'paid employment' – many of them almost not seen at all in some contexts, let alone regarded as 'real' or legal work. This process of social evaluation, in a sense part of the moral symbolism of our society, underlies this discussion of work and helps to explain why the kinds of working brought into the open here have so often remained unnoticed.

Working 'underground'

In standard economic accounts work takes place in the official economy. It is recorded in official statistics, taxes are paid with reference to it, and it forms the basis of adminstrative action and planning. But as social scientists and administrators are now incresingly realizing, a great deal of activity escapes being reported in official accounts. Much of this is cash-based and, in one way or another, illegal. It ranges from specifically criminal activity like theft or embezzlement, through work which may in itself be legal but undeclared for tax purposes, to the covert perks and fiddles found in most kinds of work. Once again this depends on the drawing of boundaries, with certain activities classified as disapproved or illegal – the exact lines of those boundaries varying of course at different historical periods and from society to society.

This kind of hidden economic activity has been classed under many different labels: work in the black or irregular economy for instance, or parallel, dual, cash, unofficial, second, moonlight or underground. Other languages have their equivalents too in *travail noir, Schattenwirtschaft* or *lavoro sommerso* (listed in Smith, 1981, p. 45). Here it will mainly be referred to as 'underground' or 'hidden'.

The existence of a 'black economy' in certain foreign countries has been remarked on for some time. Italy is often taken as a striking example of the large-scale involvement in unauthorized – often highly productive – activities, often by those who are also employed in full-time jobs in the formal economy. A 1980 survey of the extra-mural activities of Italian civil servants, for example, suggested that as well as over half of them holding second jobs, a third sold goods within ministries during working hours, while nearly the same number took early or late holidays (and thus a longer holiday because of their supervisors' absence at the main holiday time), and nearly one-fifth 'hardly ever report for work because no checks made' (Smith, 1981, p. 47). Several studies have also been made of the socialist countries in Eastern Europe where hidden economic activities outside the official State plans and policies are almost a commonplace. This facet of Soviet life, for example, receives constant comment in newspaper articles as well as research journals: not only people's use of privately owned houses and plots, but the whole system of black market activity: rule-fiddling, private entrepreneurship and illicit trading. The various accounts of this 'second economy' (e.g., Grossman, 1977; Katsenelinboigen, 1977) demonstrate well how little understanding we would have of economic activity in the Soviet Union if we confined our interest in 'work' just to that reported in the formal State economy.

Underground economic activities have often been particularly associated with underdeveloped and with socialist economies – 'getting by' outside the framework of official economic institutions and policies. More recently, however, comparative research on both industrial and non-industrial economies together with continuing sociological work on deviance have begun to focus interest on whether one can find arguably comparable patterns in Western countries.

Considering these possible parallels in our own society provides yet another dimension to the varied ways we work in our society. Some of these ways are quite explicitly illegal, some partially so, some basically legal but with certain non-reported (tax-evasive) elements to them. Of course, the exact boundaries between what is 'legal' and what is not depend not only on the actual laws in any given culture (what is legal in Britain may be illegal in the USSR and vice versa) but also on changes in the law over time. Thus what in one country or at one period of time is evaluated as illegal may be counted as legal at another place or time, and the basis for classifying particular activities as 'underground' at any one place or time has thus no universal validity. Nevertheless, it is interesting to consider some of the ways in which the concept of 'working' can be extended, and the variety of important forms of work – more or less illegal – which would go unnoticed if we concentrated only on formal employment.

It might be well to start with a brief mention of criminal work – something worth remembering even if the official employment statistics omit it. Some people make their living from activities explicitly classified as illegal: professional theft, handling stolen goods, drug trafficking, organized prostitution, 'protection' rackets, illegal child-labour, large-scale black market deals and 'organized crime' generally. Some of these activities have their legal side, but in general they are labelled as criminal; as such, they often get classified with 'criminology' and 'deviancy studies' rather than under the sociology of economic life. Yet they all arguably involve a kind of work and – whatever the official statistics, conventional academic boundaries or moral stigma involved – their significance for the economic processes of our society is now being increasingly realized.

The extent of criminal work is not known. This is inevitable for the same reason that the 'black figure' of unreported crime is unrecorded. It is made yet more difficult by the way 'criminal' work shades into semi-legal acts, and by the interaction between 'black' and other informal (but not necessarily illegal) economic activities. In a fully professional form 'criminal' work is in most countries probably the work of a small minority of people, though its interaction with amateur activities increases its importance. At any rate this is certainly one type of 'working' in the wider definition of the term.

There are also the forms of work which, while legal in themselves, are commonly reckoned part of the underground economy because they are often unreported and thus tax-evasive.

Moonlighting is one common form – a second job in addition to the 'official' job on which tax is paid and/or entitlement held to social security benefits. In some economies this is extensive. In Italy, for example, the government apparently recognize it by 'setting the hours for many public officials from 8 a.m. to 2 p.m. in order that they qualify in the Official Economy for social security benefits, and still have time for moonlighting after a mid-day meal' (Rose, 1983, p. 18). In Europe in the mid-1970s a labour force survey indicated that an average of over 2 per cent (2.7 per cent for men, 1 per cent for women) were double job holders (Alden, 1981, pp. 45–6; given that these figures rest on official statistics and that people are liable to keep rather quiet about second jobs for both tax reasons and fear of their main employers' reactions, this is almost certainly an underestimate of the numbers). Its significance is further reinforced by the fact that some tasks might not get completed without moonlighters: hairdressing, window cleaning, plumbing, decorating, taxi driving and electrical work, as well as work by telephonists, cleaners and 'bar persons'. Indeed, as Alden sums it up, 'in spite of the view that moonlighters deprive Inland Revenue of income, people holding two jobs boost national output' (Alden, 1981, p. 48).

The obvious advantage for the workers is economic – a way of supplementing personal or family income and thus raising living standards. Social reasons come in too, though. In a recent study in Cardiff, for example, where it turned out that (as elsewhere apparently) a high proportion of second job holders were teachers, 65 per cent of these 'moonlighters' did indeed give 'economic' reasons as their primary motivation. The remaining 35 per cent did not, mentioning instead a variety of motives; for example, for social or interest reasons rather than for money, at a friend's request or, at least initially, to help someone out (Alden, 1981, pp. 53–4). Sometimes too a first job can provide basic livelihood, whereas the second job (perhaps much less economically productive) is where an individual finds his or her real satisfaction: working the dustbins by day, perhaps, and playing in a rock band in the evenings.

To set against these personal advantages for the worker, there are also problems. Some trade unions disapprove of moonlighting as an encouragement to over-long hours, lack of proper qualifications or lower rates of pay. Indeed a law was passed in Belgium in 1976 to make '*travail noir*' illegal following trade union pressure (Alden, 1981, p. 49). Moonlighters can provide some employers with a useful labour source, in particular in the hotel and catering trades, but for others this pattern is awkward when they want employees to work overtime but find second-job commitments prevent this. Governments often discourage moonlighting because of lost tax and yet also have to countenance it just because underground work is hard to control and because it does, after all, provide an input to economic growth by 'this most energetic group of the labour force' (Alden, 1977, p. 30).

Indeed the greater flexibility in work hours in Western countries over recent years has led to yet further opportunities for second-job holding. Any increase in moonlighting may only be within certain limits, though, for even studies highlighting its importance suggest that only a relatively small proportion of the labour force in the EEC in the late 1970s were double job holders, and the number of second jobs in the economy may be limited (Rose, 1983, p. 18). However, the existence of this 'clandestine' employment is obviously one form of work which, though often hidden from official accounting, is nevertheless not a negligible one in many contemporary industrial countries.

Moonlighting is technically the holding of two jobs. However, there is also work that follows a similar pattern even where there is not, strictly, a second job – or rather, the 'first job' may be an ex-job and take the form of drawing unemployment benefit while the 'second' (whether full or part-time) remains untaxed and unreported. This shades into paid (but unreported) work, often part-time, taken up by someone not officially classified as 'economically active' at all (e.g. a housewife to add to the family income) or by someone who holds some 'official part-time job but enters into other paid work on the side (e.g. someone employed as a school 'dinner lady' but also, unknown to the tax authorities, working as a part-time cleaner for several hours a week). Once again, the extent of this quasi-moonlighting work is not precisely known, but at one time or another it probably forms one aspect of the working lives of a considerable number of individuals in modern industrial societies and must be familiar to most readers of this paper.

A further form of underground working may be paid activity at home. This is an extremely varied category, ranging from the 'outwork' used extensively in the garment trade to child minding, manufacturing, clerical work (an important category) or the kind of small independent business that may, it seems, be run increasingly from the home (Cragg and Dawson, 1981).

Once again, such work is not *in itself* illegal. The conditions, however, in which it is sometimes carried on may well be. Indeed some sociologists have pointed to the way in which during the Industrial Revolution workers were in a sense forced *out* of their homes so that they could be more effectively controlled in the workplace, while today a contrary move may be taking place, exploiting people at home who are free from workplace regulations, as with some of the low-paid textile and assembly homeworkers. Such work also often comes outside the tax net (sometimes evasive, though sometimes just because the pay is too low), and in this way too is part of the 'underground' economy. On the other hand, the apparently increasing importance of home-based secretarial and computer work, together with current trends in 'information technology', may mean that some forms of homework will become increasingly attractive and visible. Whether and how far home-based paid work will increase or change in the future remains to be seen, as do the implications of any such a development.

The next category, unlike the last, probably applies in one way or another to just about everyone in paid work: unofficial perks, fiddles, pilferage and undeclared 'fringe benefits'. Various lively ethnographic accounts of this kind of working have now appeared, from the systematic fiddling that one set of doorstep bread salesmen were encouraged in by their supervisors (Ditton, 1974) to the well-worn ways of pilfering or fiddling in hotel dining rooms or the docks (Mars, 1973; cf. also Zeitlin, 1971; Ditton, 1977a; Henry, 1978; Mars, 1982).

It is clear from these and similar examples that unofficial perks and fiddles take many forms. Some specifically benefit the well-paid: partially or wholly untaxed perks and benefits on top of the official salary, for example. Others are, on the face of it, against employers' interests and wishes, but are consciously connived at by both sides; or, perhaps more commonly, there is a tacit agreement that informal rewards may be winked at so long as some unspoken barrier is not transgressed. Such rewards function as a kind of additional 'invisible wage'. They may be undeclared by employers and employees alike, and run counter to the official management ethnic – indeed to many of the officially recognized conditions and relationships discussed in most industrial relations analyses – but in practice they are very much part of the real conditions of work as these are actually experienced.

Some of these unofficial rewards take the form of 'pilferage'. This means the abstracting of goods, services or, occasionally, cash, which is not quite classified as 'theft' by employers and up to a point is known to occur, but none the less lies definitely outside the official reward system and beyond a certain limit is likely to be cracked down on. We can all probably think of examples from our own observation. It includes using office telephones, stationery, photocopiers, etc., for private purposes; taking home the odd item from one's workplace, whether a shop, bakery, milk round, restaurant, office, etc., manipulating the bar takings in an hotel; inflating expense claims, and so on. Rather different on the surface, but with the same ultimate effect, is the practice in some contexts of supplementing deliberately slow progress in regular hours by (highly-paid) overtime. From the point of view of some workers, such fiddles and unofficial rewards may act not only as an additional (arguably essential) boost to wages, but also as a source of satisfaction encouraging them to put up with other less satisfying aspects of their jobs.

Some fiddles and pilferages are particularly hard to control and – for this reason among others – become more or less recognized by employers. Indeed the line between recognized wage-perks and worker pilferage is a thin and shifting one. Some benefits in kind become institutionalized, even official – 'the mature outcome of a long history of legitimizing a wage-pilferage system, especially when pilferage (as with the bus conductor's leisure time bus-pass, and the miner's coal) is particularly difficult otherwise to control' (Ditton, 1977b, p. 46). Certain perks of this kind have become visible enough to become officially noticed by the tax authorities. Others rest on unspoken agreements between employers and workers, and represent a kind of commitment between the two (or between certain individuals, as in the bread round in Ditton, 1974), in such cases shading into pilferage and fiddling.

There are some obvious problems in these invisible wage systems. They represent rewards which for the most part escape the official tax net and do not enter into the national statistics and accounts; they are a possible depressant to money wages; an informal and arguably immoral system which goes against the rational ethic supposedly characteristic of modern bureaucracy; a hidden counter to the prevailing norm that in modern cash economies employees should be paid their due wage as of right and not depend on the personal machinations of the individuals with whom they are working; and in many cases apparently not far from criminal activities.

But there are also some points to set against these problems; or rather, it is possible to look at them from a different viewpoint. One common way of analysing bureaucratic organization in modern industrial society, together with the work supposedly characteristic of such contexts, is of course to consider mainly the formal situation: the formally organized relations between management and workers, the official rules and the official line of command. Another well-established approach in sociology, though, has drawn attention to the *informal* processes within large organizations through which work and relationships are actually practised. It seems that in practice – whatever the formal ethic – informal negotiating, rewards and fiddles are often a normal part of work in modern societies. Paying attention to informal benefits, therefore, is merely to recognize what in fact is often the accepted practice.

A system of payment or part-payment in kind is actually nothing new or unusual. It has roots far back beyond industrialization and is common in non-industrial contexts. What is less often noticed is the way such forms have continued or re-formed in industrial settings too. Because of the change in the organization of work associated with the Industrial Revolution, attention became focused on what was *new*: cash wages for specific timed work. But in fact the practice of additional rewards outside the official wage structure has not disappeared, even though it is only relatively recently that social scientists have paid much attention to this.

In addition, it is worth noting the *non*-material aspects of some of these benefits. In some cases at least these are bound into a wider system of social relationships, where membership of a particular grouping or network may in itself bring a certain social satisfaction: people do not work for material reward alone. In other cases, the apparent advantage of having seemingly got 'something for nothing' or scored off the management or the tax officials can seem very satisfying. There is also the excitement and, in a sense, creativity involved in some of the fiddles and other informally, sometimes 'dangerously', achieved rewards; for some people this can be an important element to set against the otherwise dull routine and limitations of their work.

This also has some bearing on the wider question which has often vexed sociologists: why do people apparently accept the clear inequality of rewards for different types of work as it is constructed in our own – and in every other – society? The comparison with the *apparent* rewards others get for their work is one factor here. One knows one's own whole income (i.e. including the invisible benefits) but usually only the visible pay of others; thus the comparison of one's own pay with that of jobs just 'below' and even just 'above' one's own in the social hierarchy often looks more advantageous in subjective terms than it perhaps really is. Invisible earnings may thus contribute to people's acquiescence in the existing social order, as Ditton and Brown argue:

> The bricklayer can become the income equal of the executive not by ceasing to be a bricklayer, but instead by sweating on piece-rate to earn bonus, selling a few bricks on the side, underpaying his mortar boy, taking building materials home for personal use, falsifying his time-sheet, moonlighting in the evenings (without paying National Insurance or Income Tax), taking in paying guests and not declaring them to the Inland Revenue, and so on. What bricklayer, with this load of extra earnings, invisible (he fervently hopes) to everybody but himself, would not believe himself to be the income-equal of, at least, the manager of the brickworks? The 'bricklayer' is in each of us: life's hidden extras are a constant source of social stability. (Ditton and Brown, 1981, p. 527)

Given that we all probably find such activity familiar, how important is underground work? This has been looked at in various ways. First, there are questions about the effect of underground working on the economy. This is a matter of concern to economists, bankers and planners, not to speak of government tax-collecting agencies, and a number of calculations have been suggested. Not surprisingly, the answers are varied even for a single country, partly because the boundaries and interpretations of just what counts as 'underground' are fuzzy, partly just because of its hidden nature. For Britain in the late 1970s and early 1980s, for example, estimates of the size of the underground economy ranged from 2 per cent to 15 per cent of GDP, with perhaps the most commonly suggested estimates being between 5 and 8 per cent (e.g., Rose, 1983, p. 23; Outer Circle Policy Unit, 1980, p. 36; Smith, 1981) – quite a startling figure, and one that suggests that the economic significance of the 'black economy' needs to be taken seriously.

The non-economic implications of underground working are equally significant. Sociological accounts of the nature of work and of both the benefits and disadvantages of particular kinds of jobs often concentrate mainly on formal jobs and, within that, on the official pay and conditions of those jobs. It is now becoming clear, though, that if we want to understand both the variety of ways in which people work and the *actual* benefits from their work, we must take account of hidden as well as official rewards. This whole area of the *socially* significant conditions of work for employers and workers alike extends beyond the strictly economic into questions such as stability and conflict in our society – questions for which it it important to consider not some ideal management model or essentially economistic definition of work and its conditions, but how people actually operate in practice.

The domestic economy

Working outside the official economy does not just consist of illegal or 'black' activities, for it has been argued that, at least in terms of time, the 'domestic economy' is actually the most important setting for work outside the official economy. Rose, for example, estimates that over half the average productive hours of British adults are spent in the 'domestic economy', i.e. on household tasks like cooking, housework, DIY, gardening or child care, with only 3 per cent on the 'black economy' (1983, p. 29). Even if one quarrels with some of the detailed figures here, it is clear that informal working within the household is extremely important – if not central – to most people's lives, on a scale probably far beyond that of involvement in 'underground' working.

Unpaid work in the home once again tends to be invisible (another instance of the process of symbolic boundary-drawing in our society). But social scientists are now increasingly starting to recognize housework as a form of productive work even though it is still not counted in official statistics (see Chapter Six by Mary Maynard in this volume). The same point can be extended to the provision of goods and services in the home more generally, in the wider sense usually implied when people speak of 'the domestic economy'. This includes the performance at the household level by both women and men of such productive activities as house maintenance, gardening, child socialization, DIY, car maintenance, organized study, the production of clothes, food or recreation – in fact the provision within the domestic context of all the goods or services that might otherwise have been bought for cash through the official economy. It is the sum total of these that makes up the 'domestic' or 'household' economy.

One way of beginning to grasp its economic importance is to go through the various goods and services produced within the household and consider their cost if they were bought for cash (for even though they are not actually paid for, they *can* be seen as having a monetary equivalent). We can probably all think of such items fairly quickly from our own experience. Below is how one influential writer on the household economy summed it up for an American readership.

> What *is* the household economy? It is the sum of all the goods and services produced within all the households in the United States. This includes, among other things, the value of shelter, home-cooked meals, all the weekend-built patios and barbecues in suburban America, painting and wallpapering, home sewing, laundry, child care, home repairs, volunteer services to community and to friends, the produce of the home garden, and the transportation services of the private automobile. (Burns, 1975, p. 3)

When one remembers that all the items in this list *could* have been produced otherwise – through the market economy and for money – the extent of the productive work centring on the household becomes apparent. Preserving fruit or vegetables, for example, can be organized commercially, based on factory work and shop sales – in which case it enters into the national accounts relating to economic productivity, employment and national growth, and a money value is put on it. *Or* it can be carried out within the domestic economy: arising from unpaid work within the household to cultivate home-grown produce, followed by its preparation, freezing and cooking. The same result is accomplished, yet the first form falls within the official economy (and appears in economic statistics), while the second is located in the domestic economy (often ignored by economists and social scientists studying work). Similarly, people can pay to go out for meals, cooked and served for them by workers in the official economy; or they can prepare them themselves at home. They can travel using public transport serviced by paid employees, or depend on household-owned or controlled resources to walk, cycle or drive. The ill or frail can go into a nursing home or hospital – or be cared for at home. A family car or house paintwork can be maintained using paid outside workers or unpaid home labour; a broken window can be mended by a specialist paid glazier or by DIY; children can be taught skills in sport or music by professional instructors or by parents at home; adults can buy full- or part-time education for potentially marketable qualifications in formally established institutions or rely on studying at home; the garden can be dug and weeded by home-based labour or by a paid garden firm; dirty clothes can be sent to a laundry or washed at home – and so on.

The production of goods and services within one household may seem trivial at first sight. But if one tries to tot up the annual cost of such goods and services bought in the formal economy, the total sum is surprising – possibly running into some thousands of pounds for a single household. This is still more striking if one cumulates the thousands or millions of household economies (each itself relatively small) that together contribute to the national economy of any given country – something which comes home to one forcibly on a weekend visit to the thronged DIY shops and garden centres.

The total equivalent value of this domestic self-provisioning is not easy to calculate. Burns, writing for America in the late 1960s and early 1970s, gives some idea of its possible scale (the details may not all be fully accepted and of course the overall sum will not necessarily apply elsewhere or for a later period):

> How large would this invisible economy be if it could be measured in dollars? *Very* large. According to one study (Sirageldin, 1969), the total value of all the goods and services produced by the household economy in 1965 was about $300 *billion*. This was about equal to the gross national product of the Soviet Union at that time. If all the work done within the household by men and women were monetized, the total would be equal to the entire amount paid out in wages and salaries by every corporation in the United States. . . . Very, very little of this appears in conventional accountings for the gross national product.
>
> This neglect is . . . like assuming that somewhere between a quarter and a third of our total economic product does not exist – a large lump to hide under any rug. (Burns, 1975, pp. 6–7)

Using these and a number of other measures, Burns considered that, in economic terms, the American 'household economy' was about one-third of the size of the 'market economy' (Burns, 1975 p. 24).

Figures of this nature are not always very meaningful, so another way of looking at this is to consider the *time* spent. (Time is, after all, as much a scarce commodity as money, but with the extra characteristic that there is an absolute limit on how much is available.) One estimate of the number of healthy waking hours in a lifetime is 400,000 hours, of which on average only one hour in eight is overall spent in paid work, with that amount perhaps likely to fall yet further in the future. And yet, as Burns puts it, 'few sane men would suggest that these hours are the only productive work we ever do. The hours of work done *outside* the money economy rival those done inside' (Burns, 1975, p. 8).

Following this general approach, various analyses have been attempted of the time per week that people spend on unpaid housework and 'productive leisure': housework, odd jobs, gardening, shopping, child care, study, knitting, cooking and serving meals, etc. – all work likely to take up time just about every day and every week, unlike work in the official economy. Though the main cross-national comparison is not recent (published in 1972) it gives a broad picture of the order of time spent per week by the average adult on such household tasks. There is a surprising similarity, with the extremes ranging from thirty-one hours a week in Yugoslavia to seventeen hours a week in Bulgaria. For Western countries the range was twenty-seven hours a week in West Germany, twenty-two in American cities, twenty in French cities, seventeen in Belgium and between twenty-four to twenty-seven hours in Britain (Szalai *et al.*, 1972, quoted in Rose, 1983, p. 28). Some of the details are likely to have changed of course. In some countries and at some periods the hours per week in the domestic economy have probably fallen due to increased affluence allowing the substitution of bought goods and services for domestic production; in other (or at other times) they may possibly be rising due to the contraction of paid jobs in the official economy. But either way the general picture that emerges is of a large proportion of time spent on household work.

Some slightly more recent British estimates also emphasize the importance of household-based activities. Gershuny's time-budget studies (1981) form the basis of Rose's calculations that of the 168 hours available to the individual each week, the average adult had an average of sixty-one hours a week 'discretionary' time when such activities as sleeping, personal care and paid employment were subtracted; or rather, to be more specific, fifty-one hours a week for adults in full-time paid employment and eighty-eight for those not in paid work. Of these, some were spent in basically costless pastimes, some in leisure consumption that meant spending money and, finally, some in unpaid housework and productive leisure: 'activities in the Domestic Economy that produce marketable goods and services without money payment' (Rose, 1983, pp. 24–7). Of these three categories, the largest in terms of time spent (twenty-three hours per week) consisted of productive activities in the domestic economy.

Such figures should be used with caution, and will certainly need updating in due course (e.g. when the results of the 1983/4 ESRC Time-Budget Survey are available). Nevertheless, unless the overall picture is wildly inaccurate, the general conclusion must be that – quite apart from monetary value – in terms of effort and of sheer hours of the day spent on it, productive working the domestic economy is likely to be a significant part of just about everybody's working life. As such, a volume on 'work' which omitted any consideration of this form would be leaving out one of the most important types of work in modern industrial society.

Once one appreciates the, by now, rather obvious point that household working is indeed one form of productive activity in modern society, it is also apparent that this is not in general a new phenomenon (though the particular form it takes is naturally related to contemporary conditions). It is also clear that there are many parallels to this kind of work in other societies – in pre-industrial Europe, for example, or in non-industrial societies, cases well accepted in the writings of social historians and anthropologists. There is nothing strange, in fact, about the existence of the household economy in contemporary society.

Given that work in the domestic economy is widely prevalent, does this mean it always takes the same form? And are there changes in the organization of the domestic economy or in its relative importance *vis à vis* the official economy at different points of time and/or under different social conditions?

One point to consider here is the relative amount of time spent on different kinds of work by different categories of people. The main tendency in modern industrial societies (both Western and Eastern) is for women to predominate in work in the domestic economy, though the extent of the difference between men and women partly depends on just what is included as work in the 'domestic economy' (e.g. whether or not DIY and house or car maintenance are counted). This is partly due to the predominance of men in the official labour market in many (not all) industrial countries, and partly to certain socially-accepted assumptions about the roles of 'men' and 'women'. But changes in this sphere – as in others – are always possible in principle. Indeed it seems that in some Western economies there is also in practice a gradual (if slow) transfer of respective work responsibilities between men and women, with men increasingly spending a smaller proportion of their time than before on paid work and more on domestic work, and women a larger proportion on paid work and less on domestic work (Gershuny and Thomas, 1980).

Another aspect is the relation between the 'domestic' and the 'official' economy and the effect of this on people's work and lives (and vice versa). This is an area on which there are several different views. One is that suggested in the earlier short but influential analysis by Gershuny and Pahl (1980), in which the basic model is of movement between different sub-economies: as the official economy shrinks through increasing unemployment, the domestic economy expands to take its place with people producing more through unpaid domestic work (home maintenance or cooking, say) to replace what they no longer have wages to buy through the official money economy. This kind of analysis can be extended to fit with suggestions that 'post-industrial societies' may be becoming self-service economies with people producing more goods and

services from their own unpaid work rather than through money –
perhaps becoming 'deskilled' in formal jobs, but more skilled at home.

Some have developed this approach still further to suggest that the
capacity of the domestic economy to expand can cope with high rates of
unemployment without any serious lowering of the standard of living.
Richard Rose, for example, puts forward a stong version of this view for
Britain in the early 1980s.

> As macro-economic change, there is ample scope at the margin for sub-
> stitution between the Official and Domestic Economy. In a booming
> economy, people use increased earnings to spend more money on lei-
> sure consumption and to buy durable goods (refrigerators, freezers and
> dishwashers) in the Official Economy to shorten time spent on labori-
> ous tasks in the Domestic Economy. When demand for labour in the
> Official Economy slackens, individuals will spend less time in work, and
> marginal workers will be counted out of its labour force. But this gives
> more time and more incentive for individuals to produce goods and ser-
> vices in the Domestic Economy to substitute for products formerly
> purchased in the Official Economy. Activities recorded in the national
> income accounts will increase in the former circumstances, and
> decrease in the latter. *From the viewpoint of the individual, total con-
> sumption remains the same.* . . .
>
> From the viewpoint of the ordinary individual, *counter-cyclical*
> movement back and forth between the Official and the Domestic
> Economy has positive advantages. It is a strategy for getting by in an
> economy that is full of ups and downs. When the Official Economy is
> booming, a family has more money coming in, and can use that money
> to buy freedom from what are considered household chores, as well as
> to finance leisure consumption. When the Official Economy is slack,
> individuals can use their domestic resources to maintain consumption.
> (Rose, 1983, pp. 33–4)

Other approaches throw some doubt on this interpretation. The
suggestion that as one sub-economy contracts, another can expand to fill
the gap, has been questioned for both empirical and conceptual reasons.
Some recent analyses (further discussed below) suggest that the idea of
various separate and, as it were, autonomous sub-economies mutually
interacting and expanding in parallel does not really fit the facts of
economic life, and, further, that for people actually having to cope with
unemployment, turning to the 'domestic economy' may be of very
limited help if they have no cash to buy the necessary materials which
form the basis of much 'self-provisioning' (Pahl, 1984; Pahl and Wallace,
1984). This view can be extended to point to the unequal access people
may have to the fruits of informal work, so that perhaps those who lose
out in the formal labour market are also often precisely those who lose in
the domestic economy too.

On these questions there is, therefore, room for disagreement. Despite
these controversies, though, the continuing importance of domestic

work and servicing is accepted,— indeed stressed – by just about all writers on the subject, even though the detailed trends and the exact balance of choice and constraint for different categories of people (and perhaps different areas of the country) are matters of continuing debate.

Work and 'community'

It will be evident already that there are several different ways in which working outside official employment can be classified and subdivided. One differentiation suggested by Gershuny and Pahl (1980) was in terms of the household, the underground and the 'communal' economies. There are problems about these terms (and the writers themselves would not necessarily now wish to press them), but the mention of a 'communal economy' does point to another important aspect of working outside employment which has not yet been considered.

Many kinds of productive unpaid work and exchange take place not just within the household (the 'domestic economy') but also within and between wider groupings on a neighbourhood, kin or minority-interest basis. Remember, for example, the mainly unpaid work which provides informal support for friends, peers, relatives or colleagues. Similarly, the informal exchange of produce or services with neighbours, provision of unpaid services for a local church or club, work for voluntary agencies or fund-raising for local charities can all be regarded as forms of working outside formal employment. This is work which *could* have been paid but is actually carried out on an informal and voluntary basis within the 'community' – an admittedly vague concept used here to indicate the rather elastic and relative context of such work. This kind of work is closely linked in both its form and its setting to the domestic economy, as Gershuny makes clear in his outline of how he sees the 'communal' production system:

> Included in this sector are 'voluntary' or religious organizations, baby-sitting circles, transport cooperatives, housing-improvement cooperatives. At one extreme are those organisations on the verge of the formal production system – the baby-sitting circles or car pools – which operate on the basis of a quasi-money exchange, tokens or credits, and which break down if equal values are not exchanged within a relatively short period. But more generally there is only a rudimentary system of specific exchange, and the major reason for the involvement of those who carry the burdens are the intangible, symbolic, unquantified returns for their activities. . . . In extreme cases – such as making meals for sick neighbours – the form of exchange can hardly be differentiated from that within the household. (Gershuny, 1979, p. 6)

The existence of informal systems within the neighbourhood should be no surprise. Social historians have increasingly drawn our attention to this, building on 'oral history' as well as written evidence from – for example – working-class communities in Britain in the nineteenth and earlier twentieth centuries (e.g., Meacham, 1977, Chapter 2, esp. pp. 44ff; Thompson, 1975; Samuel, 1975). They explain how local people commonly drew on help from friends and neighbours in time of sickness, unemployment or distress, and how informal exchanges of goods and services between households helped to provide resources at a period when government benefits were lacking and – for many – money resources were low. For more recent periods too sociologists and social anthropologists have discovered similar informal welfare and exchange systems by the poor in local communities and urban ghettos, as well as in the rural economies of non-industrial communities where the goods and services elsewhere supplied by the state or the market have to be provided through networks of neighbours, kin and other associates.

This kind of socially-based and informal economic activity has been particularly noticed in a number of 'developing' countries. As people flock to the towns they often have to struggle through difficult material conditions with the mutual support of the local networks they develop. For such people, often living in shanty towns or desperately over-crowded slums, with few or no state services, and often little access to formal employment (or at any rate to well-paid employment), their resourcefulness in developing a local co-operative economy of exchange, provision of services and informal production of goods has made possible the flourishing and thronged local urban communities characteristic of some developing countries today (described, for example, in Lloyd, 1979). There are many instances then, from both industrial and non-industrial contexts, of locally recognized productive work and exchange based on informal and socially-recognized networks and support-systems rather than on cash or work in formal employment.

At first sight, the situation in modern urban communities would seem very different – dominated by the cash nexus, the market mechanism and the impersonality of modern urban life. But here too, as in other contexts, we can learn from historical and comparative parallels. Certainly one must not forget the differences – both in the past and the present – between different localities: it would be misleading to assume that, say, a recently-built housing estate in a new British town will have the same strong neighbourhood ties and sense of community identity as those where people have lived for generations following much the same trade (for example, some of the traditional mining centres, fishing ports or textile towns). Nevertheless, though localities certainly vary, there *are* localities in modern urban contexts where informal network and support-systems are still an important resource, and others in which they play some part without necessarily pervading the whole locality. It would certainly be a mistake to think that working within this kind of informal social and economic network is only something that happens far away or long ago. There have been a number of studies made of lower-income localities in the second half of this century (for example, several are summarized in Lowenthal, 1981, an account closely followed here). These suggest that the resource most immediately turned to for informal support in the absence of an adequate money income is often that of the extended kin. Maria Komarovsky, for example, in *Blue Collar Marriage* (1967), found that the extended family was crucial not only in helping with the socialization of children and provision of recreation and emotional support but also for economic support.

> A widowed father shares his home with a married son who pays no rent but is responsible for household expenses; a widowed mother residing with her daughter works as a waitress, paying rent and her share of the grocery bill; a widow and her bachelor brother inherited the parental home and rented rooms to a married daughter who is the homemaker for the whole group and expenses are shared.... Apart from such more-or-less permanent arrangements, relatives frequently exchange services which among wealthier families are purchased from specialists – such as housepainting, carpentry, repair, laying linoleum, building partitions, and help in moving. (Komarovsky, 1967, p. 237, quoted in Lowenthal, 1981, pp. 95–6)

Similar patterns have been found in British working-class localities. Young and Willmott's study of Bethnal Green (1957) noted the important services the mother provided for her married daughter, particularly at the birth of a second or subsequent child: the household tasks of child care, cooking, washing, cleaning, shopping, etc., had to be carried out by someone and, in the absence of paid labour, this work was normally done by the wife's mother, herself usually living close by. Through their kin relations, the Bethnal Greeners were also linked into the wider community, an area in which long-standing residence was typical. Mutual help from the wider kin is not just something in long-settled working-class areas either, for Raymond Firth and others found a somewhat similar flow of services between extended kin in their study of families and relatives in a middle-class suburb of London in the 1960s (Firth *et al.*, 1969). Again, a study of an Irish-American neighbourhood in Boston in 1974–5 found a highly developed network of support:

> In these reciprocal transactions, particularly between kin, a material good or service may flow from one individual to another but may be reciprocated by the provision of emotional or psychological support. The proximity of kin tended to be an important variable in the ability of persons in need to receive support and for persons as providers to carry out many of the types of non-monetised activities.
>
> The most commonly exchanged goods and services in Charlestown included: child care, financial assistance, meals, employment information and placement, repairs, clothing, solicited information and advice, housing information and assistance in rental or purchase, food, care for

the sick, elder care, shopping, temporary home for children, cleaning services and political favours. (Lowenthal, 1981, p. 99)

How far this kind of social support system pervades any given locality and how far it is merely a contingent personal network appears to depend on a number of factors, perhaps chief among them the type and number of paid jobs held and the age of the local area. Either way, this kind of informal support cannot be maintained without people being prepared to *work* at it – to put in time helping a neighbour in need, keeping an eye on each others' children, lending tools, exchanging produce or providing communication channels and moral as well as material support. Even informal gossip, passing on news of possible jobs (an important element in labour recruitment), or giving advice on study problems could be counted as falling within this general category of providing unpaid services – a situation, incidentally, which makes the oft-repeated advice to 'the unemployed' to move away from their own localities more costly than it might seem when it means leaving behind the hidden benefits of local support which are all the more valuable to those without money wages. The provision of these kinds of benefits and exchanges may at first sight seem far from 'work' as the term is often understood. And yet if we take the wider approach that has been followed in this unit and elsewhere, and remember that these are all goods and services which *could* have been paid for and counted within the official economy, then this alternative way of providing these within the local community – although often overlooked in the sociology of work – is certainly relevant for our general understanding of work and its incidence and conditions.

The examples so far have mostly been from locally-based activities, often in localities characterized by relatively poor monetary incomes. It is easy to see how the support given by these social networks operates to fulfil a function that, for others, may be performed through incomes from well-paid official jobs, together with access to services in the formal economy through the state or market mechanism. But attention is now also being turned to the way in which both beyond the neighbourhood and in new contexts, working outside official employment may be more widely significant than was once realized.

First, the wider extension of unemployment, as well as changes or cut-backs in certain kinds of jobs as compared to others, may also mean that the need to rely on informal and unpaid work may be increasing, not only in absolute terms but in the kinds of people who participate. Voluntary work in the locality has long been a part of higher income as well as poorer communities (see next section). But recent economic trends in many Western societies may also, some social scientists argue, be leading to a more widespread reliance on unpaid productive work *at every level*.

The inflation in the cost of material goods and of public and private services is putting restrictions on the ability of the so-called middle class to maintain their living patterns, particularly as people age. . . . If the trend of diminishing resources and declining real wages continues . . . there will need to be many readjustments in the patterns of economic coping and support which have characterised the mainstream of western capitalist society. (Lowenthal, 1981, pp. 91–2)

A second point is that the informal provision of goods and services need not just be on a neighbourhood basis (as in the relatively close-knit localities described in some of the research cited earlier). One of the characteristics often attributed to modern urban society is after all its heterogeneity, with a large number of special interest groupings and differing cross-cutting links drawing together different individuals and groups. In one way, this implies fewer close and continuing ties between those in the same locality. But the other corollary is that, in addition to neighbourhood links, there are many other ways in which people are both divided and linked together – in terms of occupation, for example, age, religion, ethnic affiliation or leisure interests.

These kinds of links too often form the basis of productive unpaid work, and of exchange and mutual assistance within an informal economic framework. Thus someone in need of certain resources which he/she prefers not to (or cannot easily, or can no longer) obtain through the official economy can sometimes turn, not just to neighbours or kin, but to colleagues, peers or members of the same church, political party, ethnic association or social club. You will probably be able to think of examples where the kind of provision of goods and services described earlier may take place not based on a locality, but on other shared interests. Informal and unpaid support for paid work (for example, a wife's informal but valuable back-up to a husband's work) also often takes place along such social networks. This work too is part of informal economic activity, for these goods and services *could* have been obtained for money even though within the context of such socially recognized and informal exchanges they are usually not monetarized.

A further context is found in the various local clubs and societies that are so characteristic a feature of British urban life – perhaps of all urban life. It is often vaguely assumed that such institutions somehow spring up and continue of themselves without anything much having to be done about them. They are not directly part of the official economy, usually have no paid officials, do not form part of the state or local administrative structure – and just seem a 'natural' and undemanding embellishment of city life. But of course anyone who has been a member or, far more, an organizer of any of these associations knows otherwise. Just as in the case of the household, such institutions do not run themselves: each involves a great deal of hard work, almost always on an unpaid basis.

Like the work of maintaining the household, this work has also tended to escape the notice of economists and even, till recently, of sociologists, who have followed the economists in focusing on paid work sold at a price within the market. But, just as time spent on unpaid productive tasks within the household is now increasingly recognized as one form of work, so too should be the time spent on unpaid activities within wider groupings and associations in the 'community'.

One aspect of this is the work done by the varied voluntary organizations to provide or supplement goods and services that might otherwise have been supplied through the commercial sector or – perhaps more to the fore in many people's thinking – by the state. In most British towns, for instance, there are local charities, old people's clubs, playgroups, mental health associations, volunteer organizations, mutual aid groups and a whole range of associations to help handicapped and disabled people, like the local branches of the Deaf Children's Society, 'Talking Newspaper', the Spastics, the Association for Spina Bifida and Hydro-cephalus, Multiple Sclerosis and the British Diabetic Association – to mention only a few. Unpaid local work is what sustains these associations.

This was well illustrated in a survey in three British towns in the mid-to late-1970s to discover the scale and variety of voluntary organizations in modern British towns (Hatch, 1980). It concentrated just on the 'social service' side and thus excluded such other associations as religious, political and recreational organizations, purely social clubs, and visual or performing arts. Even so, the numbers were striking. In one town with a total population of 58,000, for example, there were a total of 153 voluntary organizations dealing with such welfare areas as housing, mental health, the elderly, the handicapped and disabled, health and safety, children's needs and counselling (full details in Hatch, 1980, p. 42, and *passim*).

The activities of the members and organizers of these welfare-directed voluntary associations cumulatively take up a great deal of time. In the organizations Hatch studied *some* of the work of providing goods and services in the areas of health, education, social security, personal social services, housing and the environment was by paid workers, sometimes linked into national organizations with an accepted niche in the overall structure of service provision. But most of it was unpaid: 'In most localities . . . the voluntary sector is predominantly composed of a multitude of voluntary service and mutual aid groups, backed up in a few cases by paid staff' (Hatch, 1980, p. 148). This general picture is further supported by earlier 'community studies' in British towns and more recent surveys. In Birmingham, for example, there were probably about 8,000 active voluntary associations in the 1970s (Newton, 1976, p. 228), while a NOP survey carried out for the Wolfenden Committee in 1978 reported that 8 per cent of the population over sixteen claimed to have done some voluntary work in the preceding week and 15 per cent in the preceding year (Hatch, 1980, p. 52).

It is hard not to include this wider activity under 'work', in just the same way as work in the household economy. It is not illegal – and thus not part of the 'underground' or 'black' economy; it is not primarily or solely within the domestic economy (though it may be closely linked to it); but it certainly means a great deal of time spent by large numbers of people on providing and generating social services which would otherwise have to be paid for, sought from state services or not supplied at all. As Hatch sums this up:

> Already a substantial and growing minority of the population are actively involved through voluntary organisations in caring for each other and in promoting the welfare of their communities. The forms of this involvement and the organisations through which it takes place are numerous and varied. They provide channels for the expression of strong individual commitments, for a more diffuse willingness to help and for doing something about problems directly experienced by individuals themselves. By these means a significant addition is made to the resources available for social service purposes. (Hatch, 1980, pp. 147–8)

The social welfare functions of voluntary asociations have been attracting increasing interest if only because of current discussion about care 'in the community' and voluntary provision 'outside the welfare state'. In this context, it is not too difficult to see the unpaid time given to these functions as a form of work. However, a similar point can be made for the many recreational, religious and other special interest associations that are also a typical feature of urban industrial life, at least in contemporary Britain. The social value of the extensive and often time-consuming activities undertaken by members of such clubs is often less appreciated than that of the welfare associations, perhaps because the pay-off is intangible: recreational, cultural or spiritual rather than material. Certainly such activity is not normally paid or formalized. But it *is* productive activity in an analogous sense to both housework and voluntary welfare provision. And if the goods and services are less tangible, it must be remembered both that some at least could be – and occasionally are – provided on a monetary basis (paid secretaries or caterers, for example, or professional entertainers or managers) *and* that certain satisfactions and functions which cannot be easily costed may nevertheless be accepted as of high social value.

The achieving of these functions too involves a great deal of time and work. As with the voluntary welfare associations, a small proportion of this may be supported by *paid* workers (in the churches, for example). But much of the work is normally carried out on a voluntary basis by unpaid enthusiasts and supporters in their own time. That a substantial share of this is often undertaken by people without full-time formal jobs – the recently retired (a great resource in any local community), women and the part-time employed – is no reason for neglecting its significance.

Once again this is probably something that most of us know about from our own experience – but tend to forget when we come to academic analysis.

Figures from the 1978 surveys mentioned above throw some light on the extent of such activities. Those who had undertaken some voluntary work in the last year were questioned about how long they had spent. Forty per cent had spent no time in the last seven days, but 38 per cent *had* spent up to five hours, 15 per cent between six and twenty hours and 3 per cent over twenty hours, while in a 1973 study 8.1 per cent of a national survey said they had undertaken 'social and voluntary' work in the last four weeks (Hatch, 1978, pp. 4–5). It would also be interesting if one could multiply the average time and work spent on just *one* club by the number of clubs over the country as a whole. We do not know how many there are, but recent work on this so far under-researched area suggests that when one includes, among others, women's clubs, working-men's clubs, political clubs and parties, uniform groups, hobbies clubs, cultural groups of many kinds (including arts and drama), amateur operatic societies, musical groups and clubs, and sports groups, the total number must be huge (discussed in Tomlinson, 1979, among others). Nor should one forget participation in the churches – no longer a majority pursuit but still significant for large numbers of people – and the involvement necessary for the mounting of the many special interest performances and festivals. Consider, for example, the cumulative time and work that was needed to provide the following – a few perhaps with some paid support but mostly based on part-time and unpaid work outside the official economy.

> If all the performances that took place among public minority communities [in Britain] last year had been gathered together in one place, they would have kept a middle-sized theatre going for the entire year. 1975 saw two major West Indian street carnivals, processions for Chinese New Year in London, Manchester and Middlesbrough, runs for fourteen West Indian and African plays, three Bengali plays and dance-dramas, about twelve mass-attended Urdu poetry evenings, a tour of a Greek-Cypriot comic drama group, productions of three Gujarati plays, two Hindu ones and an Armenian production, and copious performances of Bengali, Cypriot, Indian, Ukrainian, Polish and Serbian folk song and dance groups . . . [and] a variety of music recitals as well as music and dance classes (Khan, 1975, p. 5; cf. also Kew, 1979)

Most of these groupings, of course, involve specialist minority interests and are only joined selectively by enthusiasts and supporters. But this is no reason to ignore the cumulative importance of the often hidden work performed by countless individuals and groups in providing these – to them – highly valued products, performances and services. In these contexts, too, work outside formal employment is one of the productive resources of British – and other – contemporary life. The same essential point was insisted on by the social anthropologist Cato Wadel as one necessary aspect of our understanding of 'work':

> A number of activities which are not termed work in common parlance are nevertheless necessary for the maintenance of widely valued institutions . . . everyday activities which, when considered in isolation may appear 'trivial' (even to the person who carried them out) and not merit the label work, when aggregated and considered in relation to formal work do constitute a prerequisite of effective institutional arrangements. (Wadel, 1979, pp. 379, 372)

From this viewpoint, the proliferation of societies, clubs and special interest groupings, often said to be one of the values of British culture, does not just happen 'naturally': it is essentially dependent on the unpaid and often unrecognized work of large numbers of individuals within the community.

Comments and controversies

So far, the discussion of informal working has been presented relatively unproblematically. That is, I have not turned aside continually to point to academic problems on particular points nor brought in many 'theoretical' references. However, it scarcely needs saying that no exposition, however factual-seeming, is without its hidden assumptions and controversies. One has already been to the fore – the assumption that it is both possible and useful to widen the scope of the term 'work' from the narrow delimitation to paid work in official employment assumed in most economic and many sociological analyses, so as to include both profitable (if illegal) activities outside the formal rules, and unpaid socially productive labour within the household or the 'community'. But there are also other controversies and qualifications that need to be mentioned briefly before concluding.

Up to a point, the presence of informal economic activity even in industrial societies and the existence of some kind of 'work' outside the official economy is not really in dispute. Indeed once the idea of informal economic processes has been entertained at all, this leads to an insight into many previously invisible aspects of social life and brings together so many areas of study that it becomes near impossible to deny their existence in general terms.

What is controversial, however, is exactly how significant these forms of informal activity are, and how they should be categorized and explained. One approach is to try to distinguish separate sub-economies within the wider economic structure, each with its own forms of work. For example, one can juxtapose the formal economy on the one side, characterized by paid employment and official measurement, and, on the other, 'the informal economy' covering all the kinds of activities discussed in this chapter. One set of differentiations amplifying this idea was Gershuny and Pahl's scheme (1980), distinguishing several different economies in Britain: the formal, the black and the household or communal (the latter sometimes subdivided). This three- or four-fold division was an influential one, leading among other things to suggestions such as those made by Richard Rose and others (see above) that people could at will shift from one sub-economy to another and thus, for example, compensate for losing out in the official economy (through unemployment) by spending more time in the domestic and/or communal economies.

There are a number of controversies here. There is the difficulty, for one thing, of envisaging autonomous sub-economies between which people could move, with one necessarily expanding as the other(s) contract(s). Perhaps even more significant, at least as suggested by some of the recent empirical research in Britain, is that switching is not so easy for everyone. As mentioned earlier, Pahl's research in the Isle of Sheppey suggests that it was precisely those households that had access to cash from the official economy (often two-earner families) that had the most opportunity to engage in informal 'self-provisioning' activities in the household economy, whereas those without jobs in the formal economy did far less in the domestic economy, not least because they could not afford many of the necessary materials. 'Our interviews', write Pahl and Wallace of their investigation into this topic in the Isle of Sheppey , 'have documented the despair of men living in their own homes, with their own tools, with time on their hands and with urgent decorating jobs staring them in the face, but without the money to buy the paint' (Pahl and Wallace, 1985; cf. Pahl, 1984). How far these findings are typical throughout the country still demands further research and this whole area may well remain a controversial one. But certainly it seems that the earlier idea that people could make a single switch from one form of economy to another if they lost their jobs is now regarded as open to question.

A different approach is not to envisage separate 'economies' of whatever kind, nor to assume that the official market economy is necessarily the dominant or most 'real' one (see Davis, 1984), but rather to draw attention to the importance of the many kinds of work and productive activities that people engage in outside formal employment. These are significant for understanding how people actually carry on their lives in practice, not only those who are unemployed or non-employed in the formal sense, but even those holding paid jobs. It is tempting to try to generalize across the different spheres of informal economic activities or draw conclusions applicable across the country at large or across all categories of people. Indeed, though there are some recurrent patterns of the kinds discussed in the chapter, one of the main positive findings is the way that the significance of working outside formal employment can vary in its meaning, importance and interaction with other economic spheres according to people's specific circumstances: the locality they live in, their life style, gender, class, ethnic affiliation, access to cash and stage in the life cycle.

This leads on to certain more explicitly 'applied' points. Social scientists studying informal economic activity have generally tried to take up a relatively value-free approach; they have refrained, for example, from moving in too freely with policy proposals based on their research. It will be clear already, however, that it is difficult to avoid a 'political' stance in one's attitude to a subject of such immediate interest to individuals, families, communities, countries – indeed to the whole world economy – however hard one tries.

The varying implicit attitudes to the existence and (probable) development of working outside formal employment have probably already been emerging in the earlier discussion. Some regard 'informal work' – or at any rate the 'black' aspects of it – as reprehensible and leading to dire results for individuals and countries. Other approaches are sympathetic to (some) work outside formal employment seeing it as a new and constructive development in industrial society, leading to new forms of entrepreneurship, the early stages of small business creation (later to be regularized in the formal economy) and the use of new technologies for home-based productive work in innovative work forms, perhaps desirable in a 'go-getting' society. A complementary function of some of the unpaid work in our society, in some views, would be to provide a necessary informal resource in otherwise difficult conditions in the official economy: a safety net in Milton Friedman's terms, for example (Smith, 1981, p. 46). Rose in particular paints an optimistic picture (1983) of the positive benefits in time of unemployment for those resourceful enough to exploit opportunities in the domestic or local economy.

A contrary view, though, is that it is precisely those who tend to lose out in the formal world of employment that also have fewer opportunities to do well in their work outside the formal economy – women in particular, and those at the bottom of the heap generally, above all in multiply-unemployed families. In such views, the apparent freedom of choice in work outside the official economy is in fact misleading since what goes on in the informal economy may in fact be 'determined by what is going on outside' (Bryant, 1982, p. 12; cf. Long and Richardson, 1978).

Some of these differences of emphasis are no doubt due to the differing countries, periods or groups focused on. There certainly are differences not just in the nature and incidence of informal work activity in different places and times but also in the relative costs and benefits to particular groups at any one period and place; so obviously no one picture is likely to apply equally everywhere. Nevertheless, the differences in assessment are probably due not only to real differences in the data but also in a measure to differing social and political assumptions: a view, to put it crudely, of the end result of the system of work outside the formal economy as ultimately supportive and open, on the one hand, or, on the other, as basically divisive, exploitative and inequitable.

This in turn leads into wider theoretical concerns both about the analysis of 'work' and about the nature and development of industrial society.

It is illuminating first to recall some of the still influential stereotypes of 'industrial society'. This is still commonly held to be typified by the centrality of paid employment, of the cash nexus, of impersonal bureaucratic norms and of the differentiation of 'the economic' from social and cultural concerns. Certainly there is some truth in this picture, but once we extend our conception of economic activity (and of work) beyond the formal economy, almost every clause in that once widely accepted characterization of industrial society is open to question. Or rather, to put it more accurately, these characteristics now emerge as both less all-embracing and more problematic than once appeared. New outlooks in the social sciences, perhaps together with current economic trends in our society, have raised questions for some of the traditional views in, for example, industrial sociology about what features of industrial society – and of work – are of central importance. As Richard Brown puts it in his illuminating overview of work past, present and future, 'what were the predominant characteristics of employment in the early 1960s and what was problematic about work then, are no longer an adequate agenda for work in the 1980s' (Brown, 1984, p. 268).

Many would now suggest that this wider approach of taking some account of the social, personal and domestic elements related to work, of the hidden rewards in paid work and of the local and unpaid working which upholds our valued social institutions, gives a more realistic and illuminating picture of how our own society (and perhaps 'industrial society' in general) actually operates. In this view, looking at work and its conditions *only* in the sense of full-time official employment is to follow one very narrow path through the broad sweep of our economic lives.

It is significant too how many of the forms and aspects of work treated here tend to be 'invisible' in the conventional wisdom of our society (a conventional wisdom not always queried as directly as it might be by sociologists). And yet they both form one significant part of the actual way work is socially organized and an illuminating example of how accepted social classifications in any given culture can, as it were, define certain forms of activity out of explicit consciousness or, at the least, as somehow less real than other forms. Once again this is an instance of the symbolic classification to be found in any culture in regard to 'work' (or indeed any centrally important moral concept). This kind of boundary-drawing is not confined to modern urban Britain either. For example, in the Shetland island of Whalsay the activities involved in crofting are not regarded as 'work' (in fact they have symbolic associations which make them of far higher value than 'mere' work – A. Cohen in Wallman, 1979, p. 265). Or again, to take a non-industrial example, the Paez peasant farmers in Columbia classify certain of their activities as 'non-work' which to the outsider would clearly be part of work: they regard agricultural tasks and wage labour as self-evidently work, but *not* selling food or cash crops, domestic activities or even walking to far-away fields to give salt to the animals: that is *visiting* your animals, not 'working' (Ortiz in Wallman, 1979, pp. 217–18). The same kind of process takes place in our own society. Thus the existence of this set of culturally-given (but perhaps changing?) symbolic classifications in our society is yet another finding to emerge from the kinds of studies reported here – in our case, symbols that are powerful enough to mislead us into classifying certain types of work which we know go on as somehow non-existent. Here is yet another way in which work is 'socially' (rather than 'naturally') organized and evaluated.

The treatment here also suggests that in studying the specific organization of work, we would do well not to confine ourselves to purely economic factors and management design, but also consider informal processes and personal links. These affect formal employment too (witness the personal obligations in fiddling systems as well as the domestic and local background which, among other things, affect how people become recruited, or not, into the labour market) and are of course particularly prominent in the non-monetarized social values of much unpaid work. This approach also throws some light on questions and controversies about the distribution of resources in our society, and about the overall organization of work and social division of labour. In making definitive comments on this we need to take account not only of people's formal occupations but also of their differential contribution in the domestic and local contexts which, in a comparable though not necessarily identical way, may also be constrained by gender, age, class, ethnic background, religion or locality. Questions about equality and inequality, furthermore, apply not just to the official employment hierarchy but also – if we want to understand how people really live on the ground – should and must lead us straight into the kind of controversies discussed here.

Finally, it should be noticed that the treatment here implies a move away from the more 'economistic' views of work typical of many earlier approaches – regarding work as fully or mainly defined by its *economic* characteristics in the context of the formal market place – to a greater emphasis on the more *cultural* context of work. It is time that, as well as paying due regard to the formal conditions of official employment, social scientists also drew attention to the informal work activities, personal links, unofficial processes, domestic and local ties and social values and symbols that form in practice so important – if 'invisible' – a part of people's working and living.

CHAPTER EIGHT

Leisure, work and unemployment: old traditions and new boundaries

ROSEMARY DEEM

Work and its boundaries

Amongst the consequences of rising levels of unemployment in industrial societies are a challenge to dominant conceptions about the boundaries of work, and a questioning of the traditional values and sentiments attached to paid employment. Established demarcations of work and leisure begin to be debated; the line between paid and unpaid work is re-examined. The widespread introduction of considerations of social divisions other than class (such as gender, ethnicity and age) into the parameters of sociological debate has also had a significant impact on our understanding and analysis of work and its boundaries. In this chapter what is proposed is an examination of the shifting nature of work/non-work boundaries in contemporary industrial societies. This exploration will suggest that such boundaries vary in their extent and clarity according not only to the socio-economic location of individuals, but also in relation to the nature of work undertaken, their gender identity, ethnic group membership, age and prevailing economic and social conditions. A consideration of the definitions of leisure, traditionally seen as something related to but distinct from paid work, is followed by a discussion about the changing nature of work/leisure connections, including an assessment of the impact of the study of gender decisions and the effects of mass unemployment on the conceptualization and study of leisure. Next the social reality of life without employment is carefully examined, before a brief investigation of contemporary contributions to a debate about whether industrial societies are becoming leisure societies. The chapter concludes by pointing out that various social and economic changes have affected and continue to influence and alter our traditional views about the connections between work and non-work and the worth attached to those two categories, to such an extent that for many people and groups there no longer exist clear boundary demarcations between what constitutes work and what does not.

Paid work itself, of course, may lead to many personal and social problems (as other chapters in this collection note) and as such has attracted much attention from sociologists. But the absence of paid work is also a major source of tension in an increasing number of industrial societies, and this too is now a major consideration and starting point for analysis by sociologists of work. This has meant an increasing focus on unpaid work (see the chapter by Maynard for a detailed examination of one form of unpaid work, housework) as well as on unemployment and leisure. Lack of paid work certainly does not always mean a life of leisure, although for some privileged social groups it may.

Unemployment may signal an end to leisure activities, as well as giving rise to problems about status, money and confidence. Even leisure can prove a source of social tension and conflict. Some groups may enjoy leisure at the expense of others: children at the (often literal) expense of parents, men whilst women do domestic work, the idle rich whilst the poor work hard. Certain social groups have long periods of leisure (the retired, school children on holiday) while others have almost none (mothers of dependent children, workaholics). What to do with leisure time may be a problem for some; for others their leisure may prove a social problem (holiday traffic jams, football hooliganism). Whilst employment has been the subject of extensive sociological theorizing and empirical study, leisure and unemployment have received much less attention, with the consequence that both their importance and theoretical development have often been underrated.

One of the reasons for this comparative neglect of leisure and unemployment by sociologists has been the extent to which the concerns of the founding fathers of sociology have dominated the discipline. The attention of nineteenth- and early twentieth-century social thinkers and writers was rarely drawn to leisure or unemployment, since these were seldom perceived of as socially important. Only when there is a sharp rise in unemployment, or insistent demands for more leisure time are made by workers, do these issues become important. In the 1930s, unemployment became a prominent social and economic concern, as did the question of education for leisure. In the 1970s and 1980s both unemployment and leisure have again assumed some importance in Western societies, and social scientists have turned their attention towards them. But the centrality of unemployment and leisure as social issues do not lie solely in what sociologists choose to study. The experience of these social conditions by people and our own common-sense notions about them are also important. For example, how do we as lay people tend to define leisure? It is likely that most readers conceptualize leisure as 'free time', 'an enjoyable activity', or 'doing what you want'. Unemployment on the other hand may be regarded as 'not having a job' or 'being on the dole'. Such definitions are obviously very much influenced by our own experience and the dominant culture of our society. If you have never been unemployed, and do not know anyone who is voluntarily without employment, the national unemployment may be less real and important to you than to someone who is currently unemployed. In pre-industrial societies unemployment was not really an issue because it is dependent on the existence of an industrial economy where some people employ labour and other people work for wages and basic subsistence or sustenance of life styles. In our society, some groups do not get much leisure; prisoners, junior hospital doctors, shift-workers, mothers of very young babies, whereas other groups have an abundance – the retired, or upper-class teenagers for instance. You may have a lot of leisure yourself – reading this book for instance; or you may have very little or only enjoy leisure at certain times of the year; for example, on holiday. This is bound to affect your views about leisure. What is 'normal' or 'given' for us is not necessarily so for others. Also, definitions of leisure are much harder to arrive at than definitions of unemployment and have taxed many theorists. And definitions of work have many pitfalls for the unwary. Yet definitions of work, unemployment and leisure are all very closely bound up in sociological analyses of what is happening to industrial societies in the second half of the twentieth century.

This chapter concentrates on leisure, work and unemployment, and the boundaries between them in modern industrial societies, particularly in Britain. The boundaries between work, unemployment and leisure can be and are theorized in particular ways, but these boundaries vary from different groups, and at different stages of the life cycle. Boundaries develop not just from individual variations and choices, but also from wider social political and economic conditions and decisions. Just as different societies have different forms of work organization and work processes, so it is possible for societies to have different boundaries or varying degrees of clarity or fuzziness between leisure, work and unemployment. Some changes affecting these boundaries can occur very quickly, for example, the development of high unemployment. Other changes may be very gradual: working hours hardly changed in Britain between 1948 and 1968, while in the USA major reductions in hours of employment occurred in the early part of this century rather than later. Nevertheless, if, following Newman (1983), we look at industrial societies now and those same societies in the nineteenth century, changes of all kinds can be observed to have occurred, and are continuing to happen.

> The basic structure of social existence is in a condition of flux. Since the beginning of industrialization, arduous, disciplined work, albeit rarely autonomous, has been the prime source of ego identification. Free time, though spontaneous and largely autonomous, has had to take second

place . . . the work and free time duality is giving way to the triad consisting of work, consumption and leisure. Secondly, whilst the work
arena enjoys partial humanization, the expanding consumption sphere
has moved in the reverse direction. And thirdly, leisure, the final refuge
for private existence, is set to act as the supreme outlet for ego gratifica-
tion. It is also where, to an increasing extent, alternative life styles are
acquiring ever greater importance. (Newman, 1983, p. 97)

But, although some groups are joining the 'leisure society', others are
patently not:

To rank the working class as equal members of 'leisure society' is clearly
absurd. Even their sole brief interlude from routinization – the annual
holiday – is subject to the grossest commercialization. In every respect,
for them the notion of spontaneous self-directed leisure existence is
even further off the mark than the contention of comprehensive household capitalization. In common with other facets of social existence,
their leisure experience is stratified and no less alienated than that of
family, life chances, or avenues for social participation. Yet, if nothing
but quantitatively, they are caught up in the incipient leisure explosion.
Already their hours of work have become fewer, and retirement a
shared expectation. Moreover, as far as trends are concerned, they
occupy a peculiar vanguard position. While they are the prime victims
of the 'new industrial revolution', as they were of the old, they also
appear as the forerunners of the leisure society to come. The technical
advantages causing most of the mass unemployment, namely, the
breakthrough of micro-technology and bioengineering, have hit them
especially hard. Prolonged loss of work has become almost commonplace. The historically ingrained 'work ethic' must make way for a
'leisure ethos' incorporating a greater emphasis on leisure experience, a
broadening of social options, the acknowledgement that non-work is a
worthwhile activity, and a shift away from activism or the intensive
revaluation of it. On present evidence this is a highly remote prospect.
Yet it is essential, if only in the interest of social stabilization. (Newman,
1983, pp. 102–3)

Here Newman is raising questions about the centrality of a 'work ethic'
to a society with high rates of unemployment and shorter working hours
for the employed. But ethics about work do not necessarily apply only to
paid work. Maynard's chapter noted that for many women housework
is a major time commitment hinged about with many constraints and
obligations, even compulsions, despite being paid. Houseworkers may
not adhere to a conventional work ethic but their work is unlikely to
diminish with unemployment or shorter hours of paid employment;
indeed it may well rise if the net effort is that members of households
spend more time at home. Young school leavers may have internalized a
work ethic, but then find no jobs available. For both housewives and the
young unemployed, increased leisure may either be impossible or too

expensive or both. Those without a permanent job may sometimes try to rationalize their situation, convincing themselves they do not need a job or can manage without. It is to these often contradictory views and concerns about work, leisure and unemployment that we will now turn.

Exploring leisure

Sociologists have often found a solution to their 'how to define leisure' problems by contrasting leisure with paid work and then examining different kinds of work–leisure relationships. Unfortunately, however, this fails to take into account those social groups outside formal paid work; housewives, the retired, the marginally employed, the young and the unemployed. Nor does this solution enable us to examine effectively how, for instance, the paid employment and work expectations of one person affect the leisure and work of others (for example, some husbands' occupational roles assume that their wives will also contribute to that role with consequent effects on the leisure and work of such wives). Even more recent work which explores the leisure/work/unemployment spectrum has sometimes failed to move fully away from the assumptions that work equals paid work, and that paid work affects only the economy, the individual who works and the groups with whom they work or are employed by. The effects of seeing all work, whether paid or not, as socially important, or the impact on the unemployed and/or unpaid workers on those who remain in employment, have not always been fully considered either. It has been argued, for instance, by Burns (1973) that the separation of leisure and paid work occurred with industrialization, in parallel with the separation of home and (paid) employment. Burns suggests that the commercialization of leisure pursuits began in the late nineteenth century, as paid working hours were being shortened. From this came the arguments about the connections of leisure with work, and about leisure being the counterpart of industrial labour. But leisure and work were not separated either at once, or totally, through industrialization for everyone, any more than were home and work (Hall, 1982). Burns himself recognizes that social class and life styles (although gender is not mentioned) may also influence leisure. He argues that leisure in contemporary societies represents a way of giving meaning to everyday life, in the same way that pre-industrial leisure, with its religious and civic festivals, gave meaning to social existence. Thus Burns is able to escape the strait-jacket of 'leisure as time free from work' in a way many other writers are not. Roberts (1976), for example, talks of leisure as being a relatively freely undertaken non-work activity, but also claims that if an activity is renumerated it does not constitute leisure. Here again is the 'leisure is the obverse of employment' argument. But if leisure is to be defined in relation to work, it must be so defined in relation to *unpaid* work as well as employment and must relate to the quality and enjoyable nature of the activity as well. Furthermore, it needs to be recognized that not everybody is in a position to compartmentalize their work and leisure time. Leisure is itself, of course, not simply a 'chosen' non-work activity. There are many other dimensions of leisure to be taken into account. Leisure and work may be combined (the housewife who listens to the radio whilst she irons, the factory worker who daydreams whilst on the assembly line). Leisure is rarely 'freely' chosen, and nearly always involves constraints. Nor is it necessarily an energetic or definite activity; doing nothing, 'staring out of a window' or just sitting down, can all be construed as leisure. Where 'free' time is available for leisure, the quality of that time may be poor; a nurse or doctor on call, a woman at home in the evenings expected to be ready to tend children, wash clothes or make drinks. Whilst some sociologists argue that leisure has become commercialized, others claim it is something which remains personal and private. Leisure can be linked not just to individuals or to particular social groups, but also to communities and to the home. Gender, age, life cycle and ethnicity are all important determinants of leisure experiences and leisure time. So too is the economic, political and social climate of any given society.

Leisure then is notoriously difficult to define; no writer or researcher has found a satisfactory definition. But leisure as a 'social problem' continues to occupy many social scientists, as well as educationists and politicians, the more so as unemployment increases. Roberts, Noble and Duggan (1982) argue that although leisure may be a kind of experience, a particular type of activity or play, and/or a type of time, leisure is no one single 'thing', but has been created through the fusing in industrial societies of free time, play and opportunities to do things for the intrinsic satisfaction. For the time being let us assume that leisure is something personal, meaningful and enjoyable, which is 'chosen' (but not always without constraints) time and/or space and/or activity outside of employment, unpaid work and life obligations.

Much of the discussion by sociologists about leisure, and about the relationship between leisure and culture, has centred around the connections between class and leisure. This has been particularly the case in studies of youth culture, where the emphasis has usually been on the distinctive nature of working-class youth cultures and the forms that those cultures take. In the more general study of leisure and culture, the emphasis has sometimes been on the ways in which class determines or influences life-styles and cultural styles. For example, the definition of culture has been described as a way of life of a particular class, group or social category (Johnson, 1979). Working-class cultures have come in for more scrutiny than middle-class ones and the necessity of linking cultural to community studies has been well emphasized. It has been counter-argued that class is playing a decreasing role in understanding social phenomena such as leisure. Parry (1983), however, points out that writers in the latter category still make use of evidence which demonstrates class differences and inequalities in leisure.

There are quite considerable differences between the Marxist approach to class, leisure and culture, and that of the pluralists. Critcher (1979) argues that many studies of working-class life emphasize passivity: working-class people are those to whom things happen. Some such studies may thus divert theoretical questions into policy recommendations, by defining certain kinds of working-class life as problematic. Critcher emphasizes that it is important to see the centrality of the relationship between changes in material life and the forms of working-class consciousness and culture:

> There were important changes in the nature of British society in the post-war period, the proper significance of which has never been adequately assessed. Mr Gaitskell's list – 'the changing character of labour, full employment, new housing, the way of life based on the telly, the fridge and the motor-car and the glossy magazines – have all affected our strength' – did point to something real. Changes were often misrepresented, but they were real enough, especially in comparison with the immediate past. The comparison with society before the war not only gave empirical verification for the apostles of progress; it was also a lived experience of improvement for a whole generation of working people. A situation of full employment, whatever inequalities persisted, was eminently preferable to mass unemployment; the extension of 'welfare', however skeletal, promised some right to security compared with the degradations of pre-war poor relief (even if the means test remained at the heart of the system); the pulling-down of slums and the substitution of houses with decent living space and bathrooms was a measure of improvement even if rents began to spiral and new estates seemed 'unfriendly'; the ownership of a car, a fridge and vacuum cleaner provided partial relief from domestic drudgery and access to new enjoyments, even though each one would need replacing almost before it was paid for. (Critcher, 1979, pp. 15–16)

In Critcher's view, then, there are strong connections between changes in living standards, jobs, pay and working conditions, and culture, including leisure. Class *is* an important component of leisure. But this is not the same as defining working-class culture as a social problem because, or in so far as, it differs from middle-class culture.

The pluralist position on the other hand, whilst not totally denying the significance of class to leisure, argues that other factors are more or as important. Marsland (1982) claims that young people may have common leisure interests which override the effect of gender or class differences existing between them, but even he is unable to deny that social divisions have an effect.

In particular, it has been argued that, in terms of class, race and sex, there is so much structural differentiation in the total life-world of young people that the fact of youth itself, and of the general significance of leisure associated with the generalized category of youth, is at best of relatively trivial importance ... or even, strictly speaking, fictional. ...

This kind of argument seems to me dangerously false, and its exponents blind to facts about the human condition generally and about contemporary society in particular. Nevertheless, it contains an important element of truth. For the life – including the leisure – of young people of different classes, races and sexes is manifestly and strongly differentiated. (Marsland, 1982, p. 308)

Another pluralist, Roberts (1981) also suggests that social class differences are an inadequate or unimportant basis for explaining leisure activity differences. But he goes on to review research evidence showing that there are still class-based differences in leisure, although all these amount to is to point out how middle-class people 'do more', that income is an important predictor of leisure activity and that attitudes to leisure are to an extent the products of experience and opportunity. Roberts concedes also that low income groups are the least active in outside the home leisure.

In nearly all of the analyses of class/leisure connections, there is an assumption that class (whatever the difference in theoretical perspective of the respective writers) relates to paid work, the economy and life chances. It is also nearly always assumed that the class position of family groups is determined by the status or position of men; women are frequently left out of class analysis. Unpaid work, especially that done by women, is rarely taken into account when discussing class, culture and leisure, although gender considerations are crucial to an understanding of all three phenomena.

Social variations and differences between women's and men's leisure activities have been recognized and known about by social scientists for many years. But it has largely been left to feminists to raise the issues of gender and leisure as problematic. Yet societal divisions of labour, which allocate certain work tasks to women and others to men on the basis of assumed gender appropriateness, affect *all* social institutions and activities. The difficulty of compartmentalizing much of the unpaid work which many women do may also make it hard to study female leisure in the same way as male leisure. Leisure and work are certainly linked, but not always in the manner which researchers have assumed on the basis of studies of males. Women participate less in sport and have less leisure of all kinds than do men, and female leisure is more often of a home-based, domestic kind than is the case for men.

Class differences clearly interact with gender divisions to influence leisure. But all women, regardless of class position, have in common a number of characteristics which may in certain sets of circumstances override other economic and social divisions between them:

(i)   The major responsibility assumed by women for unpaid domestic labour and child care in households.
(ii) The general political, economic and ideological oppression of women by men (sometimes called patriarchy).
(iii) The inferior position of women in the labour market.
(iv) The sexism and discrimination suffered by most women in the educational system.
(v)   The treatment of women by state institutions, often based on assumptions about male breadwinners and female dependence. State policy itself may, of course, be contradictory, emphasizing both formal equality between the sexes and the essential place of women in the home.
(vi) The representation of stereotypes of feminity and images of women in the mass media and in other cultural forms.
(vii) The politics of sexuality and the control exerted by men over women on the basis of sexual politics. This is sometimes exercised through the threat of sexual harassment, rape and assault, and at other times by husbands or male cohabitees controlling when 'their' women go out, or by the *de facto* 'barring' of many male social spaces to women (working men's clubs, pool rooms, rugby clubs, etc.).

It has been argued (and I would agree) that gender constrains women's leisure experiences to a much greater extent than it constrains men's experiences. You may disagree, believing that gender constraints operate as strongly on men as they do on women. Certain activities and leisure concerns are sometimes considered inappropriate or unsuitable for men (for example, knitting, sewing). But does male sexuality influence male leisure? Are there certain places men fear to go because of fear of sexual attack or harassment? What are the responsibilities which men have, which might affect their leisure (paid employment, car maintenance)? How are men represented in the media and in sports? Is a male rugby player considered in the same way as a male skater, for example?

Whatever the answers to these questions, empirical evidence tends to demonstrate that the obligations, work tasks and life-styles of women are influential in ensuring that for the majority of women leisure has less life significance than it does for men. Such leisure as women do enjoy often takes different forms from that of men, with emphasis on 'doing nothing', home-based pursuits, women-only clubs and organizations, adult education, and activities which can incorporate children (Deem, 1982a and 1982b). There are, of course, exceptions to this pattern; for example, single, highly-educated, car-owning women with well-paid jobs and no children, for whom leisure experiences and the significance of leisure are comparable to that found among men. Use of time is an important aspect of leisure and those who can separate off portions of their lives (into work and life-obligations, etc.) generally have more 'free' time than those who cannot. For many women this compartmentalization of blocks of time is not really possible. Some theorists have argued that as dependent children mature, and housework responsibilities diminish, women are able to enjoy more leisure. But studies of men and women in the later life-cycle stages seem to indicate that women and men continue to have different experiences of leisure (Edgell, 1980).

Another powerful social division between groups is age. School children, adolescents and old-age pensioners are three age-divided groups whose lives and work are likely to be very different to the majority of other people in society, and this in turn influences their leisure. The impact of age upon leisure is most clearly recognized for the young. Theorists of all persuasions are convinced that youthful leisure is a different phenomena than it is for the middle-aged and elderly. But whilst Marxists maintain that youth cultures are still connected, however loosely, to adult class cultures, pluralists are more likely to argue that youth itself overrides other considerations.

The elderly have received rather less attention from sociologists of leisure, but other research studies point to the general poverty, boredom and homebound nature of many old people's lives. R. N. and R. Rapoport (1975) address the age issue by looking at family life and leisure in different stages of the life cycle, but argue that there are variations even within a single life stage. However, Parry (1983) notes the criticism levelled at the Rapoports of devoting more attention to *intra*-generational factors than to *inter*-generational ones. Roberts, Noble and Duggan (1982) suggest that the rise of unemployment amongst the young requires us to reappraise the theoretical and empirical relationships between work and leisure. They claim that young people without formal employment may themselves be engaged in redefining the boundaries between leisure and work.

Most attention in age-related studies has been focused on the watersheds between entry to employment and retirement. It is harder to claim that age affects leisure as much in between those two extremes, which is perhaps why the Rapoports' study opts for the life cycle instead. Sport is one area where age may have a dramatic, although unnecessary effect. Sport participation often decreases with age, but spectating, and non-competitive sports can be enjoyed by people of all ages.

Although class, gender and age are now usually recognized as major influences on leisure and work, race is seldom given the same treatment, and many writers or researchers still make little or no mention of it. Yet it is recognized that ethnic minority groups, especially black ones, may experience significantly different life chances and styles compared with white ethnic minorities, especially in terms of their education and employment opportunities. Marsland (1982) argues that:

Leisure might seem to be a trivial component of these problems, compared with racism, heavy unemployment and ineffective schooling. But this would be a false conclusion. Truancy from the stigmatizing environment of school, intolerable pressure from severe and hostile families, and expulsion from the dying job-market all have the effect, especially on Afro-Caribbeans, of forcing them into compulsory leisure. Their leisure time is precisely where these problems find their major expression. (Marsland, 1982, p. 309)

One might want to take issue with Marsland's notion of compulsory leisure which seems to negate most of our previous discussion about the concept of leisure as meaningful time, space or activity. But nevertheless his main point is well made: that racism and unemployment are likely to have an effect on the leisure/work boundaries of ethnic minority groups. One of the problems ethnic minority groups may face in their pursuit of leisure is that their own cultures are not adequately catered for outside their immediate social networks. This is a problem found not just in the youth service but also in schools, workplaces and within the community generally. Prevailing notions of integration and acculturation often mean 'becoming like white people'. Hence, leisure opportunities for those who are unwilling to adopt the norms and values of white bureaucracy may be limited. But ethnic minority organizations, where they exist, can play an extremely supportive social role for ethnic minority groups in both leisure and work.

One should be careful not to assume that ethnic minorities have the most deprived or deficient leisure experiences of all social groups. As Pearson (1978) points out, we should not make the mistake of labelling anyone's way of life as deprived or stunted, without evidence that the people concerned feel that way. Furthermore, different social divisions do not always act in a cumulative way. Some young, female, black, working-class girls may have enjoyable leisure experiences whilst not all white, male, middle-aged, middle-class men necessarily do. Additionally, the term ethnic minority covers a diverse collection of social groups whose cultures are extremely heterogenous and one cannot assume that all ethnic minority groups will have the same attitudes to, interest in and experience of leisure. Material poverty, language and cultural barriers, prejudice and discrimination may all play their part in shaping the work/leisure boundaries of ethnic minority groups and these factors vary for different groups.

So far we have examined concepts of leisure, and the possible interrelations between leisure and four important social divisions: class, gender, age and race. It has been stressed that the relationship between leisure and work is by no means as unproblematic as many researchers would claim, and that we need to look carefully at both concepts especially in periods of rapid social and economic change. Next we need to consider in more detail some of the connections between leisure and work.

Leisure and work

I have already stressed that it is important for sociological analysis to treat work/leisure boundaries flexibly, since whilst these are relatively compartmentalized for some, for others they overlap or are indistinguishable. Furthermore, it has been noted that work includes not just paid employment in a formal job, but also participation in the informal economy, and unpaid work too. But only feminist perspectives, and those deriving from the study of the young unemployed, make general use of more all-encompassing definitions of work. There is often an implicit belief among social scientists and society at large that paid employment is more important than leisure, because the former is much more structured and is financially rewarded. It may be useful, before examining research on work and leisure, to consider briefly some of the major theoretical approaches to the leisure/work issue.

One prominent view is that which sees leisure as reward for work. This position is largely a functionalist one, for example, as put forward by Roberts (1981) and Dumazedier (1974). It sees leisure as having major functions, such as recreation, the free development of the individual and recuperation. Leisure can be a way of helping individuals adjust to their particular social situation without threatening social stability. For most people employment is unrewarding, boring and frustrating, but also inescapable. Leisure is seen as fulfilling individuals, in recompense for other more unsatisfying aspects of life, especially (paid) work.

An alternative perspective talks about the relationship between leisure and the process of civilization in industrial societies. This perspective is a rationalizing or Weberian one adopted principally by Elias and Dunning (1969). These two argue that leisure is a rule-bound activity, which involves a different balance between the emotions than does work, a balance which cannot be understood simply by equating leisure with non-work or by polarizing leisure and work. Leisure and its development are seen to be part of a more general 'civilizing' process, which decreases the role of instincts and emotions in motivating behaviour, taking place in contemporary societies. Elias and Dunning construct a typology of modern spare-time activities, ranging from private work and family management, to sociability and play activities. They argue that leisure today is influenced as much or more by pre-capitalist influences as by capitalist ones, and is changing in form, becoming more highly organized and bureaucratic as a result of the 'civilizing process'.

A third approach is both historical and Marxist. The work of Clark, Critcher and Johnson (1979), sees the development of leisure as a struggle between the working class, employers and the state to re-achieve leisure time lost with the onset of industrialization. Class is seen as central to culture in the widest sense as well as to the narrower concept of leisure, with leisure both being used by the ruling classes as a way to reproduce healthy and rested labour power, but also used by the working classes as a way to achieve some autonomy. Employment is seen to occupy a central place in culture, both as a focus of identity and because it occupies so much time.

The feminist approach argues that most established theory has concentrated on the compartmentalization of male leisure and paid work. Such an approach, contests the CCCS Work Group (1980), cannot adequately deal with many women's lives, where such compartmentalization is often impossible. There is agreement amongst feminist researchers that women's leisure is different from men's, and that its extent is often defined in relation to the demands made upon women by male jobs and by men and children making space for their own leisure. Even work by non-feminists, for example Edgell (1980), shows that whilst in middle-class families as a husband's career progresses and children grow up, more time may be released for leisure by both partners, if there are a large number of children or children of widely differing ages, if a wife returns to employment, or if both spouses are highly identified with their work and family roles, an increase in leisure time is unlikely. Hobson (1981) argues that women with young children are often severely restricted by their domestic responsibilities. Hence their small amount of leisure often consists of activities approved by husbands; for example, bingo, rather than dancing or the pub which women themselves might prefer. For some women leisure is neither a reward for work nor a rule-bound play-like activity. Furthermore, neither working-class trade unions nor other struggles through the women's movement have yet won housewives time free from their working day, even though the nature of housework has changed over the past hundred years, as Maynard notes elsewhere in this volume. Women's leisure or its absence is often strongly influenced by the unspecified nature of their domestic responsibilities, their inferior power position in relation to men and their lower propensity than men to be in well-paid jobs, to own or drive a car or to have large amounts of clearly identifiable free time.

A relatively new theoretical approach focusing on young people without full-time jobs, has been developed by Roberts, Noble and Duggan (1982) in opposition to the belief that unemployment is a situation in which no leisure and only misery and boredom exist. Whilst these researchers do not claim that young people enjoy being unemployed, they do argue that for those teenagers who are able to earn some money through jobs in the informal economy, there has developed a flexible use of time which enables some young people to combine leisure and enjoyment with work.

Let us now turn from theoretical perspectives to more empirically-based work. One approach is to explore leisure as a clear counterpart of employment. Such research by sociologists has shown that income and available time are not the only effects of work on leisure. Jobs can also influence how individuals choose to spend their income and leisure time. Some studies have argued that certain occupations are a way of life rather than simply a way of working:

> The title of a well-known study of miners, *Coal is our life*, illustrates this point. In his study of job specialisation among factory workers, Friedmann offers a series of arguments about how routine work encourages distinctive uses of leisure, all with the end result, though achieved in different ways, of making boring jobs tolerable. He argues that some individuals use leisure to compensate by devoting spare time to hobbies and handicrafts which employ skills and talents denied outlet in employment. An alternative response to boring work, according to Friedmann, is to carry the stoicism required to make a monotonous job tolerable into leisure, thereby lulling oneself into a state of indifference towards life and society in general. Another way of becoming reconciled to monotonous work that Friedmann discusses involves using leisure to escape into fantasy, emotional release and amusement that repress the individual's awareness of unhappiness. In his now classic study, *The Organisation Man*, Whyte argues that many aspects of domestic and community life in middle-class suburbs are explicable in terms of the modern business corporation's demands upon the life and personality of the salaried employee. The analysis of white-collar work presented by Wright Mills incorporates the claim that the sensitivity to status generated in this type of employment leads to characteristic uses of leisure, such as emulating the life-styles and consumption patterns of the upper middle classes. (Roberts, 1981, pp. 53–4)

Other research cited by Roberts has documented the existence of social class differences in leisure pursuits and interests, both in Europe and the USA, suggesting that superior financial resources generally allow middle-class people to engage in more and more expensive activities than their working-class counterparts. Roberts also considers research showing that there are spill-over consequences of jobs for individuals' leisure preferences. For example, leisure may compensate for work, or it may be an extension of work-related interests, knowledge and skills. Some occupations have very definite consequences for community development and friendship networks. Roberts suggests that available research demonstrates that leisure has to some extent been freed from work determination, but that the work–leisure couplet is still an important, interactive and reciprocal one.

A very different kind of research, focusing on sport, violence and the civilizing process, has been adopted by Elias and Dunning (1969), whose theoretical perspective has already been considered. Forces determining leisure are seen to predate industrialization, with the quest for excitement in leisure being one important factor shaping modern leisure pursuits. Much of Dunning's work has been on male team sports (Dunning and

Sheard, 1979), with emphasis on the control of violence through sport, and the democratization and bureaucratization of sport in contemporary societies.

It is not that Dunning and Sheard see no relationship between industrialization and sport, or employment and leisure. Rather their research draws attention to some rather different aspects of sport and leisure, some of which stem from developments occurring before, during and after industrialization, including the autonomy of the British ruling classes from the monarchy, which allowed less-ritualized sports to develop. In societies where this autonomy was not present, court society was the major sphere for highly stylized sports, as for instance in France. Dunning and Sheard argue that, for example, rugby has become a relatively 'civilized' and less violent sport than it was once. Nevertheless, it retains violent elements, just as soccer does, albeit through soccer-hooliganism rather than in the game itself. At the same time industrialization has increased the 'serious' aspects of sport, such that fewer groups now take part in sport for 'fun'.

Research by Dunning and Elias and Dunning and Sheard suggests that the social transformation of societies into urban industrial nation-states results in shifts in power between groups. This in turn leads to the emergence of 'multi-power control' within and between groups in all spheres of life, including sport. For some, sport has become a form of employment.

> This means, for example, that top-level sportsmen are not and cannot be independent. That is, they no longer play solely for themselves but as representatives of wider communities such as cities, counties and nations. As such, they are expected to produce a 'sports-performance', i.e. to produce the sorts of satisfactions that the controllers and 'consumers' of the sport demand, e.g. the spectacle of an exciting contest or the validation through victory of the 'self-image' of the community with which the controllers and/or consumers identify. The 'material density' of modern sport works in the same direction. That is, the sheer numbers of people involved means that high achievement-motivation, long-term planning, strict self-control and renunciation of short-term gratification are necessary in order to get to the top. Moreover, given the impersonal character of the modern nation-state, sport has come to form an important channel for obtaining recognition, i.e. of having individual and group identities validated, not simply in a local context but nationally and even inter-nationally, a process in which the mass media play an important part. (Dunning and Sheard, 1979, p. 279)

Dunning and Sheard argue that the cultural centrality of leisure and sport have increased in contemporary industrial societies, as a result of six interacting determinants:

> They are: (i) the fact that sport is not linked necessarily to the division of labour; (ii) the changing balance between work and leisure; (iii) the

growing secularization of beliefs and social institutions generally; (iv) the function of sport as a source of mimetically generated excitement; (v) the fact that it becomes a key enclave for the expression of masculine identity; and (vi) its function as a means of social integration. (Dunning and Sheard, 1979, p. 280)

The work of these writers and researchers is very much more complex than the research cited by Roberts, and includes the leisure/work polarization as only a small element of the social processes contributing to the development of modern sport and leisure.

A third empirical approach shows leisure to be an integral part of culture, but also demonstrates that it is one way in which the labour force and its characteristics (acceptance of boring paid work, for example) are reproduced. As with Dunning and Sheard, much of the emphasis is on leisure as a male cultural form. Willis (1977) in his study of a group of male working-class school pupils argues that the 'lads' anti-school culture represents in itself a glorification of manual labour and adult working-class culture. A somewhat similar culture he suggests is also found amongst manual workers on the shop floor. Based on observation of the latter group Willis (1979) further argues that employment plays a central role in culture, and that cultural relations, struggles and forms at the point of production are important determinants of male working-class culture. Such culture, argues Willis, takes place in conditions set by others, where labour is detached from individuals, often meaningless and directed towards the generation of profits for employers. Under these conditions, the work tasks themselves are often celebrated and centrally related to notions of competence to carry out those tasks.

Distinctive forms of language and jokes are a hallmark of certain kinds of shop-floor culture. Willis quotes from a worker on track production of car engines:

> They play jokes on you, blokes knocking the clamps off the boxes, they put paste on the bottom of the hammer you know, soft little things, puts his hammer down, picks it up, gets a handful of paste, you know, all this. So he comes up and gets a syringe and throws it in the big bucket of paste, and it's about that deep, and it goes right to the bottom, you have to put your hand in and get it out. . . . This is a filthy trick, but they do it. . . . They asked, the gaffers asked Charlie to make the tea. Well it's fifteen years he's been there and they say 'go and make the tea'. He goes up the toilet, he wets in the tea pot, then makes the tea. I mean, you know, this is the truth this is you know. He says, you know, 'I'll piss in it if I mek it, if they've asked me to mek it' . . . so he goes up, wees in the pot, then he puts the tea bag, then he puts the hot water in. . . . He was bad the next morning, one of the gaffers, 'My stomach isn't half upset this morning.' He told them after and they called him for everything. 'You ain't makin' our tea no more.' He says 'I know I ain't not now.' (Willis, 1979, p. 193)

Studies of women differ from the research done on men both because they take gender characteristics seriously and because they indicate different experiences and perceptions of work and leisure. It is not only Willis's work which had led feminist theorists to claim that much research about leisure and culture applies only to men. It is also the existence of the unspecified nature and uncertain time-duration of domestic responsibilities and the existence of male patriarchal power relations over women at a number of levels including the workplace, the home and public places. The following group of women from a National Housewives Register group express some of their feelings about the difficulties of arranging leisure thus:

> Most of us don't drive or if we do, we can't often have the car . . . buses are expensive and difficult to get on and off if you have young children . . . we can't go out with our husbands much as that requires a baby-sitter, time, and money, as well as energy and somewhere nice to go . . . husbands do help with the housework, by washing dishes for example, but often not as much as before the kids arrived; reading or knitting or sitting down at home during the day is difficult for long as children need a great deal of time and often distract your attention . . . husbands do work hard at their jobs but when they have finished those for the day . . . they don't have to think . . . 'can I go out', they just go without thinking . . . there's the carpet to hoover, will Jane wake up . . . what can we have for tea tomorrow . . . women's work doesn't just finish at a given time. (Deem, 1982b, p. 10)

Leisure for other than single women occurs much more infrequently than it does for men. For married women, their leisure is often tailored closely to their husband's job and working hours. As one woman in Hunt's (1980) study of a small industrial village says:

> Janet Austin: We don't go out when he's on afternoons, but when he's on days we can get a babysitter and go out in the week. We'll perhaps go down Newcastle for a drink. If there's anything on at the pictures we go, it's not often, but if there's anything on that everybody's to go and see, like 'Jaws', that was a laugh. I want to go and see 'Earthquake' as well. And when he's off on Sunday we make up for it. On Sunday–he gets one day off in fourteen – yesterday we went to Southport. We were off at half past seven. We took piles of sandwiches, and we were back about half past eight. We were just going to have a relaxing evening and the 'phone rang. He'd got to go to work. I was just going to do a curry as well. I went to bed early. (Hunt, 1980, p. 49)

Hunt found that other women in the village spent much of their time alone or with just their children for company.

Most of the full-time houseworking women in Hunt's study appreciated the flexibility of their unpaid jobs, because occasionally it allowed them to stop their housework and go out to the park or watch

TV. Nevertheless, the advantages of this flexibility were often overlaid with guilt feelings about children and undone housework. Even women with older children, and who have managed to develop non-home based leisure, may find guilt a problem. Members of a branch of the Business and Professional Women's Club expressed it like this in a research study I conducted:

> Even though we have more time now than when our children were young, women's leisure occurs less often than men's . . . we are never really free from commitments . . . is looking after a pet or cooking a meal for your husband's business colleagues leisure? (Deem, 1982b, p. 11)

Women in full-time paid work in middle-class 'dual career' families, do not necessarily find things easier than women from households where there is only a male wage-earner even if domestic help is available. Mrs Harris, for example, researched by the Rapoports (1976), is a full-time designer, but if her husband wishes to give a dinner party it is Mrs Harris who must give up her evening and come home early from her job to cook and prepare:

> On Wednesday my husband has some business associates he particularly wants to bring home. I shall cook on Tuesday evening and prepare for Wednesday and come home early on Wednesday in order to be adequately ready. . . . I think one just has to be a leap ahead. . . . (Rapoport and Rapoport, 1976, p. 254)

The drawing in to the work–leisure analysis of unpaid work both complicates but also assists our understanding of how and why leisure and work might be linked. The more work an individual has, and the more unspecified the work tasks are, the less time, energy and space remain for leisure, even though time can or may be used more flexibly where working hours and tasks are not fixed.

For the final empirical perspective we turn to a piece of research on young people who are formally unemployed, but who may find paid work in the informal economy from time to time. Such research purports to show that changes in industrial societies, especially rises in unemployment, have new and possibly radical consequences not only for our thinking on how work and leisure are related, but also for our view of the unemployed. Unpaid work or casual work may replace a full-time job for some groups of people, especially teenagers. Roberts, Noble and Duggan (1982) argue that this necessitates a fresh look at theories about leisure. The young unemployed people studied by them were not in the main either bored or regarded themselves as stigmatized, especially where unemployment was a predicament shared by large numbers of their friends and peers.

We have now examined a number of different theories and empirical studies of leisure and work. Some of these express long-held views of sociologists about leisure and work; others represent radical new departures. Taken together, all of these suggest, whether explicitly or implicitly, that the boundaries between leisure and work are not fixed for all time, and that not only variations in social and economic conditions, but also major social divisions, from ethnicity to gender, have a major impact on work and leisure. Contributions from feminists, and from studies of youth culture and the young unemployed, have played a particularly important part in opening up debates about work and leisure to include unpaid work, and to dispel the traditional notions about the relationship of leisure to all kinds of work. The study of adult unemployed people is also something which sociologists have recently begun to take seriously, and it is to this which we now turn.

Life without employment

We have already begun to raise some searching questions about the importance of paid work, unpaid work and leisure to women and men in industrial societies. In this section the major focus will be on the experiences of those who have no major form of paid employment to occupy their unpaid time.

The term 'unemployed' is itself not without complications. As Roberts, Noble and Duggan (1982) have noted, the formally unemployed may nevertheless be engaged in some kind of employment on a casual, or illegal, home-working, or part-time basis. This issue is raised in more detail by Finnegan in the previous chapter. Furthermore, some houseworkers may be looking for paid employment (although if they are married women with young children they may be 'discouraged' from registering for employment). Other houseworkers may regard themselves as being fully engaged in work albeit without pay. Some paid workers may be employed on a seasonal or periodic basis, especially those involved in the tourist and holiday business and in agricultural or horticultural work. Some groups may be without paid employment but not seeking work – the retired, and school leavers awaiting entry to higher or further education. So although unemployed literally means 'without employment', a more useful and workable definition might be 'Those without a formal paid occupation and actively seeking a job'. But even this does not solve all the possible problems; some people may have given up hope of finding a job and adapted to their jobless situation as best they can; others, particularly married women and mothers, may be constrained by social and economic expectations about their appropriate place into believing that they are non-employed rather than unemployed. Between the late 1970s and early 1980s there was in Britain a definite upward trend in unemployment rates for adults and young people. There is no space here to talk about the economic and political reasons for that rise in employment. But high unemployment does generate social problems, and its social consequences are likely to be different from the social consequences of full employment. The social implications of unemployment affect not only the unemployed but also the still employed, the households of the unemployed, children still at school, the education system, and our general conceptions of work and leisure. High unemployment also raises questions about the future of paid work in society and of policies and directions for leisure itself; for example, leisure may be used as a means of alleviating the problems of the unemployed.

The consequences and effects of unemployment upon people are mediated by a number of factors, including alternative sources of household income, gender, ethnicity, the extent of regional/local unemployment and the perceived possibilities of obtaining a job. The social situation of unemployed people varies enormously, from the young female school leaver who has never had a job, to the sixty-year-old man who has lost his job of forty-five years standing through the closure of a firm. As Sinfield (1981) points out, unemployment is not equally distributed across all groups in society; if it were, then the social effects might be better understood and more sympathetically dealt with. Those most likely to become unemployed in the first place are the low-paid, the youngest and oldest adults, people from ethnic minorities, the disabled and handicapped, the unskilled and inhabitants of depressed areas.

The young, the past middle-aged, the least skilled, the disabled and ethnic minorities are much more likely to become part of the long-term unemployed (defined officially as those out of employment for more than one year). Long-term unemployment itself has very considerable financial effects, social effects (greater feelings of rejection and stigmatization) and health consequence (Miles, 1983).

Some psychologists have examined unemployment as a series of stages; the long-term unemployed experience all of these but others perhaps only one, if a new job is found fairly quickly. Hill (1978), for example, delineates three stages:

(i)   the initial response to unemployment: traumatic perhaps but often seen as a chance to experience freedom and have a holiday;
(ii) the intermediate phase: individuals start adjusting to their new identity and low status and may feel psychologically debilitated, depressed and lazy, but there is still hope of finding a job;
(iii) settling down to unemployment: not having a job becomes a way of life, and anxiety, struggles and hope may all subside. This is the stage that the long-term unemployed are most likely to reach.

Unemployment then does not affect everyone equally, and we now need to consider some of the variables which can influence the experience of unemployment.

The first variable to be explored is that of age. Youth unemployment is not a new problem for Western industrial societies, but during the late 1970s there began to develop in Britain, and in other European countries, an extreme imbalance between those students coming out of compulsory schooling and the jobs available to them. There are a number of reasons why youth unemployment may reach considerable heights, including a bulge in the birthrate coming on to the labour market, a drop in unskilled jobs, a decline in apprenticeships, and competition between young people and adults for the same jobs because there are fewer vacancies and/or because adult rates are payable to teenagers. Employers may show reluctance to take on young inexperienced workers when they can employ older experienced mature workers instead. Many attempts are made by governments and other agencies to deal with the problem of youth unemployment, but despite these efforts (which are often short- rather than long-term) there remain large numbers of young people without jobs in many Western industrial societies. Whilst Roberts, Noble and Duggan (1982) argue that the young unemployed are not necessarily bored, or unhappy, other writers claim that the young unemployed do suffer these fates. This is implicitly recognized in special schemes which seek to provide structured leisure opportunities for adolescents who are neither at school nor in employment (Carrington and Leaman, 1983). Some teenagers may join the informal economy and others turn to having babies, but the rest may well experience boredom, despair, pressure from their parents and a difficult life. Furthermore, the informal economy is not necessarily either an escape or an unpoliced unregulated paradise. As Cohen (1982) points out, the jobs done by teenagers in the hidden economy are often an extension of those done whilst still at school – paper rounds, the milk round, casual work in factories, shopwork – for very low pay. The experience of long-term unemployment by the young may mean that their teenage years without paid work stretch into an adult life without prospect of jobs, so that their whole social experience is different from that of their parents, with poverty and joblessness remaining hallmarks of their adult lives.

But it is not only the young who suffer as a result of unemployment. Colledge and Bartholomew (1980) in a large-scale survey of the adult unemployed found that a quarter of those interviewed thought their failure to obtain work was related to their age. Being older and unemployed may mean loss of pension rights when retired, and increasing poverty, or the using up of a lifetime's savings. There is likely to be a feeling that life can only get worse, that there is no status or worth in being an individual without a job. But the problems of the older jobless is often dismissed as inevitable in a recession. Early retirement schemes are used by employers who need to make people redundant as a way of masking the real nature of redundancy. Early retirement *is* acceptable to some, but to others it is not. Townsend (1979) has shown that in the late 1970s nearly two-thirds of elderly people over sixty-five lived on the margins of poverty. People in their fifties thrown out of work can quickly join these poverty margins:

> Married couple with one child. Husband 59 years old, unemployed since June 1980.
> 'I find it very hard to make ends meet with only £34 to keep my wife aged 45 and a daughter aged 13 and myself. My wife and I do not spend money on anything but essentials but every week I have to use savings to pay my rent. They are very nearly all gone.' (Burghes and Lister, 1981, p. 93)

A second variable affecting the experience of unemployment is disability. The disabled number disproportionately amongst the unemployed. Yet this group are given little official attention and where special employment opportunities are provided, they are often in sheltered workshops rather than ordinary places of employment. The disabled may face extreme prejudice in trying to get employment, even though in Britain large firms are supposed to employ a certain quota of disabled workers. For the chronically sick rather than those who have long been disabled, the impact on their lives is not always apparent immediately, and there may be attempts to 'wish away' the effects of physical incapacity and ill-health.

> Mr Coxon: For the chronically sick Mr Coxon, the full impact of unemployment had crept up only slowly over the years. 'At first I didn't realize. I thought I would be all right and go back to work, but when you can't do a full-time job, you can't do this and you can't do that, then you can't go to work really. I mean I thought I could go to work, because I've been after jobs. I've been after a job a couple of years ago, I've been after a driver's job, driving a big fifteen tonner, up in Finchley, and that bloke took me out on test. I had a nice drive around the houses, I took it back, and he said "Do you know another driver to go up to Liverpool?" I said "Yes, my son-in-law." He said, "All right, I'll give him a job an' all", he said "£20 a week", and I came home and told my son-in-law, but he said no. I think he didn't want to take it on because he knew I couldn't go to work. I could have got a job like that, got a job anywhere. Now I can't because they've brought in the H.G.V. licence. You see, and the tying over and the sheeting over, I can't do that. I could drive all right, do driving all right. It's all heavy lifting on them jobs, such as like delivering televisions. Just imagine me getting a job like that where you cart televisions up to the top of buildings. It'd kill me. It'd kill me with empty hands going upstairs, let alone televisions. You see I can't do the driving and unloading. I'm going to mess myself up unloading.' (Marsden, 1982, pp. 161–2)

Ethnicity is a third variable important in helping to understanding the experience of unemployment. Even in times of relatively full employment, ethnic minority groups have suffered disproportionately from discrimination against them by employers. Some ethnic minority groups experience more problems than others; Sinfield (1981) and Walker (1981) both note that West Indians have a particularly difficult time. Ethnic minority women may also find employment very hard to obtain. Gender segregation of the labour market affects this particular group, clearly, but another factor affecting many ethnic minority men as well as women is skill, since this is an important determinant of employment chances. Those with least skill have least chance of work. Other significant factors include cultural and language difficulties. Where ethnic minority groups do obtain employment they are often exploited. As one employer due to the fact that they are unable to get work elsewhere. They neither mix well nor speak the language well, hence, they are easy victims of this society. They simply have to take what is offered to them.' (Hoel, 1982, p. 87)

Gender has already been mentioned as something which mediates the impact of unemployment. Much of the literature on unemployment deals only with men, or with men and single women. Men are depicted as losing confidence in themselves, suffering boredom and depression. The experience of women who are unemployed are considered likely to be significantly different from those of men, often for the same reasons that their leisure differs. Women have different roles and responsibilities, and are often in inferior power positions to men in society as a whole.

There have been a number of debates about whether women are losing their jobs as fast as or faster than men. But there is more agreement on reasons for female unemployment: the recession hitting traditional sectors of female employment such as textiles, clothing and footwear, and the impact of new technology, plus the tendency for part-time workers to be made redundant before full-time workers. Individual and societal ambivalence about women's dual role in the home and the labour market means that women employees often form part of 'natural wastage' from employment. Some groups of women, particularly those from ethnic minority groups and in low-paid jobs, may accept that redundancy will affect them, or certainly not believe in 'jobs for life' as some men do. Wood (1981) in a study of women volunteering for redundancy at a computer centre owned by a multi-national company, found that some of the women who volunteered saw redundancy as an opportunity to do something else. This included having a baby and looking for different kinds of work. The firm was not seen as a bad employer, and the major concerns were uncertainty and loss of friends, rather than job loss, since most of the women did not expect or want to be employed for life in the same firm. But women facing redundancy at another firm studied by Wood emphasized that their jobs were economically necessary as a vital contribution to their household budgets. Women were often aware that their husbands were also vulnerable to unemployment too, hence making their own jobs even more important. Wood then sees some differences between male and female responses to redundancy, but argues that we cannot assume that women will necessarily be less concerned about unemployment.

It can be claimed that women who lose their jobs have more options culturally available to them than men have. But those options are not always attractive, or long-term, and the degree of social and economic dependency that certain options entail (childbirth and raising children, marriage, domestic work, unpaid voluntary work) is not necessarily preferable in all respects to having a job. Nevertheless, in a climate where it is still sometimes argued that married women should give up their jobs to men, it would hardly be surprising if some women were able to rationalize their unemployment even though they would not and have not 'chosen' to be unemployed. For married women whose husbands are unemployed, having a job at all may make the household financially worse off through loss of benefits since the social security system in Britain still makes assumptions about the supremacy and entitlement to benefits of men. Men may also feel threatened if they are unemployed whilst their wives remain in jobs. Chappell (1982) quotes two case-studies of unemployed men who are unhappy with the thought of having a working wife. The first example concerns a household with a handicapped child, James.

> Staying at home with James (when he's not at the day centre) hasn't done much for Joe's paternal instincts, either. He has to watch him all the time. 'Now he knows what I have to put up with,' says Pauline. 'Joe's not domesticated at all. His mum brought him up to be waited on by women, didn't she, love? But now he's pig sick of the house and the kids.' (Chappell, 1982, p. 76)

The second concerns a couple with young children whose move to find secure employment misfired when redundancy struck.

> Adrian won't allow Christine to go out to work. It's partly male chauvinism, partly practical. 'Why should she have the job while I have to sit at home?' he says. On the other hand, if she got £45 a week working in a shop, they'd only lose most of it off their dole money. (Chappell, 1982, p. 78)

The effects of unemployment upon people are far from uniform, and not only gender but the other variables we have already discussed – age, race and disability – also influence the likelihood and impact of job loss. Initial reactions to redundancy are often different to the responses later on when the redundancy money (if any) has run out and job searches have proved unsuccessful. At first having 'free' time is often a bonus, but later it can begin to pall. Hobbies enjoyed whilst employed may be too expensive on a reduced income; hours spent, albeit unwillingly, at a job become even more monotonous when there is no longer a job to do. Men often resent doing housework although they may be forced into it if their wives remain employed. For most social groups then, unemployment is not received well, and gives rise to many difficulties and problems, ranging from loss of confidence, through cessation and truncation of friendship networks and social activities, to considerable poverty and deprivation. Being without paid work certainly does not mean that life is all leisure. It is not only financial losses the present problems.

The strong emphasis on occupations as a focus of identity can have a major effect, compounding loss of status with reduction in income. Unequal power relations between the sexes can also exacerbate the effects of unemployment. Men may reject or resent domestic obligations and object to wives remaining in or entering employment. For similar reasons, women may sometimes feel that their right to a job is less than a man's. The young unemployed may consider that schooling has been a waste of time and that there is no future without a job. Almost no one enjoys unemployment. Many writers talk about the possibilities of a leisured society, or the potential for developing education for leisure in the absence of jobs, but this is in sharp contrast to the realities of unemployment for many.

Towards a leisure society?

Changes in the economy and in society relating both to unemployment and to the hours of paid employment normally worked raise a number of wider issues than have so far been considered. One such important issue is whether we are moving towards a leisure society. We need first to consider why this question is currently receiving so much attention from social scientists. One answer is the level of unemployment amongst young people and adults. Another is the advent of technology, especially micro-electronic and micro-computer varieties, which can displace human labour power from many areas of productive activity (Arnold, 1981). A third reason may lie in the concerns aroused about adolescents and black people after the urban riots of summer 1981 in several major British cities (Hall, 1981). These riots were seen by some to be a consequence of unemployment, racial discrimination, poor living conditions and a lack of constructive ways to use 'free' time. However, as Carrington and Leaman (1983) point out, whilst there has been much speculation about how people spend time released from employment, there has been little consideration about how additional leisure will be financed and resourced. As we have already noted, the long-term unemployed can quickly enter poverty if they are dependent on state benefits (Burghes and Lister, 1982). Women without jobs have no or few financial resources with which to pursue non-home-based leisure pursuits.

The young unemployed rarely have much money either. Certainly national funds and efforts have been put into schemes designed to keep school leavers and unemployed adolescent 'off the streets' (Carrington and Leaman, 1983). Unemployed workers' centres have also been established in some areas, usually with TUC backing, and sometimes with local authority or MSC support. But these schemes are a long way from the idealistic visions about leisure societies in which everyone will do much less paid work, and be 'free' to enjoy a large number of leisure pursuits; less time spent in employment does not automatically lead either to more 'free' time. Studies of women and leisure (Talbot, 1979; Deem, 1982a and 1982b) suggest that time 'freed' from paid work is often taken up with many other obligations and responsibilities, leaving even less time for leisure.

Arguments about leisured societies are not new. Holroyd in 1942 wrote confidently that 'the amount of time spent by an adult in gainful occupation is growing shorter and, in consequence, his [*sic*] leisure is longer. The increasing mechanization of industry and many other factors, such as the decay of craftsmanship, all demand in their different implications that increasing study be given to the cultural and social conceptions of education' (Holroyd, 1942, pp. 9–10). This could equally well have been written in the 1980s. Holroyd's idea of 'education for leisure' is still very much with us, as the work of Jenkins and Sherman (1981) shows. Not that the idea of a leisure society necessarily appeals to some of the individuals towards whom it is aimed.

> They talk on television about the leisure society. God help us, that's all I can say. If there's one thing the lads round here don't need it's leisure. Leisure means institutionalised unemployment. For ever. What a nightmare 'In loving memory of the working class. Fell asleep around 1980 . . .' (Community worker, 20s). (Seabrook, 1981, p. 11)

What may be new and different about the 1980s, however, is the extent to which leisure is seen as an appropriate concern for state and public intervention, with the legitimation of seeking to make leisure 'an act both of compulsory consumption and social control' (Fergusson and Mardle, 1981, p. 80).

Jenkins and Sherman, in two books *The Collapse of Work* (1979) and *The Leisure Shock* (1981), present a series of arguments in favour of a leisure society and how this can be achieved. They talk of displacing the work ethic with a blurring of the work/leisure distinction, arguing that long hours of paid work are now no longer essential to an individual's survival and that most people do not enjoy work or its related commitments. But, suggest the authors, we must plan carefully and manage the 'leisure shock' rather than let it manage us. Instead of people gaining most leisure time when they are least able to use and enjoy it (at retirement or with redundancy), we should ensure that everyone has sufficient leisure time all their lives.

Jenkins and Sherman consider the commercialization and passive nature of much modern leisure, claiming that what is needed instead is a more constructive use of leisure. This would mean the present distinctions between (paid) work and leisure, which see work as good and leisure as passive or sinful, disappearing. Hours of paid work could be shortened and shared out between the adult population, with a basic assumption that everyone will be financially secure whatever the extent of their involvement in paid work. All would be engaged in activity and usefulness, but not necessarily in the same way as now. Means of achieving this are suggested, in studying how it can be financed, but it is noted that it may mean an end to people's rising expectations, and a cessation of financial motivations for work.

Some of the policies put forward by Jenkins and Sherman include developing a concern for the constructive use of leisure within the educational system for children, teenagers and adults. They argue that we need to become a more 'caring' society (for the old, the sick, the handicapped) thus creating more activities, but not necessarily more *paid* work. Imaginative environmental craft and industrial projects are advocated; for example, the development of inner cities, housing and transport systems and the production of crafts and other goods. Co-operatives are seen as one way in which these projects might be organized. New forms of the arts, and fresh locations for sports and recreation are seen as other projects. All their proposals are seen as a constructive way to deal with high unemployment rates which might otherwise generate misery, poverty and boredom. Jenkins and Sherman advocate we should stop seeing tasks and activities in the context of the traditional work/leisure dichotomy. They are also reasonably optimistic that such a society can be achieved.

The case against a leisure society

Roberts (1981) is much less optimistic in outlook about the prospects of a leisure society. He argues that neither the optimistic 'society of leisure' nor the pessimistic leisure society, because of 'limits to economic growth' and 'ecological calamity', would be functional or useful on their own. Roberts contends that some long-term projections – such as the effects of new technologies on employment, ecological and economic disasters (the end of fossil fuel, for example, or the effects of pollution), the collapse of work and a new found interest in constructive leisure amongst the population – may not occur in quite the forms envisaged by the commentators. Leisure will not, Roberts says, abolish the economic problem of scarcity, increase democracy or add meaning to empty lives. Paid work is seen by him as likely to continue, although not necessarily in its present form. But he accepts that leisure may offer some possibility of fulfilment for people's lives.

Carrington and Leaman (1983) go further than Roberts and argue that we must be sceptical of notions that we can create for young people a society of structured leisure to replace the world of paid work which is largely closed off to them. They point to many recent initiatives by the police, local authorities, central government and the Sports Council in relation to sport rather than work innovations. These have often put forward sport or recreation as a way of channelling the energy of unemployed adolescents into constructive activities. Carrington and Leaman claim that an underlying philosophy of such schemes is that while both employment and leisure are essential to the quality of life, if individuals are short on one of these criteria (paid work) larger doses of leisure can compensate for the absence of work. The assumption made by Jenkins and Sherman amongst others is that a leisured society will be paid for through increased productivity. How, say Carrington and Leaman, are activities of increased leisure to be paid for in a situation where the new 'leisure class' is growing whilst the numbers in paid work are declining?

The authors critically examine 'increased participation in sport' schemes, and ask why sport has been given such an important role in social engineering. Sport may merely embody existing societal values and beliefs, hierarchies and the principles of meritocracy. Sport is often rule-bound like paid employment, and similarly requires discipline, effort and 'skill' as well as deference to authority. It may be used to 'civilize' people, but sport and leisure are not necessarily likely to be any more successful than any other strategy in bringing stability to the young unemployed, for example, in inner cities, unless accompanied by more far-reaching economic and social changes which alter the conditions which originally led to unemployment and to urban riots.

A further viewpoint opposing the notion of a leisure society is that expressed by Newman (1983). Newman views with scepticism the idea that leisure embodies simplicity, autonomy and personal liberation, compensating for the routinization of other aspects of life, and suggests that leisure itself may well become routinized. Debates about a leisure society, Newman notes, often occur in a sociological vacuum, without class or power being taken into account, although such factors are clearly important.

The arguments for and against a leisure society are by no means conclusive, irrespective of which perspective their proponents adopt. Certainly there is at present no industrial society where there are strong indications of a move towards a leisure society for all groups regardless of position in the social hierarchy. Rather, the evidence appears to point towards a polarization between the unemployed, or low paid who have time but little leisure or income, and the employed who have money, leisure and compartments of time in which leisure may legitimately be enjoyed. The two sides to the leisure society debate throw into sharp relief some of the issues and themes of this chapter. These have included how work and non-work are socially organized, what influences operate on the boundaries between work, leisure and unemployment, and how shifts in those boundaries are determined. There has also been a central concern with the connections between patterns and relationships of inequality, and work, leisure and unemployment. It has been shown that the notion of what is, and what is not work is an extremely complex issue which cannot be easily answered or dealt with. It has also demonstrated that there is no straightforward and simple way in which to define and study either leisure or unemployment. Further, it has been suggested that conventional and traditional sociological themes and studies may provide an inadequate means through which to understand the totality of work and non-work connections. Feminist perspectives, for instance, and studies of youth culture have made an important and far-reaching new contribution to the debate. Finally, the chapter has argued that life-styles, leisure and unemployment and the ways in which people do or do not compartmentalize their lives, are as important to a consideration of paid and unpaid work as the degree of conflict and resistance in work or the work place, or the varieties of employment which exist in contemporary and past societies.

BIBLIOGRAPHY

Alden, J. (1977), 'The extent and nature of double jobholding in Great Britain', *Industrial Relations Journal*, 8.

Alden, J. (1981), 'Holding two jobs: an examination of "moonlighting" ', in S. Henry (ed.), *Can I have it in cash? A study of informal institutions and unorthodox ways of doing things*, Astragal Books, London.

Andors, S. (1977), *China's Industrial Revolution*, Martin Robertson, Oxford.

Appelbaum, E. (1979), 'The labour market', in A. S. Eichner (ed.), *A Guide to Post Keynesian Economics*, Macmillan, London.

Armstrong, P. (1984), 'Competition between the organizational professions and the evolution of management control strategies', in K. Thompson (ed.), *Perspectives on work*, Heinemann, London.

Arnold, E., Birke, L. and Faulkner, W. (1981), 'Women, electronics: the case of word processors', *Women's Studies International Quarterly*, vol. 4, No. 3, pp. 321–40.

Beechey, V. (1982), The sexual division of labour and the labour process', in S. Wood (ed.), *The Degradation of Work*, Hutchinson, London.

Benston, M. (1980), 'The political economy of women's liberation', in E. Malos (ed.), *The Politics of Housework*, Allison & Busby, London.

Berger, R. (1972), 'Factory Management in China', China Policy Study Group, Broadsheet 9, August.

Berger, S. and Piore, M. (1980), *Dualism and Discontinuity in Industrial Societies*, Cambridge University Press.

Berk, R. and Berk, S. F. (1979), *Labour and Leisure at Home*, Sage Publications.

Berk, R. (1980), The new economics; an agenda for sociological research', in S. F. Berk (ed.), *Women and Household Labour*, Sage Publications.

Berk, S. F. (ed.), (1980), *Women and Household Labour*, Sage Publications.

Bettelheim, C. (1978), 'The Great Leap Backwards', in C. Bettelheim and D. Burton (eds.), *China Since Mao*, pp. 37–130, *Monthly Review Press*, New York.

Beynon, B. and Blackburn, E. (1972), *Perceptions of Work: Variations within a Factory*, Cambridge University Press.

Beynon, H. (1973), *Working for Ford*, Penguin, Harmondsworth.

Blackaby, F. (ed.), (1979), *De-industrialisation*, Heinemann, London.

Blackburn, R. M. and Mann, M. (1979), *The working class in the labour market*, Macmillan, London.

Blackler, F. H. M. and Brown, C. A. (1978), *Job design and management control*, Saxon House, Farnborough (Hants).

Blauner, R. (1964), *Alienation and the worker*, Chicago University Press.

Bose, C. (1982), 'Technology and changes in the divisions of labour in the American home', in E. Whitelegg *et al.* (eds.), *The Changing Experience of Women*, Martin Robertson, Oxford.

Bosquet, M. (1980), 'The meaning of job enrichment', in T. Nichols (ed.), *Capital and labour*, Fontana, Glasgow.

Bradley, K. and Hill, S. (1983), ' "After Japan": the quality circle transplant and productive efficiency', *British Journal of Industrial Relations*, vol. XXI, No. 3, November, pp. 291–311.

Branca, P. (1975), *Silent Sisterhood*, Croom Helm, Beckenham (Kent).

Braverman, Harry (1974), *Labour and Monopoly Capital, Monthly Review Press*, New York.

BLPG (Brighton Labour Process Group) (1977), 'The Capitalist Labour Process', *Capital and Class*, 1, pp. 3–26.

Bromley, R. and Gerry, C. (1979), *Casual work and poverty in Third World Cities*, Wiley, New York.

Brown, R. (1984), 'Work: past, present and future', in K. Thompson (ed.), *Work, employment and unemployment*, Open University Press.

Brugger, W. (1976), *Democracy and Organisation in the Chinese Industrial Enterprise, 1948–1953*, Cambridge University Press.

Bryant, J. (1982), 'An introductory bibliography to work on the informal economy in Third World Literature', in J. Laite (ed.), *Bibliographies on local labour markets and the informal economy*, Social Science Research Council.

Burawoy, Michael (1978), 'Towards a Marxist Theory of the Labour Process', *Politics and Society*, 8.

Burawoy, Michael (1979), *Manufacturing Consent: Changes in the Labour Process under Monopoly Capitalism*, University of Chicago Press.

Burghes, L. and Lister, R. (1982), *Unemployment: who pays the price?* Child Poverty Action Group, London.

Burns, Scott (1975), *The household economy. Its shape, origins, and future*, Beacon Press, Boston.

Burns, T. (1973), 'Leisure in industrial society', in M. Smith, S. Parker and C. Smith (eds.), *Leisure and Society in Britain*, Allen Lane, Penguin, London.

Carrington, B. and Leaman, O. (1983), 'Work for some and sport for all', *Youth and Policy*, vol. 1, No. 3, Winter, pp. 10–15.

Cavendish, R. (1985), 'Women on the line', in C. Littler, *The experience of work*, pp. 105–16, Heinemann, London.

Centre for Contemporary Cultural Studies Work Group (1980), 'Women and leisure', paper given to the British Sociological Association Leisure Study Group, University of Birmingham, January.

Chappel, H. (1982), 'The family life of the unemployed', *New Society*, 14 October, pp. 76–9.

Charles, N. (1983), 'Women and trade unions in the workplace', *Feminist Review*, Winter.

Chaytor, M. (1980), 'Household and kinship: Ryton in the late sixteenth and early seventeenth centuries', *History Workshop Journal*, 10.

Chen, N. and Gallenson, W. (1969), *The Chinese Economy under Communism*, Edinburgh University Press.

Child, J. (1984), 'Managerial Strategies, New Technology and the Labour Process', in D. Knight *et al.* (eds.), *Job Redesign: Organization and Control of the Labour Process*, Heinemann, London.

Clarke, J., Critcher, C. and Johnson, R. (eds.), (1979), *Working Class Culture*, Hutchinson, London.

Cockburn, C. (1983), *Brothers: male dominance and technological change*, Pluto Press, London.

Cohen, P. (1982), 'School for dole', *New Socialist*, January/February, pp. 43–7.

Cowan, R. S. (1976), 'The "Industrial Revolution" in the home: household technology and social change in the 20th century', *Technology and Change*, vol. 17, No. 1, January.

Cragg, A. and Dawson, T. (1981), *Qualitative research among homeworkers*, Department of Employment Research Paper.

Craig, C., Garnsey, E. and Rubery, J. (1983), 'Women's pay in informal payment systems', *Employment Gazette*, April.

Craig, C., Garnsey, R. and Rubery, J. (1984), *Pay in Small Firms: Women and Informal Payment Systems*, Department of Employment Research Paper, forthcoming.

Craig, C., Rubery, J., Tarling, R. and Wilkinson, F. (1982), *Labour market structure, industrial organization and low pay*, Cambridge University Press.

Cressey, P. and McInnes, J. (1980), 'Voting for Ford: Industrial Democracy and Control of Labour', *Capital and Class*, 11, pp. 5–33.

Critcher, C. (1979), 'Sociology, cultural studies and the post-war working class', in Clarke, Critcher and Johnson, op. cit.

Dalla Costa, M. and James, S. (1980), 'The power of women and the subversion of the community', in E. Malos (ed.), *The Politics of Housework*, Allison & Busby, London.

Davidoff, L. (1976), 'The rationalization of housework', in D. Barker and S. Allen (eds.), *Depen-*

dence and Exploitation in Work and Marriage, Longmans, Harlow.

Davidoff, L. *et al.* (1976), 'Landscape with figures; home and community in English society', in J. Mitchell and A. Oakley (eds.), *The Rights and Wrongs of Women,* Penguin, Harmondsworth.

Davis, J. (1984), 'Rules not laws: outline of an ethnographic approach to economics', in Roberts *et al.* (1984), *New approaches to economic life,* Manchester University Press.

Deem, R. (1982a), 'Women, Leisure and Inequality', *Leisure Studies,* vol. 1, No. 1, pp. 29–46.

Deem, R. (1982b), 'Women's Leisure – does it exist?', unpublished paper given to the British Sociological Association's Gender and Society Conference, University of Manchester, April.

Delphy, C. (1977), *The Main Enemy,* Women's Research and Resources Centre, Feminist Information Centre, London.

Ditton, J. (1974), 'The fiddling salesman: connivance at corruption', *New Society,* 28 November 1974.

Ditton, J. (1977a), *Part-time crimes: an ethnography of fiddling and pilferage,* Macmillan, London.

Ditton, J. (1977b), 'Perks, pilferage, and the fiddle: the historical structure of invisible wages', *Theory and Society,* 4.

Ditton, J. and Brown, R. (1981), 'Why don't they revolt? "Invisible income" as a neglected dimension of Runciman's relative deprivation thesis', *British Journal of Sociology,* 32.

Doeringer, P. (1967; 1980), 'Determinants of the structure of industrial type labour markets', in A. Amsden (ed.), *The Economics of Women and Work,* Penguin, Harmondsworth.

Doeringer, P. and Piore, M. (1971), *Internal Labor Markets and Manpower Analysis,* D. C. Heath, Lexington, Massachusetts.

Dore, E. (1974), *British Factory – Japanese Factory: the Origins of National Diversity in Industrial Relations,* Allen & Unwin, London.

Dumazedier, J. (1974), *Sociology of Leisure,* Elsevier, Amsterdam.

Dunning, E. and Sheard, K. (1979), *Barbarians, Gentlemen and Players,* Martin Robertson, Oxford.

Edgell, S. (1980), *Middle Class Couples,* Allen & Unwin, London.

Edwards, Richard (1979), *Contested Terrain,* Heinemann, London.

Edwards, R., Reich, M. and Gordon, D. (eds.), (1955), *Labour Market Segmentation,* Lexington Books, Massachusetts.

Elias, N. and Dunning, E. (1969), 'The question for excitement in leisure', *Society and Leisure,* No. 2, pp. 50–85.

Elias, R. and Mann, B. (1982), *Women's Working Lives: Evidence from the National Training Survey,* Institute for Employment Research, Coventry.

Elson, D. and Pearson, S. (1981), 'Nimble fingers make cheap workers', an analysis of women's employment in Third World export manufacturing, *Feminist Review,* No. 7, pp. 87–102.

Evrard, P. *et al.* (1977), *Petite agriculture et capitalisme,* INRA, Paris.

Ferguson, R. and Mardle, G. (1981), 'Education and the political economy of leisure', in R. Dale *et al.* (eds.), *Education and the State Vol. II: Politics, Patriarchy and Practice,* Barcombe, Falmer Press, Lewes.

Firth, R., Hubert, J. and Forge, A. (1969), *Families and their relatives,* Routledge & Kegan Paul, London.

Fox, Alan (1974), *Beyond Contact,* Faber & Faber, London.

Fox, A. (1980), 'The meaning of work', in G. Esland and G. Salaman (eds.), *The politics of work and occupations,* Open University Press.

Freedman, M. (1976), in 'The search for shelter', *Labour Markets: Segments and Shelters,* Ch. 7, Allanheld Osman.

Friedman, A. (1977a), *Industry and Labour: class struggle at work and monopoly capitalism,* Macmillan, London.

Friedman, A. (1977b), 'Responsible autonomy versus direct control over the labour process', *Capital and Class,* No. 1.

Galbraith, J. D. (1974), *The Economy and the Public Purpose,* André Deutsch, London.

Gallie, D. (1978), *In search of the new working class: automation and social integration in the capitalist enterprise,* Cambridge University Press.

Gardiner, J. *et al.* (1980), 'Women's domestic labour', in E. Malos (ed.), *The Politics of Housework,* Allison & Busby, London.

Garnsey, E. (1981), 'The Rediscovery of the Division of Labour', *Theory and Society,* 10, pp. 337–58.

Gavron, H. (1968), *The Captive Wife,* Penguin, Harmondsworth.

Gershuny, J. I. (1978), *After industrial society?* Macmillan, London.

Gershuny, J. I. (1979), 'The informal economy: its role in post-industrial society', *Futures,* February.

Gershuny, J. I. (1981), 'Changement des modeles de loisir, Royanume Uni. 1961–1974/5', *Temps libres*, 4.

Gershuny, J. I. (1982), 'Household tasks and the use of time', in S. Wallman *et al.* (1982), *Living in South London*, Gower, Aldershot.

Gershuny, J. I. and Miles, I. D. (1983), *The new service economy: the transformation of employment in industrial societies*, Frances Pinter, London.

Gershuny, J. I. and Pahl, R. E. (1980), 'Britain in the decade of the three economies', *New Society*, 3 January.

Gershuny, J. I. and Thomas, G. S. (1980), *Changing patterns of time use. Data preparation and some preliminary results, UK 1961–1974/5*, Science Policy Research Unit, University of Sussex, Brighton.

Giddens, Anthony (1982), 'Power, the dialectic of control and class structuration', in Giddens, Anthony, and Mackenzie, Gavin (eds.), *Social Class and the Division of Labour*, pp. 29–45, Cambridge University Press.

Ginsberg, S. (1976), 'Women, work and conflict', in N. Fonda and P. Moss (eds.), *Mothers and Employment*, Brunel University Management Programme.

Goldthorpe, J. H., Lockwood, D., Bechhoffer, F. and Platt, J. (1968), *The Affluent Worker: Industrial Attitudes and Behaviour*, Cambridge University Press.

Gordon, D. M., Edwards, R. and Reich, M. (1982), *Segmented Work, Divided Workers; the Historical Transformation of Labor in the United States*, Cambridge University Press.

Grossman, G. (1977), 'The "second economy" of the USSR', *Problems of Communism*, 26.

Hakim, C. (1979), *Occupational Segregation*, Research Paper No. 9, Department of Employment, London.

Hall, C. (1979), 'The early formation of Victorian domestic ideology', in S. Burman (ed.), *Fit Work for Women*, Croom Helm, London.

Hall, C. (1982), 'The Butcher, the baker, the candlestick maker: the shop and the family in the industrial revolution', in E. Whitelegg (ed.), *The Changing Experience of Women*, Martin Robertson, Oxford.

Hall, S. (1981), 'Summer in the city', *New Socialist*, September/October, pp. 4–7.

Hamilton, P. (1984), 'The Incorporation of Agriculture Within Capitalism', in Thompson (ed.), (1984), *Work, Employment and Unemployment*, Open University Press.

Hamilton, P. (1985), 'Small Farmers and Food Production in Western Europe', *International Social Science Journal*, No. 105.

Hamilton, P. (ed.), (forthcoming), *Socio-Economic Change in Rural Society 1945–80: Britain and France*.

Harrison, J. (1973), 'The political economy of housework', *Bulletin of the Conference of Socialist Economists*, vol. 3, No. 1.

Hart, K. (1973), 'Informal income opportunities and urban employment in Ghana', *Journal of Modern African Studies*, 11.

Hartmann, H. (1981), 'The family as the locus of gender, class and political struggle: the example of housework', *Signs*, vol. 6, No. 3.

Hassan, D. (1982), 'Small-Scale Agriculture and Capitalism: the Status of Milk Producers', in Hamilton (ed.), (forthcoming).

Hatch, Stephen (1978), *Voluntary work: a report of a survey*, Volunteer Centre, Voluntary Organizations Research Unit, London.

Hatch, Stephen (1980), *Outside the State. Voluntary organizations in three English towns*, Croom Helm, London.

Henry, Stuart (ed.), (1981), *Can I have it in cash? A study of informal institutions and unorthodox ways of doing things*, Astragal Books, London.

Hewitt, M. (1958), *Wives and Mothers in Victorian Industry*, Greewood Press.

Hill, J. (1978), 'The psychological impact of unemployment', *New Society*, 19 January.

Hill, Stephen (1981), *Competition and Control and Work*, Heinemann, London.

Hobsbawm, E. J. (1968), *Labouring Men*, Weidenfeld & Nicolson, London.

Hobson, D. (1981), 'Young Women at home and leisure', in A. Tomlinson (ed.), *Leisure and Social Control*, Brighton Polytechnic.

Hoel, Barbo (1982), 'Contemporary clothing "sweatshops", Asian female labour and collective organization', in J. West (ed.), *Women, Work and the Labour Market*, Routledge & Kegan Paul, London.

Holroyd, G. H. (1942), *Education for Leisure*, E. J. Arnold, Leeds.

Horn, P. (1975), *The Rise and Fall of the Victorian Servant*, Gill & Macmillan.

Howe, C. (1979), 'The Modern Economy', in C. Howe (ed.), *Studying China*, School of Oriental and African Studies, London.
Hua, G. (1983), *A Small Town Called Hibiscus*, Panda Books.
Humphries, J. (1977), 'Class struggle and the persistence of the working-class family', *Cambridge Journal of Economics*, vol. 1, September, pp. 241–8.
Hunt, P. (1980), *Gender and Class Consciousness*, Macmillan, London.
Hunter, I. and Mulvey, C. (1981), *The Economics of Wages and Labour*, Macmillan, London.
Hyman, Richard and Brough, Ian (1975), *Social Values and Industrial Relations*, Basil Blackwell, Oxford.
Jenkins, C. and Sherman, B. (1979), *The Collapse of Work*, Eyre Methuen, London.
Jenkins, C. and Sherman, B. (1981), *The Leisure Shock*, Eyre Methuen, London.
Jiang, Zilong (1984), 'Manager Qiao Assumes Office', in Littler (ed.), (1985), *The Experience of Work*, first publ. in *People's Literature*, July 1979: trans. Wang Mingjie.
Johnson, R. (1979), 'Three problematics: elements of a theory of working-class culture', in J. Clarke *et al.*, op. cit.
Jones, B. (1982), 'Destruction or redistribution of engineering skills: the case of numerical control', in S. Wood (ed.), *The Degradation of Work?* Heinemann, London.
Kahn-Ackermann, M. (1982), *China: Within the Outer Gate*, trans. D. Fernbach, Marco Polo Press.
Kaluzynska, E. (1980), 'Wiping the floor with theory – a survey of writings on housework', *Feminist Review*, No. 6.
Kamata, S. (1982), *Japan in the passing lane*, Allen & Unwin, London.
Katsenelinboigen. A. (1977), 'Coloured markets in the Soviet Union', *Soviet Studies*, 29.
Kelly, J. E. (1982/4), 'Economic and structural analysis of job redesign', in J. E. Kelly and C. W. Clegg, *Autonomy and control at the workplace*, pp. 21–50, Croom Helm, London.
Kelly, J. (1982b), *Scientific management, job redesign and work performance*, Academic Press, New York.
Kelly, J. (1984), 'Management's redesign of work: labour process, labour markets and product markets', in D. Knights *et al.* (eds.), *Job redesign, organization and control of the labour process*, Heinemann, London.
Kerr, C. (1964), *Industrialism and industrial man*, Penguin, Harmondsworth.
Kew, S. (1979), *Ethnic groups and leisure*, Sports Council and Social Science Research Council, London.
Khan, N. (1976), *The arts Britain ignores: the arts of ethnic minorities in Britain*, Community Relations Commission.
Komarovsky, M. (1967), *Blue-collar marriage*, Random House, New York.
Kumar, Krishan (1979), 'The social culture of work: work, employment and unemployment as ways of life', *New Universities Quarterly*, 34.
Kusterer, K. (1978), *Know how on the job:* Westview Press, Boulders.
Laite, Julian (ed.), (1982), *Bibliographies on local labour markets and the informal economy*, Social Science Research Council, London.
Lazonick, W. (1978), 'The Subjection of Labour to Capital: The Rise of the Capitalist System', *Review of Radical Political Economics*, vol. 10, No. 1.
Lazonick, W. (1979), 'Industrial relations and technical change: the case of the self-acting mule', *Cambridge Journal of Economics*, vol. 3, September.
Lee, D. (1982), 'Beyond deskilling: skill, craft and class?' in S. Wood, *The Degradation of Work?* Heinemann, London.
Le Roy Ladurie, E. (1979), 'Peasantry', in the *New Cambridge Modern History*, vol. XIII, Cambridge University Press.
Liang, Heng and Shapiro, J. (1983), *Son of the Revolution*, Chatto & Windus, London.
Linhart, R. (1985), 'The Assembly Line', in C. Littler, *The Experience of Work*, pp. 117–31, Gower, Aldershot.
Lipsey, R. *An Introduction to Positive Economics*, 5th edn., Weidenfeld & Nicolson, London.
Littler, C. J. (1982), *The development of the labour process in capitalist societies: a comparative analysis of work organization in Britain, the USA and Japan*, Heinemann, London.
Littler, C. R. (1984), 'Soviet-Type Societies and the Labour Process', in K. Thompson (ed.), (1984), *Work, Employment and Unemployment*, Open University Press.
Littler, C. (ed.), (1985), *The Experience of Work*, Gower, Aldershot.
Littler, C. R. and Lockett, M. (1983), 'The Significance of Trade Unions in China', in *Industrial Relations Journal*, vol. 14, No. 4, pp. 31–42.
Littler, C. R. and Salaman, Graeme (1984), *Class at Work*, Batsford, London.

Lloyd, Peter (1979), *Slums of hope? Shanty towns of the Third World*, Manchester University Press.

Lockett, M. (1981), 'Self-Management in China', in *Economic Analysis and Workers' Management*, vol. 15.1.

Lockett, M. and Littler, C. R. (1985), *Management and Industry in China*, Heinemann, London.

Long, N. and Richardson, P. (1978), 'Informal sector, petty commodity production, and the social relations of small-scale enterprise', in J. Clammer (ed.), *The new economic anthropology*, Macmillan, London.

Lowenthal, M. (1981), 'Non-market transactions in an urban community', in S. Henry (ed.), (1981), op. cit.

Low Pay Unit Review: various issues published by the Low Pay Unit, 9 Poland Street, London, W1V 3DG.

Lupton, T. and Bowey, A. (1974), *Wages and Salaries*, Penguin, Harmondsworth.

McBride, T. M. (1976), *The Domestic Revolution*, Croom Helm, London.

Macfarlane, A. (1978), *The Origins of English Individualism*, Basil Blackwell, Oxford.

Mann, M. (1973), *Worker on the Move*, Cambridge University Press.

Manwaring, A. (1984), 'The extended internal labour market', *Cambridge Journal of Economics*, vol. 8, No. 2, pp. 161–87.

Manwaring, T. and Wood, S. (1984), 'The Ghost in the Labour Process', in D. Knights *et al.*, *Job redesign: organization and control of the labour process*, pp. 171–96. Heinemann, London.

Mao, Zedong (1975), *Mao Tse-Toung et la construction de socialisme*, Editions du Seuil, Paris.

Mars, G. (1973), 'Hotel pilferage: a case study in occupational theft', in M. Warner (ed.), *The sociology of the workplace*, Allen & Unwin, London.

Mars, G. (1982), *Cheats at work. An anthropology of workplace crime*, Allen & Unwin, London.

Marsden, D. (1981), *Workless*, Croom Helm, London.

Marsland, D. (1982), 'It's my life: young people and leisure', *Leisure Studies*, vol. 1, pp. 305–22.

Martin, J. and Roberts, C. (eds.), (1984), *Women and Employment: A lifetime perspective*, Department of Employment, HMSO.

Marx, Karl (1954), *Capital: A Critical Analysis of Capitalist Production*, Lawrence & Wishart, London.

Marx, Karl (1968), 'Wages Price and Profit', in Marx and Engels, *Selected Works*, pp. 185–226, Lawrence & Wishart, London.

Maurice, M., Sorge, A. and Warner, M. (1980), 'Societal differences in organizing manufacturing units: a comparison of France, West Germany and Great Britain', *Organizational Studies*, pp. 59–86.

Mayo, E. (1949), *The Social Problems of an Industrial Civilization*, Routledge & Kegan Paul, London.

Meacham, S. (1977), *A life apart: the English working class 1890–1914*, Thames & Hudson, London.

Melman, S. (1974), 'The myth of autonomous technology', in N. Cross *et al.*, *Man-made futures*, pp. 56–81, Hutchinson, London.

Miles, I. (1983), 'Is unemployment a health hazard?' *New Scientist*, pp. 384–6.

Mill, J. S. (1862), *The Principles of Political Economy*, vol. 1, Routledge & Kegan Paul, 1965 edn.

More, C. (1982), 'Skill and the survival of apprenticeship', in S. Wood (ed.), *The Degradation of Work?* pp. 109–21, Hutchinson, London.

National Union of Mineworkers (1980), Delegation to China: Report, mimeo.

Nelson, D. (1975), *Managers and Workers*, University of Wisconsin Press, Wisconsin.

Newby, H. (1977), *The Deferential Worker*, Penguin, Harmondsworth.

Newby, H. (1979), *Green and Pleasant Land?* Hutchinson, London.

Newby, H. (1983), 'European Social Theory and the Agrarian Question', in P. Hamilton (ed.), (forthcoming), op. cit.

Newby, H. (1984), 'The Work Situation of the Agricultural Worker', in Littler (ed.), (1985), *The Experience of Work*, Heinemann, London.

Newman, O. (1983), 'The coming of a leisure society?' *Leisure Studies*, vol. 2, No. 1, pp. 97–109.

Newton, K. (1976), *Second city politics. Democratic processes and decision-making in Birmingham*, Clarendon Press, Oxford.

Nichols, T. (ed.), (1980), *Capital and labour*, Fontana, Glasgow.

Nichols, T. and Armstrong, P. (1978), *Workers Divided*, Fontana, Glasgow.

Nichols, T. and Beynon, H. (1977), *Living with capitalism*, Routledge & Kegan Paul, London.

Noble, D. (1977), *America by design: science, technology and the rise of corporate capitalism*, Alfred A. Knopf, New York.

Oakley, A. (1974), *The Sociology of Housework*, Martin Robertson, Oxford.

O'Toole, James (1981), *Making American Work: Productivity and Responsibility*, Continuum, New York.

Outer Circle Policy Unit (1978), *Policing the hidden economy. The significance and control of fiddles*, OCPU, London.

Outer Circle Policy Unit (1980), *Measuring the hidden economy. A review of evidence and methodologies* (Michael O'Higgins), OCPU, London.

Pahl, R. E. (1980), 'Employment, work and the domestic division of labour', *International Journal of Urban and Regional Research*, 4.

Pahl, R. E. (1984), *Divisions of labour*, Basil Blackwell, Oxford.

Pahl, R. E. and Wallace, C. D. (1984), 'Forms of work and privatization on the Isle of Sheppey', in B. Roberts, R. Finnegan and D. Gallie (eds.), (1984), *New approaches to economic life*, Manchester University Press.

Palmer, B. (1975), 'Class, Conception and Conflict', *Review of Radical Political Economics*, vol. 7, No. 2, pp. 31–49.

Parkin, F. (1974), 'Strategies of social closure in class formations', in F. Parkin (ed.), *The Social Analysis of Class Structure*, Tavistock, London.

Parry, N. (1983), 'Sociological contributions to the study of leisure', *Leisure Studies*, vol. 2, pp. 57–81.

Pearson, L. F. (1978), 'Non-work time: a review of the literature', Birmingham University Centre for Urban and Regional Studies Research Memorandum, No. 65.

Penn, R. (1982), 'Skilled manual workers in the labour process, 1856–1964', in S. Wood (ed.), *The Degradation of Work*, pp. 90–108, Hutchinson, London.

Phillips, A. and Taylor, B. (1980), 'Sex and skill', *Feminist Review*, No. 6, pp. 79–88.

Pinchbeck, I. (1930), *Women Workers and the Industrial Revolution*, Routledge & Kegan Paul, London.

Pollert, A. (1981), *Girls, Wives, Factory Lives*, Macmillan, London.

Rapoport, R. and R. N. (1975), *Leisure and the family life cycle*, Routledge & Kegan Paul, London.

Rapoport, R. and R. N. (1976), *Dual career families re-examined*, Martin Robertson, Oxford.

Rawski, T. G. (1979), *Economic Growth and Employment in China*, Oxford University Press.

Reich, M., Gordon, D. and Edwards, R. (1980), 'A theory of labour market segmentation', in A. Amsden (ed.), *The economics of women and work*, Penguin, Harmondsworth.

Roberts, B. (1978), *Cities of peasants. The political economy of urbanization in the Third World*, Arnold, London.

Roberts, B., Finnegan, R. and Gallie, D. (eds.), (1984), *New approaches to economic life: economic restructuring, unemployment and the social division of labour*, Manchester University Press.

Roberts, C. and Woods, S. J. (1982), 'Collective bargaining and job redesign', in J. Kelly and C. W. Clegg (eds.), *Autonomy and control at the workplace: contexts for job design*, Croom Helm, London.

Roberts, K. (1977), *The Fragmentary Class Structure*, Heinemann, London.

Roberts, K. (1981), *Leisure*, 2nd edn., Longmans, London.

Roberts, K., Noble, M. and Duggan, J. (1982), 'Youth unemployment: an old problem or a new lifestyle?' *Leisure Studies*, vol. 2., No. 1, pp. 83–96.

Robinson, J. (1977), *Changes in America's Use of Time: 1965–1975*, Cleveland State University Press.

Rose, R. (1983), *Getting by in three economies: the resources of the official, unofficial and domestic economies*, Centre for the Study of Public Policy, University of Strathclyde, Glasgow.

Rosenbrock, H. H. (1985), 'Engineers and the Work that People Do', in Littler (ed.), (1985), *The Experience of Work*, op. cit. First publ. in IEEE Control Systems Magazine, 1/3 September 1981.

Rothschild, J. (1983), 'Technology, housework, and women's liberation: a theoretical analysis', in J. Rothschild (ed.), *Machina Ex Dea: feminist perspectives on technology*, Pergamon Press, Oxford.

Routh, G. (1980), *Occupation and Pay in Great Britain*, Oxford University Press.

Rubery, J. (1978), 'Structured labour markets, worker organization and low pay', *Cambridge Journal of Economics*, vol. 2, No. 11, pp. 17–36; reprinted in A. Amsden (ed.), (1980), *The Economics of Women and Work*, Penguin, Harmondsworth.

Salagen, M. (1983), *Love and power in the peasant family*, Basil Blackwell, Oxford.

Samuel, R. (ed.), (1975), *Village life and labour*, Routledge & Kegan Paul, London.

Samuelson, P. (1980), *Economics*, 11th edn., McGraw-Hill, New York.

Scott, R. (1976), *The Female Consumer*, Associated Business Programmes.

Seabrook, J. (1976), 'Unemployment now and in the 1930s', in B. Crick (ed.), *Unemployment*, Methuen, London.

Secombe, W. (1974), 'The housewife and her labour under capitalism', *New Left Review*, No. 83.

Segalen, M. (1985), 'The Household at Work', in Littler (ed.), (1985), *The Experience of Work*, Gower, Aldershot; extract from *Love and Power in the Peasant Family*, trans. S. Matthews, Basil Blackwell (1983), first publ. Flammarion, Paris, 1980.

Sinfield, A. (1981), *What Unemployment Means*, Martin Robertson, Oxford.

Sirageldin, I. (1969), *Non market components of national income*, Survey Research Centre, University of Michigan, Ann Arbor.

Smith, A. (1976 edn.), *The Wealth of Nations*, Oxford University Press.

Smith, Adrian (1981), 'The informal economy', *Lloyds Bank Review*, 141, July.

Stone, K. (1974), 'The origin of the structures in the steel industry', *Review of Radical Political Economics*; reprinted in Edwards, Reich and Gordon (eds.), (1975), *Labour market segmentation*, D. C. Heath.

Strasser, S. (1982), *Never Done: A history of American housework*, Pantheon.

Szalai, A. (1972), *The Use of Time*, Mouton.

Talbot, M. (1979), *Women and Leisure*, Social Science Research Council/Sports Council, London.

Taylor, F. W. (1947), *Scientific Management*, Harper & Row, London.

Taylor, Frederick (1972), 'The Principles of Scientific Management', in L. E. David, and J. C. Taylor (eds.), *Design of Jobs*, pp. 27–31, Penguin, Harmondsworth.

Thompson, K. (ed.), (1984), *Work, Employment and Unemployment*, Open University Press.

Thompson, Paul (1975), *The Edwardians*, Weidenfeld & Nicolson, London.

Thompson, P. (1983), *'The nature of work*, Macmillan, London.

Thompson, P. (1984), 'The labour process and deskilling', in K. Thompson (1984), op. cit.

Thrall, C. A. (1982), 'The conservative use of modern household technology', *Technology and Culture*, vol. 23, No. 2, April.

Thurow, Lester C. (1981), 'Death by a Thousand cuts', *New York Review of Books*, vol. XXVIII, No. 20.

Tilly, L. and Scott, J. (1978), *Women, Work and Family*, Holt Rinehart & Winston.

Tomlinson, A. (1979), *Leisure and the role of clubs and voluntary groups*, Sports Council and Social Science Research Council, London.

Townsend, P. (1979), *Poverty in the United Kingdom*, ch. 13, Allen Lane, London.

Trist, E. L. and Bamford, K. (1951), 'Some Social and Psychology Consequences of the Long-wall Method of Coal Getting', *Human Relations*, vol. 4, pp. 3–39; reprinted in T. Burns (ed.), (1946), Penguin, Harmondsworth.

Unger, J. (1975), 'The Politics of Wages in the Socialist States: an Enquiry into the Origins of Inequalities', Institute of Development Studies Discussion Paper, 88, University of Sussex, Brighton.

Vanek, J. (1974), 'The time spent in housework', *Scientific American*, November.

Wacjman, J. (1983), *Women in Control*, Open University Press.

Wadel, C. (1979), 'The hidden work of everyday life', in Wallman, S. (ed.), *Social Anthropology of Work*, Academic Press, London.

Walder, A. (1981), 'Some Ironies of the Maoist Legacy in Industry', *The Australian Journal of Chinese Affairs*, 5, pp. 21–38.

Walker, A. (1981), 'The Level and distribution of unemployment', in L. Burghes and R. Lister (eds.), op. cit.

Walker, Charles R. and Guest, Robert H. (1952), *The Man on the Assembly Line*, Harvard University Press, Cambridge, Mass.

Walker, K. E. and Woods, M. (1976), *Time Use: A Measure of Household Production of Family Goods and Services*, American Home Economics Association.

Wallman, S. (ed.), (1979), *Social anthropology of work*, Academic Press, London.

Weber, E. (1977), *Peasants into Frenchmen*, Chatto & Windus, London; first publ. Stanford University Press, 1976.

Webb, S. and Webb, B. (1926), *Industrial Democracy*, Longmans, Green & Co., London.

Westergaard, J. H. (1970), 'The Rediscovery of the Cash Nexus', in R. Miliband and John Saville (eds.), *The Socialist Register*, Merlin, London.

White, G. (1982), 'Introduction: the New Course in Chinese Development Strategy: Context, Problems and Prospects', in J. Gray and G. White (eds.), *China's New Development Strategy*, pp. 1–16, Wheatsheaf Books, Brighton.

Wilkinson, B. (1983), *The shopfloor politics of new technology*, Heinemann, London.

Wilkinson, F. (ed.), (1981), *The Dynamics of Labour Market Segmentation,* Academic Press, London.

Wilkinson, F. and Tarling, R. (1982), 'The movement of real wages and the development of collective bargaining in the period 1855 to 1920', *Contributions to Political Economy,* vol. 1, Cambridge Political Economy Society.

Willis, P. (1977), *Learning to labour,* Saxon House, Farnborough.

Winter, M. (1979), 'Family Farming and the Development of Capitalism', Open University internal research paper.

Wood, S. (1981), 'Redundancy and female employment', *Sociological Review,* vol. 29, No. 4, pp. 649–82.

Wood, S. (1982), 'Introduction', in S. Wood (ed.), *The Degradation of Work?* pp. 11–22. Hutchinson, London.

Wood, S. (1985), 'The flexibility of recruitment systems', *British Journal of Industrial Relations,* forthcoming.

Wood, S. and Kelly, J. (1982), 'Taylorism, responsible autonomy and management strategy', in S. Wood (ed.), *The Degradation of Work?* Hutchinson, London.

Wootton, B. (1955), *The Social Foundation of Wage Policy,* Allen & Unwin, London.

Xue, Muqiao (1981), *China's Socialist Economy,* Foreign Languages Press, Beijing.

Young, M. and Willmott, P. (1957), *Family and kinship in East London,* Penguin, Harmondsworth.

Young M. and Willmott, P. (1975), *The Symmetrical Family,* Penguin, Harmondsworth.

Zaretsky, E. (1976), *Capitalism, the Family and Personal Life,* Pluto Press, London.

Zeitlin, J. (1979), 'Craft control and the division of labour engineers and compositors in Britain, 1890–1930', *Cambridge Journal of Economics,* vol. 3, No. 3, pp. 263–74.

Zeitlin, L. R. (1971), 'A little larceny can do a lot for employee morale', *Psychology Today,* June.

Zimbalist, A. (ed.), (1979), 'Case studies on the labor process', *Monthly Review Press,* New York and London.

Index